COLLECTED POEMS

1954–2004

COLLECTED POEMS

1954–2004

IRVING FELDMAN

 SCHOCKEN BOOKS • NEW YORK

The selections from *New and Uncollected Poems* orginally appeared in the following publications: *American Scholar*, "The Return of the Repressed"; *Crayon*, "The Needy Rich Are Always with Us," "Ideologue," and "Versions of Proteus"; *The Forward*, "Culprit Conscience"; *Grand Street*, "Arslan & Arpad: On the Question of Craft"; *Gulf Coast*, "Say Pardon"; *Kiosk*, "Gigsburg"; *Light Year '87*, "[Sic] Transcript Gloria, or The Body Politician"; *The Literary Imagination*, "Old Ivy and Arsenic"; *Long Shot*, "Prometheus at Fourteen" and "The Weakest Hands Seize the Heaviest Ax"; *Metre*, "Speed of Words" and "State of the Union"; *Michigan Quarterly Review*, "When the Lion Dies"; *Northwest Poetry Review*, "Came to Nothing"; *Paris Review*, "Chaos Theory, or Karmic Chutzpah," "Man with Blue Catarrh," and "To a Grave, Unquietly"; *Poetry*, "For J.M., His Poems" and "Fifteen Minutes"; *Smartish Pace*, "The Brother"; *Southwest Review*, "The Interruption"; *Yale Review*, "Dance in the Dark," "Poem with Refrain," "Don't You Admire Me?," and "Happening."

Grateful acknowledgment is made to the following for permission to reprint previously published material:
Grove/Atlantic, Inc.: *Beautiful False Things* by Irving Feldman. Copyright © 2000 by Irving Feldman. Reprinted by permission of Grove/Atlantic, Inc.
The University of Chicago Press: Poems from *The Life and Letters* by Irving Feldman (The University of Chicago Press, 1994). Reprinted by permission of The University of Chicago Press.

I am deeply grateful to Deborah Garrison,
who has made this book possible.
—I. F.

Library of Congress Cataloging-in-Publication Data
Feldman, Irving, 1928–
[Poems. Selections]
Collected poems, 1954–2004 / Irving Feldman.
p.   cm.
Includes index.
ISBN 0-8052-4229-5
I. Title.
PS3511.E23A6 2004
811'.54—dc22   2004042769

www.schocken.com

Printed in the United States of America
First Edition

9 8 7 6 5 4 3 2 1

To

GAIL
and
SABRINA *and* FERNANDO
and
NATASHA *and* ALEXANDER
and
CHERYL *and* ED
and
STU *and* HARRIET

Oh why
is the soul sent on errands
in the dark? with its list
of names, its fist of pennies,
its beating heart?

CONTENTS

From *LOST ORIGINALS* (1972)

From *TEACH ME, DEAR SISTER* (1983)

ALL OF US HERE (1986)

From *THE LIFE AND LETTERS* (1994)

From *BEAUTIFUL FALSE THINGS* (2000)

NEW AND UNCOLLECTED POEMS

From *Works and Days*

The Prophet

I am your stone. I seek the center.
Lean back, bend over, I know one way.
You cannot move. I weigh. I weigh.
I am your doom. Your city shall not burn.
The flood has gone by, the fever passed.
Get home. Empty the square
As your hearts are empty. Only I am there.
Everywhere. I bring all things down.

Your eyes wander to the ground.
You yearn for density, the solid,
You want blocks, you want the hardest matter:
Clay will not do; granite, not marble.
Your souls crave no room. All is brought together.
You shall be as stone and wedge yourselves down.
Where all things are one.

Non-Being

And all about him rock—with heavy grayness as of a sigh.
And yet Prometheus saw the sardonic humor of the place,
How the mountains tilted back their heads against the sky
And twisted out a smile; a smile passed on his face.

After a thousand years he thought he saw the joke,
And began, almost nostalgically, to giggle; even his joints
Felt a certain lightness, it took so little to provoke
A knee, merely, say, the wryness of two opposing points.

Another aeon passed and he laughed outright;
He felt himself, in fact, the universal satirist,
The final glittering of the rictus of cosmic spite.
So nothing really mattered; and his mirth bubbled off in mist.

What terrible cackle bounds blatant through the vale?
O come to the mountain and see a suit of clothes on a nail!

Arabian Night

This place, these women talking after dinner,
before they rise to bless goodnight, I should
know them, their stories of the past: sorrows,
children, the dead; those very tales, yes!
sisters, mother, aunt, still as they were,
at the white table in the darkening room
—genies of familial memory, who,
convened, becalmed, by nearness and the night,
rub from a boy's tender pride or impudence,
or cousin's guile, or uncles' merriment
—so innocent, so unredeemed!—
a steady, timid spell against the night.

And I who sit like night at the window
and cannot enter except I become a child
—that light has gone, they cannot conjure him,
not for all their burnished hearts' lamp!

In other lands, striving in chains, he builds
but cannot grow; and I have come in his stead.
And here one is, Time's prosaic Sinbad
returned from dull adventures in the years,
ancient changeling, impostor of a life,
—my treasure flotsam, debased, befouled,
I cannot ransom forth the light, or save
this drifted past abandoned on a hill.

Become the porter of my history,
what can I do but toss this black bag down,
share the relics I've got, knock, return,
like any prodigal—holding out
tarnished gifts to strangers: some guilt,
merely sentimental; a little childish loyalty;
a little useless pity.

A Poet

From earliest age he'd shown himself an adept of décor
And could not be anywhere long but he was onstage
And obtrusively would produce from pockets a window, a door,
A table and chair, strike a pose, and say, "This is Rage."
And accompanied this attitude with prelude and postlude,
Or pointed heavenward to certain platonic flats
Awaiting their *entrée,* or seemed to engage a feud
With spirits under the floor, who were, in fact, under his hat.

I think he wanted to convince us our lives are papers
(Or that his was not) written over with the same old word
And folded up into gay little party favors
That go *pop!* and tell an ominous fortune if tugged too hard.
(It may be we *are* much minuscule literature.)
Articulate he was, but mistrusted eloquence,
For *that* pretends that something is real and, like Nature,
Can crumple one's performer's-smile with easy indifference.

An unpleasant shipwreck; though for this situation,
Too, he had a name somewhere in his everpresent valise.
For everything, he felt, was named already in the lexicon
Of public dreams—awkward, sad, and noble like his properties.
O perhaps he'd been a desolate child who'd murdered by fact,
Named his toys and thought them dead because respondent to his
        strings.
No matter, for now he could be seen at the end of his act
Grinning, grabbing up the tray, and scampering into the wings.

Well, and if he liked to pretend, at times, that the wind
He'd invoke to mow down a house of cards was not from his deck
And had not also, like all his gods, been machined,
Every magician believes that Chaos is the finest trick.
In his Master File of Forms, Norms, and Storms, he sought
        Repose.
But nameless death came and blew them all into a weather,
Deceived, deny it who will, by his Apocalypse-Pose.
It is to be doubted we live as well or die better.

Goya

MAN

The soldiers bear a sack,
A white sack without a tear;
The soldiers are in black.
For the rest, the plain is bare.
And what else *should* be there?

They carry the sack,
They do the best they can;
One in his arms, other on his back.
Are these animals? their bag of bran?
No. They are men. This is a man.

"SE APROVECHAN"

"They take advantage"—the soldiers need clothes,
While corpses don't, who have their repose
And nakedness like a second birth,
And nose-down sniff new science from the earth.
So what if nakedness admits the crows!

Such handsome athletic figures,
Twenty centuries of nudes! which now the soldiers
Like bungling apprentices of the muse
Or drunken helpers in a museum cellar,
Yank and tug at to uncover.

And doing so, give that hopeless bric-a-brac
A little of the rhetoric of passion back.
A giant tree with haunches of a mother,
In her anguish torn and flowering and black,
Rears up!—but the head is out of the picture.

OTHER MUTILATIONS: DISASTERS OF THE DEAF

Not sound, no—that's not his—they steal
The silence, their machines have sucked the space

Out through his ears, *his* space, *his* silence, unloosed
The inner volumes of his body; hopeless to feel
Within himself, and in a place.

The eye reposeless; here surfaces crack,
And his eye-bewildered, weighted with trying to hear,
Aghast, in the ragged depths, before the huge dim spook
Of skin and stones, the *them!* the horror: the hacked
Cadaver of his space. But right, or left, a lane there

Is winding out of the present toward a nowhere,
A something or nothing, all white or all black,
Not his or theirs—but escape! an inward ear.

THE DUELISTS

We look at masker, mask, and think: tree/root,
Face/soul. A pretty word-game wherewith
The world's made one; which these masks refute,
Saying: white/black—surface of no depth,
Depth without surface, as: bare foot/empty boot.

See, the darkness fills an eye or stains
Across a mouth, and their swordpoints daze the air
Like black flies buzzing here/there
That light and leave and touch, as on two windowpanes,
To learn what world of blackness a little mask contains.

THE NIGHTMARES

O Beauty! O . . . but that no longer twists.
Better these after-all harmless succubi
With noses you can grip with both fists,
And dwarfs with humps like a witch's saddle,
Outrageous hairy runts who come knee-high
And No-faces sketched in on a paddle,
And Hot-feet who jump up and down, hop hop,
And cackle and cry and bite their hands, and stop.

        .   .   .

Little children, in fact. O may they now come
Unto us, bringing their tantrums of delight;
O, in this banal twilit delirium,
May these idioms, crotchets, slips of the brush
Come daub their mimicries of our human fright.
Well then, is it asking too much
To have, before the frozen night of terrors,
Such charming playmates as these lively errors?

SATURN

Is it ambition leads him there?
The witty artist starts in air—
Where exclusion, balance, order disclose
An ethereal and delicious pose,
And intimate a phantom doggie and
Imagined feet that stray or stand
Beneath the portrait of a doll.
An art of seeming not to fall.

But hunger brings one back to earth:
To carnival maskers, madmen, clowns,
Dark hordes of cobbleheaded crones,
—The riotous fictions of rebirth—
And odd bones the war has left around;
So much to feed those starving wits,
To be gotten down. But somewhere's a ditch
Of blackness always dropping underground

—To where the monster, lit by a chthonic glow
And having eaten the charming *cogito*,
Now lifts a bloody torso like a toy,
As if, poor thing, there was only one joy.
At the bottom of all, this preposterous end
That wit cannot define or passion comprehend.
And the black holes in the fiercely rounded whites . . .
But be careful! don't touch it!—*it bites.*

The Lost Language

I have eaten all my words,
And still I am not satisfied!
Fourteen thousand and twenty blackbirds
Hushed under my side.

And when I think of what I have written
Or might have and can and shall write
—My life, this appetite,
But how shall I eat the food I've forgotten?
And think of how my envy like a lust
Kept me up all night with its tease,
And how the night unveiled a noble bust
When I thought of glory—but that doesn't please.
So much ambition,
And so little nutrition.

Après le déluge, moi.
There it is, all the sad tale—
A perfect postdiluvian male,
And other humanist ta-ran ta-ra.
For, after all, it's only disgrace,
At the very best, to outlive
(Half-monadnock, half-sieve)
The saddest thing in the life of the race.

And when I think how many fathoms deep
Debris of that mighty birth . . .
O then there were words in the earth
That were the things they named
And lay like manna in easy reach,
And when you spoke, there was speech.

·　·　·

Very hungry and not a little ashamed,
For passion is no longer food,
I have taken up again,
In ghostly parody, pot and pen,
And sit to gnaw my chattering brood.

One cup of Lethe and it's always too late.
Where are you, *O liebe brayt?*

From *The Pripet Marshes*

Prologue

I in the foreground, in the background I,
and the stone in the center of all,
I by the stone declaiming, I
writing here, I trundling in
the moody mountain scene, the cardboard
couples, the dusty star, I turning
from the page, my hand staying moonlit,
my pen athwart the light, I dimming
the moon with cloud, the scene then pensive,
uneasy, and seated colossal
on Earth's round brink I, my head bending
my hand back at the wrist, thinking,
thinking . . . And, still by the stone, I
attent to my declamation, taking it down.

So the mind above its theater, on
restless wing aloof, circles
in a thin ether of pain. And I
the more outside holding the global
thing at arm's length, the sphere withdrawing
its rounded perfection. Night falling
there, I prompt the little towns to wink,
show faces sudden at windows, peering
from the radiant blocks; I transmit
the earnest domestic effulgence to
the endless stars, I declare those lives
indispensable, good, and I think, I think. . . .

The stone, too, floats off, swaying its wide
circle, taking the all along. I
bodiless, watching it go, sipping
the transparent pain, the void, sending
my message after it. It goes off,
gathering the starlight to itself.
And does not shrink. I afterward
melancholy, thoughts thinking . . .

Artist and Model

After Picasso's Suite de 180 dessins

THE ABDUCTION

I

Carefully, he set an easel out,
a page (white), which made the site
a cave, thrusting who had been
beside him, she, seized, captured, beyond the plane,
yet not forever into shadow.
On his side, he, O in a motley of loss—chattering
secretive, sad febrile, sick animal,
credulous sly, monkey pensive. And she,
cast away and dormant, lying-in, a model,
sample, sign pointing mysteriously
from the darkness outward to herself,
what she was, is, still to be, beyond the cave.

THE SUBJECTION

2 She

And not less is, cannot be more,
all center, surface, herself,
continuous simulacra rising
outward to this form, what here she is,
offered in the cave, there flying and glinting
on a hill, spume aloft and facet,
and in the forest there on all
the trees at once dazzled like a wind.

3

And does she think? What thought is possible
to that body's absolute curve, head, its
supple repose? Then, if anything,
a rhythm of becomings, herself, her
innermost, most infinitesimal
simulacrum in triumph on waves
of rosiness riding to her skin.
Quickly, this ease he translates

to opportunities, discovers answers,
landfalls, clues to a something hidden
where he has left the leavings of his brush
—in armpits and legpit a splotch,
trickle of hair: three sapient beards.

4   *Monkeyshines*

To his glance opening, teasing
to a gaze nowhere repulsed, never
satisfied, eludes, confuses him,
she, so and thus, grave, serene.
And he is cross, tracking this endless clue
to a secret that doesn't exist: her
inside, her other side. And persists, embarks,
paddling his little cave, sail sighting,
Mozambique, Madagascar, still sail,
searches under a buttock, along a thigh,
near ear, dodging among the points
of view, *Qua qua*, chattering, followed by:
spoor of anecdotes, vestigia, mask-droppings.

5

He has his way, his trade—and this,
his maker, set its thumbprint on him,
mark of its power, swirling the lines
of his face over his smock down the page,
where his profile's squiggle is justified,
stayed, in a few satirical dots.
And she, naked, absolute, posing only
the problem of unity—by which light
he recognizes he is grotesque, perverse,
embarks on his dialectic, hopping
about in festinate fury, seeking
a slur, a total perspective, to create
beyond the work her, her garden
without labor, to repossess that innocence.
Ignorant, she stands. Stymie. On his brow
finger delves furrow, there between
the worn bumps of horn, warts of thought.

6

He will set her to work. She listens, stares,
puts on the masks. And why not?—flesh
accommodates, and welcomes home the wanderer.
All ports are one port; the door opens, the bed's
page blank. Another mask. Again, here
in the cave where she remains to furnish
the world to her keeper's cell, subjects
for the endless busyness of mind and hand.
Smiling a myopic squint of mouth,
taking his peek-a-boo of masks for
the gestures of her inwardness, confessions,
expressions, he lays back her head
for abandon or tilts her elbow for offense.
She, upon request, cradles a breast with her hand,
"Like so?" And he, "Hold it!" commands,
snaps to attention like a thumb.

7

As thought will, his haunts the depths,
groundswell, the crucible of pressure,
where the monstrous shape flashes into
the universe of rhythm. So,
trawls his net of lines, hunting
the sunken old Venus, the model's other,
her brine-beaten vestige. And up it comes,
thumping the cave's keel, enormously
beyond its calyx reaching, sublime,
out of the cave, brilliant, defined,
world that, quicker than fish-petal, fin,
flares piquant in the periscopic eye.

8   *Monkey Art*

The purpose of a line is to create
a transparency, a foreshortening of
the total perspective, that what is not
seen can be imagined there where it veers
around and slopes against the backward
space—of the mind, alas! Imitation
is magic, abuse of her good kindness

that requires man's sinew, man's breath
to bring (strike! sing!), declare her to herself.
Stuffed with possession, her effigy
cramping in the perambulator
of his mind, he strides about,
refines her to ovoids such and such, hatches them
as schemes that telescope down
to mines of Babel. He looks through,
yes, he sees it, at last! a navel.
Or is it mountains on the moon?

9   *His Monologue*

Cheap tricks, these scribbles and dots,
data to tick, tickle in mental
IBM: breast, nipples, nose. And these
polarities, parallels, rhymes,
dialectics, symmetries; this "like,"
this "stands for"—scum and froth
of convention, squibble and quibble,
boundaries of the mind,
its dark court where fools (two) (Thesis?
Antithesis?) banter a shuttlecock
across a net and call it phoenix,
cry, *My* phoenix. Only the court endures,
persists beyond the badinage of rebirth.
Ground of the mind! Arbitrary lines!
Under the game reclines, out
of its plane, she, reposing, ungraspable:
foothold, mountain, sky.

10   *He Speaks of Her Accommodations*

What I have sought, passage outward
into the garden, where, terror surrendered,
the soul reverts in a shower of seed
—this she presents, dreaming
salvations, appearances, answering
at cave's mouth, tower window,
vocations of hammer, stylus, string,
and shows, in every pose, her happy accident:
trou: trouvaille, the lucky hole-in-One.

II

With passage of the voice, the thing evoked
drifts back to itself, silence; unblinking
attention, the note sustained until
it screams, only this can hold it here.
All magic fails, the uneasy metaphor
of lines collapses; and ancient
jackanapes must have her all, his feeble
arms cannot gather her greatness,
receding, seemingly poised somewhere
else seemingly beyond flesh.

But now he will enter, deposit his
inwardness, make her soulful, think,
swell with pathos, crumble
to characters and roles—and daubs
her every, her most minute, apparition
with monkey ink.

12 *After*

And, at the last, only ink is, a sea
of sighs and signs, cave darkness, dark
petroleum pool whose old metamorphoses
come, in slow turmoil, surface
rainbow, surface of fire. Of fire
he thinks, living in a charred moment
after the power, seeking the moment
before it shined. And makes another
line, sign: vestige of the power gone,
pointing a power to come
where she, regnant, entire, toward herself
lightly draws him with powerful repose.

"Portrait de Femme"

After Picasso

I

Somewhere between our nervousness and
our admiration, she sits in her portrait
—*une femme*, with two noses, in a striped blouse,
being poked fun at, feeling doubtless
herself honored by this satirist so famous
no one laughs anymore, she, the chosen
one, of flippered arms and perfunctory fingers,
a visage clawed in colors, one heartless
breast a blank circle, on her vase-stem
neck imposed, a brow like Gibraltar's.
Maybe it is Dora Maar—"charming, talented,
vivacious"—composed here on a collapsing
chair between three jokes (on the flesh,
on vanity, on painting)—whose iron mouth
and clear fixated gaze betray to all
the world only the fiercest equanimity.

2   The One Verity

Flesh is what, exactly? And the spirit—"witty,
vivacious, provocative"—livening it,
what? Mysteries rendered negotiable by
a sly counterfeiter who's countersigned her Maar,
merely, having, ungently, reinvented her all
—one lady, in one chair—and cashed her in
for the small change of relation, except:
the imagined horizontal connecting to one eye
corner the next. The rest is paint.
Behind the eyes on the goblet-head, defined
by the jest of unkiltered metamorphoses, is:
a liquid just level, precariously still. This
not to spill a life long while providing witty
vivacity with vivacious provocation—this
is perhaps the soul and quite enough
to make dear Psyche weary, bright Eros weep.

3   *Who Is Dora? What Is She?*

Perhaps on such a day as this—but
in France in 1936, before,
that is, the War and other events
now too infinite to list (though
out-of-doors the oak whispers not
and the birds exist much as
they did and will) came and went
like that and like this, all things
that time bore and then dismissed
—before the War perhaps, on such
a day as this, Dora Maar (let us
say "Dora Maar," for who would be
anonymous? and her name was all
she really wore) sat in a chair
in 19 and 36 with a wish fierce
and commonplace to be mysterious,
to survive and to thrive, to be a success
and be good, and be covered
with paint like a kiss,
eternally, in nineteen hundred thirty-six.

In Time of Troubles

In time of trouble, prophets
abound: excrement of stone,
rushing from hallways, ardent
and spastic in the spotlight of their auras.
Mumming children yowl on the street,
women in aprons follow after,
wailing, the dinner's turnip
and paring knife waved in their hands.
And the half-mad feel the key wince round,
released from their hutches, bolt out
into the street, direct the traffic.
Around the prophets all hunch, hushed
to hear the headline scale the sheer walls
of their throats: "Gr-r-eat-est!" It is the circus

of pestilence. Convulsed, gurgling,
the murderous martyrs drop
away to their holy pratfalls.
Void next: sudden of the street corner:
where machine guns connect
with a wicked wisecrack.
The crowd like cards fanned, flying.
On high bridges and high buildings
vague figures lean, leap out
over the treetops. The looters, however,
do not observe the holiday,
keep their wits,
quietly
from door to door . . .

The Messengers

To those (only to those?)
who abandon all, yes,
to the great abandoners
unliving their lives,
the ecstatic messengers come
unconscious of their tunics'
heartbreaking expressive fall,
their gusty disheveled curls,
their cheeks puffing as if
one second more they will
lift their trumpets and call.

Radiant, they, and always
earliest arriving
to precede the lavish day
like the light prophesying
at dawn, lighting nothing
for nothing yet is born,
they are almost turning
to go, almost are gone,
already spoken the word

delightfully their faces shine,
and fullness of the day
in a blaze of trumpet metal:

See how I love my life!
Faithless,
you have loved your lives too little.

The Double

On other cloudy afternoons
you will be sitting here, or pacing
the rooms, your restless words
unuttered. I put you there now
so the drama may continue, with poplars
invoking the wind outside, the lamplight
slowly focusing to a pencil point.
Here, it is murdering an angel
in the very center of everywhere. This same
joy shall be yours, drawing the blood out
among these mazes that continue
always, under the aspects
of a cloudy day.
                    Mysterious the mazes
of those afternoons through which
the red leaves sweep, your own hand
tracing joyfully there another life
to live you on afternoons like this.

The Return

Was this life? Good, let it come again!—NIETZSCHE

Did you speak those words?
But if your life were given you again . . .
—But as another turning of the maze,

or the same maze a second time;
and not the struggle you wanted,
but intricate escaping whispers
that hint (or simulate) a mystery,
and bring you (your enemy retreating,
scattered among lurkings, absences)
toward a struggle deflected
through minute, imperative clashes,
till, circling on the infinite threshold,
your weariness and your way unite;
past, future connect in a dream
there is no adversary, no ending. . . .

Yet suppose that on this
your own occluded morning
(with the wind idly revolving,
the rain oppressing the streets
with impetuous disdainful imminence),
suppose that over and over
your life returns,
mingling in a radiant moment
those turnings, those doorways and days,
your mumbled street of mazes
flashing down in the singular falls!
And you, perplexed in the roaring
of the simultaneous syllable,
go blind,
            unable to recall
the name of life
                —as this day
(on your own cloudy morning,
the wind idling, turning,
the rain above the streets withheld)
you turn,
under the momentous, pouring body,
and search the doubtful passageways
(repeated, dividing), unaware
that from the first your cry was answered,
and your life, and lives, are here.

Scene of a Summer Morning

Scene of a summer morning, my mother walking
to the butcher's, I led along. Mountains
of feathers. My breath storms them. Angry feathers.
Handfuls. The warm gut windings stinking.
Here, chickens! Yankel, the bloody storeman,
daringly he takes the live animals
in vain. Yankel, a life for a life! Eternal
morning too young to go to school. I get
a hollow horn to keep. Feathers, come down!
Gone. The world of one morning. But somewhere,
sparkling, it circles a sunny point.

Incredible the mazes of that morning,
where my life in all the passages at once
is flowing, coursing, as in a body
that walked away, went.
                              Who writes these lines
I no longer know, but I believe him
to be a coward, that only one who escaped.
The best and bravest are back there still,
all my Ten Tribes wandering and singing
in the luminous streets of the morning.
Unsounded the horn! And silence shudders
in the center of the sunny point,
heart-stopping at dawn.
Enormous my thieving hand in the ancient sunlight
no longer mine. Littering through my fingers,
drifting, the Ten Tribes there, lost forever.

The Pripet Marshes

Often I think of my Jewish friends and seize them as they are and
    transport them in my mind to the *shtetlach* and ghettos,

And set them walking the streets, visiting, praying in *shul*, feasting
    and dancing. The men I set to arguing, because I love dialectic

and song—my ears tingle when I hear their voices—and the girls and women I set to promenading or to cooking in the kitchens, for the sake of their tiny feet and clever hands.

And put kerchiefs and long dresses on them, and some of the men I dress in black and reward with beards. And all of them I set among the mists of the Pripet Marshes, which I have never seen, among wooden buildings that loom up suddenly one at a time, because I have only heard of them in stories, and that long ago.

It is the moment before the Germans will arrive.

Maury is there, uncomfortable, and pigeon-toed, his voice is rapid and slurred, and he is brilliant;
And Frank who is good-hearted and has the hair and yellow skin of a Tartar and is like a flame turned low;
And blond Lottie who is coarse and miserable, her full mouth is turning down with a self-contempt she can never hide, while the steamroller of her voice flattens every delicacy;
And Marian, her long body, her face pale under her bewildered black hair and of the purest oval of those Greek signets she loves; her head tilts now like the heads of the birds she draws;
And Adele who is sullen and an orphan and so like a beaten creature she trusts no one, and who doesn't know what to do with herself, lurching with her magnificent body like a despoiled tigress;
And Munji, moping melancholy clown, arms too short for his barrel chest, his penny-whistle nose, and mocking nearsighted eyes that want to be straightforward and good;
And Abbie who, when I listen closely, is speaking to me, beautiful with her large nose and witty mouth, her coloring that always wants lavender, her vitality that body and mind can't quite master;

And my mother whose gray eyes are touched with yellow, and who is as merry as a young girl;
And my brown-eyed son who is glowing like a messenger impatient to be gone and who may stand for me.
I cannot breathe when I think of him there.

And my red-haired sisters, and all my family, our embarrassed love bantering our tenderness away.

Others, others, in crowds filling the town on a day I have made sunny for them; the streets are warm and they are at their ease.

How clearly I see them all now, how miraculously we are linked! And sometimes I make them speak Yiddish in timbres whose unfamiliarity thrills me.

But in a moment the Germans will come.

What, will Maury die? Will Marian die?

Not a one of them who is not transfigured then!

The brilliant in mind have bodies that glimmer with a total dialectic;
The stupid suffer an inward illumination; their stupidity is a subtle tenderness that glows in and around them;
The sullen are surrounded with great tortured shadows raging with pain, against whom they struggle like titans;
In Frank's low flame I discover an enormous perspectiveless depth;
The gray of my mother's eyes dazzles me with our love;
No one is more beautiful than my red-haired sisters.
And always I imagine the least among them last, one I did not love, who was almost a stranger to me.
I can barely see her blond hair under the kerchief; her cheeks are large and faintly pitted, her raucous laugh is tinged with shame as it subsides; her bravado forces her into still another lie;
But her vulgarity is touched with a humanity I cannot exhaust, her wretched self-hatred is as radiant as the faith of Abraham, or indistinguishable from that faith.
I can never believe my eyes when this happens, and I want to kiss her hand, to exchange a blessing.

In the moment when the Germans are beginning to enter the town.

But there isn't a second to lose, I snatch them all back,
For, when I want to, I can be a God.

No, the Germans won't have one of them!
This is my people, they are mine!

And I flee with them, crowd out with them: I hide myself in
    a pillowcase stuffed with clothing, in a woman's knotted
    handkerchief, in a shoebox.

And one by one I cover them in mist, I take them out.
The German motorcycles zoom through the town,
They break their fists on the hollow doors.
But I can't hold out any longer. My mind clouds over.
I sink down as though drugged or beaten.

To the Six Million

But put forth thine hand now, and touch his bones and his flesh . . .

I

If there is a god,
he descends from the power.
But who is the god rising from death?
(So, thunder invades the room, and brings with it
a treble, chilly and intimate, of panes rattling
on a cloudy day in winter.
But when I look through the window,
a sudden blaze of sun is in the streets,
which are, however, empty and still. The thunder
repeats.) Thunder here. The emptiness resounds
here on the gods' struggle-ground
where the infinite negative retreats,
annihilating where it runs,
and the god who must possess pursues, pressing
on windowpanes, passing through.
Nothing's in the room but light
wavering beneath the lamp
like a frosty rose the winter bled.
No one is in the room (I possess nothing),
only power pursuing, trying
corpses where the other god went,

running quickly under the door. In
the chill, the empty room
reverberates. I look from the window.

✦

There is someone missing.
Is it I who am missing?
And many are missing.
And outside, the frozen street extends
from me like a string, divides, circles,
with an emptiness the sun
is burnishing.
               In the street
there is nothing, for many are missing,
or there is the death of many
missing, annulled, dispossessed,
filling the street, pressing their vacancy
against the walls, the sunlight, the thunder.
Is a god
in the street? where nothing is left
to possess, nothing to kill;
and I am standing
dead at the window looking out.

✦

What did you kill? Whom did you save? I ask
myself aloud, clinging to the window
of a winter day.
                  Survivor, who are you?
ask the voices that disappeared,
the faces broken and expunged.
I am the one who was not there.
Of such accidents I have made my death.

Should I have been with them
on other winter days in the snow
of the camps and ghettos?
And on the days of their death that was

the acrid Polish air?—
I who lay between the mountain of myrrh
and the hill of frankincense,
dead and surviving, and dared not breathe,
and asked, By what right am I myself?

Who I am I do not know,
but I believe myself to be one
who should have died, and the dead one
who did die.
Here on the struggle-ground, impostor
of a death, I survive reviving,
perpetuating the accident.
And who is at the windowpane,
clinging, lifting himself like a child
to the scene of a snowless day?

✦

"Whatsoever is under the whole heaven
Is mine." Charred, abandoned, all this,
who will call these things his own?

Who died not
to be dying, to survive
my death dead as I am
at the window (possessing nothing),
and died not to know
agony of the absence,
revive on a day
when thunder rattles the panes,
possessed by no one;
bone and flesh of me, because
you died on other days
of actual snow and sun,
under mists and chronic rain,
my death is cut to the bone,
my survival is torn from me.
I would cover my nakedness
in dust and ashes. They burn,

they are hot to the touch. Can my
death live? The chill treble
squeaks for a bone. I was
as a point in a space,
by what right can I be myself?
At the window and in the streets,
among the roots of barbed wire,
and by springs of the sea,
to be dying my death again
and with you,
in the womb of ice, and where
the necessity of our lives is hid.
Bone and flesh of me,
I have not survived,
I would praise the skies,
leap to the treasures of snow.

  II

*By night on my bed I sought him whom my soul loveth: I sought him,
but I found him not.*

*I will rise now, and go about the city in the streets, and in the
broad ways I will seek him whom my soul loveth. . . .*

What can I say?
    Dear ones, what can I say?
You died, and emptied the streets
and my breath, and went from my seeing.
And I awoke, dying at the window
of my wedding day, because
I was nowhere; the morning that revived
was pain, and my life that began again was pain,
I could not see you.
    What can I say?
My helpless love overwhelmed me,
sometimes I thought I touched your faces,
my blindness sought your brows again,
and your necks that are towers,
your temples that are as pieces
of pomegranate within your locks.

Dead and alive,
your shadows escaped me. I went
into the streets, you were not there,
for you were murdered and befouled.
And I sought you in the city,
which was empty, and I found you not,
for you were bleeding at the dayspring
and in the air. That emptiness
mingled with my heart's emptiness,
and was at home there, my heart
that wished to bear you again, and bore
the agony of its labor, the pain
of no birth. And I sought for you
about the city in the streets, armed
with the love hundreds had borne me.
And before the melancholy in the mazes,
and the emptiness in the streets,
in the instant before our deaths,
I heard the air (that was
to be ashen) and the flesh
(that was to be broken), I heard
cry out, Possess me!
And I found you whom my soul loves;
I held you, and would not let you go
until I had brought you
into my mother's house, and into the chamber
of her that conceived me.

Dear ones, what can I say?
I must possess you no matter how,
father you, befriend you,
and bring you to the lighthearted dance
beside the treasures and the springs,
and be your brother and your son.
Sweetness, my soul's bride,
come to the feast I have made,
my bone and my flesh of me,
broken and touched,
come in your widow's raiment of dust and ashes,
bereaved, newborn, gasping for

the breath that was torn from you,
that is returned to you.
There will I take your hand
and lead you under the awning,

and speak the words it behooves to speak.
My heart is full, only the speech
of the ritual can express it.
And after a little while,
I will rouse you from your dawn sleep
and accompany you in the streets.

Song

So you are

Stone, stone or star,
Flower, seed,
Standing reed,
River going far

So you are

Shy bear or boar,
Huntsman, death,
Arising breath,
Stone, stone or star

So you are.

From *Magic Papers*

Magic Papers

Before we came with our radiance
and swords, our simulacra of ourselves,
our injurious destinies
and portable exiles,
                              women were here
amid incredible light that seemed
to have no source, that seemed suspended.
And so they moved majestically,
like the months, forward without
straining, not toward their goals
yet carrying them as they went,
their round limbs seeming
to exemplify what they did,
leaning out of windows, stepping from
or through doorways, bending to uncover,
lifting on their palms, carrying and
setting down, pausing to converse,
turning to where we were not yet,
saying, Here we live the victory
of the senses over the senses.

                    ✦

Taken, hurried into exile,
excited and flushed, chosen, delighted,
the bride beckons and inclines;
Desire me! her eyes say; her hair
is combed and set in token of her reign
and servitude, her departure, her suffering.
And the day's head splits the darkness,
breaks forth, bruises her womb;
she screams; he burns and rises.
He carries a message across the sky
from darkness into darkness,
mounting furiously toward vengeance,
falling asleep so soon, and drops
the magic paper with the magic word
that falls into the chimney, into the fire

that burns the darkness, that also goes out
and no one is saved, no one the same.

◆

I remember this: the window
rinsed clear, the droplets,
rainbabies clinging there;
the day is vexed with boredom
and correction; light shining
over here cuts like a knife;
suddenly I know I will never
again be happy in my life.
They slide, they roll down in streaks of light.
Sword in hand, the crying children,
their faces bunched like fists,
storm the highest ramparts of heaven.
What else is there to do
on miserable days like this?

◆

I have lost the ability to sleep.
Conscience stabs my night through the sheet.
Murderer! He stabs again.
I feel for her, body draped in darkness,
defenseless, sobbing, trying
to sleep, trying to bring forth the day.
What is to be done?
I should have killed the bastard where he stood!
I make up a story without end.
The night is bleeding to death on me.
I have lost everything.
My open eyes keep open the night,
she clings to my lids.
Sleep would dishonor the dead;
I struggle to be born,
covered with blood my battering head,
my thought is misinterpreted.

I do not speak the language of this place.
I am innocent.
I scream.
If my voice itself could be
a stream intelligent of light!

✦

I am the father of rainbabies,
shepherd of jewels, of jews,
of boys in holiday skullcaps,
shining and white.
                        With studious rapture
I lean over their gleaming shoulders
and behold the texts of light.
What pressure holds these brilliant scholars?
The swelling unison of their breaths
expounds the lesson, Light!
They say it right!
They want to run out and play;
they shimmer, they stay,
so many! they multiply,
they dazzle, translating the glory hidden
in the chill, in the thunder of voices
from the street.
                        I tap my finger
on the pane; they slide,
they run down in streaks of light.
I rage, I cannot understand my rage.
I shake the window and splash them
into darkness.
                        Am I the devil?
My seed is running toward the sea.
I laugh like hell, like hell I laugh.
I am the father who cannot reach them,
I am the sons who cannot be reached
and everlasting darkness floating between.

✦

At twilight, mocking the season,
November in May is cold
and gleaming, excited, slithers,
lashing its darkness
over the glistening street;
the demon hangs in the tree,
laughing, eating the light,
then arches her body to show
her incredible extruded hole;
spewing, sucking back
her spew, pale belly up,
she lies with me like the Nile.
Conceive in me, she shrieks,
do not deny my womb!
From hole to hole, there is
no heart, harbor, nothing at all.
My word floats off, lost sail
dandled on the greasy wave.
So many scholars drowned!
Her gross tail pounds her turd
into a semblance of children.

◆

My struggle to escape the idiot,
his suckers that starve my senses,
his placental calm, his resemblance to me;
he is brainless,
he is undifferentiated,
he is always there,
he is inedible,
he is faithful to the order of things,
he has no shape,
he is obsolete,
he is slippery,
he can't even say quack.
My twin, my caul.
I refuse to be two.
Use your knife, you fool! a voice says.
The one who remains will be I,

the other is another sex.
Where I cut free, the pain in my side
surpasses understanding.
I gasp for clarification.
What is reality?
The earth leaps on me.

✦

Illness is the land for which the warriors
set out, from which return, cured, the doctors say,
of their extravagant need for reality.
The efficacy of substitutions has taught
them the existence of generalities
and boredom, that is to say, death.
They lie—the need is not extravagant,
there is no cure, I never returned.

✦

Despair is frivolous.
               Therefore
is there laughter in Sheol,
the hiccuping of drunken actors.
They vomit in their graves.

Only our shallowness saves us
from being crushed by the knowledge
of our shallowness.

What is the depth for which I thirst?

✦

I make up a story without end

of the dying child who lifts
his crippled chest, his heavy thighs;
he migrates through the earth,
hunting his lost children.

They seep, they run away.
November comes, it clogs the air,
paralytic season of rain, of chaos
and asthma. Lying on his side,
he goes white in spots like a candle;
he mourns himself everywhere
and covers the earth with his traces.
Nothing holds him; discontented,
he rolls, he plunges.

Every day in each new place, he rests
in his litter, withered and golden;
messengers flash across the heavens,
blazing with the seed they bear;
infallibly, their speed hurls them past,
but from their glowing arcs they look at him.
He sees it all: their dazzling transport,
the blue sky, their tranquil diligence,
their gaze, the seed, the sun, their breathing,
the joining of heaven and earth.
There! he thinks, there should go I.
And his sole descendants, his childish tears,
splash down and waste themselves here
on this inhospitable earth of ours.

✦

I am embarrassed. I mumble.
I blush. I am ashamed.
Before whom, stupid? Yes,
I am stupid. I look down.
I hold my hand over my mouth.
I am tongue-tied. I am too much,
I cannot.
It is comforting to be stupid,
to be confused, to look down,
to say, I do not know my name,
I am someone else's child.
I would be swept away
if I were not so burdened.

Speak to me, say
what I cannot say
that I may hear it said,
that I may say it.
I wish to unburden myself.
Kiss me. My voice
is thick, is mud,
my depth of anguish is
my depth of reservation.
I detest the wryness of my voice,
its ulteriority, its suffering
—only what is not lived
can suffer so. I wish
to give birth to the deep,
deliver myself of
this darkness, this devil.
I know the words.
I must learn to speak.

◆

After the blood,
the violence and flowing,
after conception,
the women enter the stream,
they wash and purify,
they prepare themselves;
their distended wombs, between
two waters, divide
heaven from birth.
My voice itself
a stream of light
to bathe your bodies
and behold your eyes.
Look in me! and see
what you were before
you came out of Zion
into exile
for our sakes.

The Word

Holding the book before his shining eyes,
he reads aloud to the prince from the sacred
texts and the profane. Clear afternoon
on an amiable terrace, beyond which: a garden
whose leisurely country gesture (its unfurling
stream, its waving boughs) companions
the ceremonious twittering of cadences

of volumes that recite, within a spreading
geography of obstacles and accidents,
the fortunes of many or two or all
parted and lost, rescued, rejoined,
of persons discovered, disguises thwarted,
random journeys toward importunate destinies,
and evil that recoils against itself
—the tales inflecting such rambling peace
as the garden discloses. All of which he reads
aloud, holding the book before his shining eyes,
while, far off, a white bird, arriving,
darts above the loftiest of the pines.

The sacred tomes, however, repeat endlessly
the one word "bread," which, with shining eyes,
he reads aloud over and over.
A bread that escapes the mouth, that dilates
in the air, transparent to the sky,
the stream, the trellised walks—so sweet,
the bread of all these, the unconsumable
one, invisible, unheard, it is
spoken bread, the uttered silence of bread
that, reverently, he reads aloud, holding
the book, as always, close before his shining eyes.

Psalm

There is no singing without God.
Words sound in air, mine
are flying, their wombs empty.
Whining for the living weight, they bear
themselves, a din of echoes,
and vanish: a subsiding
noise, a flatulence, a nothing
that stinks.
The glory of man shall fly away like a bird
—no birth, no pregnancy, no conception.

A people dies intestate, its benediction
lost. And the future succeeds, unfathered,
a mute, responding to no sign,
foraging its own fields at night,
hiding by day.
            Withheld in the unuttered
blessing, God labors, and is not born.

But if I enter, vanished bones
of the broken temple, lost people,
and go in the sanctum of the scattered
house, saying words like these,
forgive—my profaneness is
insufferable to me—and bless, make fertile
my words, give them a radiant burden!
Do not deny your blessing, speak to us.

Colloquy

I have questioned myself aloud
at night in a voice I did not
recognize, hurried and
disobedient, hardly brighter.
What have I kept? Nothing.
Not bread or the bread-word.

What have I offered? Rebel
in the kingdom, my gift
has wanted a grace. I am crazy
with the brutality of it.
What have I said? I
have not spoken clearly,
not what must be said,
failed in using, in blessing.
I have wanted long to confess
but do not know to whom
I must speak, and cannot
spend a life on my knees.
Nonetheless, I have always
meant to save the world.

Girl Singing

The partridge, the russet bird,
lies gently on the cutting board
between the blue bowl
and the sea-green decanter.
And a young girl is singing,
"A partridge in a pear tree,"
adding in a free contralto
all those increments that return
always to the partridge in
the pear tree. Perhaps she has
only now turned from the mirror
or put her diary aside,
roused unknowing by a second life
she has received from the russet bird.
It is like some genre painting
come alive with a touch of blood.
I note this without irony,
and I intend no danger.
One tress hanging down,
she bends over it as over
a baby she is going to powder.

I do not know for certain
that she is serenading the bird,
or why our spreading increments,
like a pear tree of winter,
retrace, between a bowl of one color
and a decanter of another,
the crooked steps to the russet root,
while somewhere a free contralto,
perched with two lives in an auburn tress,
clothes the tree with populous song

—as I am here in a winter scene
reasoning and yet with delight,
my voice, beyond me, conjoining
with hers in the floating air;
and it is sweet to be
the bright cold sky
in winter time and any time,
and all the snow that lies between,
and the partridge and the pear tree.

Dressing Hornpout

1

The squared black massive head yanked
down draws the innards with it
and the slit skin, which droops
now, draggled, saddish coat tails.
The head has: obvious whiskers of eight
strange, curling barbels; three
nasty spines; two tiny
nearly sightless eyes. The lissome
delicious body lies exposed.
This she has done.

2

And now she ranges them side by side
on wax paper: pink little gentlemen

put to bed, with pretty tails
like raven polls fresh from the bath,
neatly combed, glistening, and stiff.
Her head tilts to one side pleasantly
for so tender and unabashed a nakedness.

3

Tidy in nothing else, a primitive
aesthetic has induced her to prod
them gently here and there toward a more
perfect symmetry. All is well!
Her smiling revery is occupied
with numbering them again and again,
for all is well.

4

Dead, still their bodies arch and flip.
Heartless, headless, in what darker,
more perilous water their wandering?
A marvelous thing!
But generally are well-behaved,
and lie still to be admired in
a wholly admirable way in their not
unattractive death. How well
they can endure being looked at!
And aptly answer her passionate gaze
by staying put.

5

Joy of the fish in his leaps,
his startled bolting, his water swilling
and low lying in the settled slime.
And other joy, of ours, in what
precipitates his narrow blood
into a less recondite, a larger
universe. Prey and morsel coincide
in death. In its relation to eating,
death is a mode of kinship, for we
are not a species that eats its food

in a tempest of wings, or wriggling,
or squealing down our throats,
yet are consanguine with all we eat.

6

Yes! the huntress returns to her lair,
dignified and wise her amble,
her mien solemn and attentive
as a courting dog's. I imagine
her quickening approach. A joyous law
hastens her stride and she is obedient.
How lovingly she carries the morsel!
It almost seems she mothers it.
The cat goes in her special trot,
a dead mouse between her jaws.
A string of tail is all that shows,
yet kitten could not be safer there.

7

And now besprinkles them liberally
—her gestures grow expansive and free—
with salt, garlic powder, and pepper,
and rolls them firmly in a coarse flour.
It is neither grueling labor nor exacting
work, and a quiet, profound pleasure.

8

A woman stands before a chopping
board, in her bloodied hands a small
cleaver. Subtly violent odor
of fish, and droplets of sweat distilled
by the heating oven, which she wipes
away with her forearm. The kitchen's
only season is summer. Somewhere
a mystery is in preparation,
but here is all the evidence.
One has done worse than fall in love
with such plainly capable hands.

Four Passages

Hot Saturday expands toward twilight,
Spacious and warm. Their train, at the end of the line,
Haltingly departs from Coney Island,
And settles, after an initial whine,

To a lulling commotion, with which they, too, move,
He sixteen, she almost a year older;
They have been swimming and are in love,
And sit touching and rocking together.

Exercised and sober, their bodies are
Rested, tingling, refreshed and grave, compel
The tautened skin; he is freckled,
Her complexion of the Crimea

Is healthy olive-and-rose, her frequent smiles
Transcend what is perhaps a pout or the faint
Ruminative suckling of a child;
A severe and orphan dress disdains

The completed opulence of her body. Stretching,
They vie in banter with sunburned strangers nearby,
Break off, having acquitted themselves
With honor. Pride completes their pleasure.

They are indeed proud: of being lovers,
Of their advanced and noble sympathies,
Their happiness, their languorous wit
That mocks at dignity, ripens pleasure,

And candles the failure in these faces, then
Restores their opacity with kindly justice
—Imagining their competence exceeds
Every foreseeable occasion.

. . .

These are young gods defining love, banqueting
On glances and whispered smiles and amiable
Raillery, and believe inexhaustible
Their margin for error, and summon back

The solicitous waiter, command another course
Of immortal tenderness and levity,
Drunk and dazzled with love, twining fingers
On a summer evening after the War.

Fixed in force, the train persists on the ways,
Its windows intersect the streaming darkness;
Their expanding revery engages
Almost the first apparent stars.

A cunning and subterranean will
Even now detaches them toward other destinies,
Misery, impatience, division that shall
Complete their present and mutual ignorance.

MEETING HALL OF THE "SOCIEDAD ANARQUISTA," 1952

The rough wooden floor impedes the dancers,
Who, unable to glide, move by steps,
And, warmed by Gallo wine, gain speed, their pleasure
Neither false nor excessive, though uncertain.
Too sparse for the loft, the rest, making many,
Crowd the phonograph and wine jug on the table.

Folded chairs are ranked along a wall;
Atop the shelves, the dying pamphlets,
Absolute with ardor and fraternity,
Receive New York's gray intermittent soil,
Dust. A few Spaniards with weakened eyes
Desiccate in the fadeout of history.

Tonight, under the toneless light
Of usual selves, young friends have made
This party to welcome home a friend,

A woman fiery-looking, childless, and stubborn.
Embarrassed by gloom, she sits on the floor
And smiles her description of famine in Italy.

These two who dance have met since parting, yet,
Because she has come alone, because he, too, is,
Like one recently divorced, freshly marketable,
Novel with the glamor of commodity,
A vividness revises his elder desire,
Selects her cropped hair with loving recurrence.

Her response is rare volubility,
Her conversation challenging, obscene,
Embittered or descends to jokes or glorifies
Giving, pictures Nietzsche dying for want of love.
It is quite certain she does not like him, certain
She wishes to please. Her caricature boringly enacts

A passion genuine and chaotic. Wearing red,
At twenty-four having desired, having failed
To be reborn a Negro, Israeli, Gypsy;
Devastated by freedom, her uncompleted soul
Retains its contact with psychosis and with
The incredible softness of a woman.

Her manic vehemence drops. Dances off, gazes,
And says he looks sad, and to restore his spirits
Offers the nursery of this body she
Exhibits and dislikes; her pity and her guilt,
Like children deprivation has misled,
Hold hands tenderly, without affection.

Before night ends, forgotten at two by a mad
Mother, dragged along by her father, lodged
With orphans, she jumps, denuded, gleaming,
Nervous, from the bed, and producing
Her repertoire of wifeliness,
Asks would he like a book to read.

Three walls are tin enameled; on the fourth,
a spreading country all sienna and curves
offers in conventionally edible style,
and half-eaten already, glory that is Greece:
a bit of marzipan sitting on a hill
—it is the Parthenon; beside it, Delphi's vale
whose lovely oracle from her picnic table,
foretelling free food, expensive manners,
teaches the very gods not to grab,
while lots of girls, consuming the sun's output
of yellow, dance madly over the flowers, or caress
those half-human heads upon their human laps;
symmetrical and white, a splendid mountain
overlooks it all, though shaken, it might seem,
by inspired tremors from the artist's hand
which fluttered like a bacchant who commends
Pasha's friendly pilaf and *beautiful* wine.

Dull, but fathers, and exotic in a faintly
swarthy way, and practical about their women
who can't let anything alone with their long noses
and short fuses, and dish-busting politics,
and their big mouths and spitefulness and vanities
—vaguely indifferent, they take in the dancer's lousy
American style, from whose disorder they infer,
by casual and well-known processes, the exact degree
of her voluptuary value: how hot in bed,
and with careful Mediterranean lucidity
thank their gods she's no Greek's daughter
earning so little for showing her stuff. Roused
from their revery of sensuous shade,
they shout advice, encouragement, praise, keeping
one eye cocked at what figure they might cut
and wondering if she's maybe not there in the head.

Intolerant of the abstract ritual,
Her dancing too portentous to entertain,

Inept, overt, offensively familiar,
Breathless in the burdened unreality,

She fights toward the pure, the undemanding
Air, toward flight, aching to inspire endless
Rebirth, a plenum taut with plentitude,
Of her virgin children the virgin child; messenger

Struck dumb, nailed to the stage, staggers
Through attitudes that crazily conflate
Sexual homilies with moral coquetry;
Her gestures heave, labor to translate

The unreality: tempt, placate, challenge,
Exclude toward a universe of love and giving . . .
Unaware that her sacrifice proceeds
Beyond her power to surrender. The audience

Stirs, its attention irregular, vague,
Its judgment unfavorable, its indifference,
Like the gods', capricious but final.
The tiny uterine increments transcend

Her body: a stillness flickers, neither
Reposeful nor dancing, the emptiness
Affirms itself in repeated nothings
At one with the judgment upon her.

PARTY ON EAST TENTH STREET, 1955

Their party has romance for its occasion,
A courtship of roses, Saturday's roses
Hilarious now in the violet air
And whom the dance encounters with loves
In a folly of poses gravely swimming, alluding to,

Deferring always to them, though importunate
Sometimes, begging their arms, their tresses, their kisses.
        Kisses
Of the rose, how little they endure! consumed

In movement, their plays revived as the air's
Repeated caresses that pursue with music

The weakening, dizzied roses faster, farther
Through misleading groves of alarms and despairs.
How cold there, frightful and lonely! till they cry aloud
And are consoled, while the music slows, by a voice
Lost and found in the voices of their hulloing loves.

The roses brighten and withdraw;
look down, smooth, correct,
amplify their persons,
these speaking modesties
of linen or of silk
wherein are nursed and hidden
the infant revelations
whispered to their beating hearts.
Given and giving this
only, untouchable elsewhere
but touched by a mothering voice,
because of whom
the roses love and are lovable,
having consoled their despairs and tears,
their fragile lament, and made coherent
the gaze of discoursing intelligence
that dallies brightly now among the roses
and their loves, and in the party's
boisterous charade invokes
a mother invisible below
the blood that gathers at the root,
the light that wakes the flower's
flower.

What strange animals we are!
                            Responding
to slaps and losses, teasing, kisses; eager
for contest, for smiles of shared intelligence;
witless, disheartened, drooping in solitude,
desiring sights, and the seeing of other eyes;
nourished by news and touches, crowding

the air with spirits and revenant loves;
asking of things what beings they possess;
compounding the soul of others or dividing
in a drama of voices, preferring guilt
to terror, terror to isolation.

Of hunger and thirst a king dies amid
fountains and gardens.
                              An infant, isolated
within the circling intelligence of love,
has died.
                      What strange animals we are!
                                                  Smiling
with the roses, held in their garden glances, he
receives intelligence of her, husbandless,
motherless mother. One now and now together,
they mime her gestures—goes
wandering, the infant across her arms
offered in the empty street.
Does not know how to feed it. They squeak
its little cries. Their eyes glaze. It sickens
and dies, curling like a leaf
amid their banquet of smiles.
They hide-and-seek,
cannot let her go. They clothe
themselves in her chill. Starlight
has estranged their faces.
Recurs, surviving in a stupor
beyond heartbreak, gnawing
her blue, delicate, negative
lip; she does not cry
or turn away: radiant with
no seeable light, breathless revenant
absenting in a poverty of desolation.
                                              From such
it shall be taken to the very conclusion
of time without mercy or remission.
                                        This one
is interesting: scrubbed pink yet oddly drab,
her articulation foreign slightly and

indistinct, direct, awkward in the dance,
stocky, broad-basined, touched with a violet glow,
and wanting, he knows, to be taken home.

Around each rose a specter glows
Bluish and biting, after the fine
Electric wit departs from it.
Odor of ozone concludes the feast
And leaves the rose its cold repose.
Spreading in darkness, the specter is the rose.

AN EPILOGUE

She has been met by others since.
They say she gardens for a living,
her manner hearty and masculine,
was married for a time, sleeps
around, though less now than before,
is given still to brooding and rages,
but faces middle age with greater
equanimity than she lived her youth,
has altered her name and has good
color, dresses better, preserves
an interest in the theater, is less
vulgar, somewhat commonplace,
and more optimistic than not.

Dunkerque 1951

Lazy or careless, he drops
out of this life to those lives
—too dry to nourish, thin for shelter—
where the animal cry, leaning forward
—quick, dangerous, nonplussed—lingers

at low tide, and over the noonday beach
they come running, in the distance flowers
but whores when they arrive

at shipside in wet bathing suits,
hugging their purses and clothes:
Blondie, Red, and crazy Lulu
foulmouthed, swindling, ready to fight.
Breathless over cigarettes, among
the sailors gone green between desire
and spite—hungover, underfed,
lowest of the low,
they fly at the men, clawing
their rancid face with the gull's
covetous voice, unremitting, voracious.

His soul set spinning to starve and freeze,
stranger nothing fits and nothing feeds.
Or is it—stupidly—at once
insensitive and fastidious?

The Father

No voice declares from heaven. Must
we, too, acquiesce in the appalling
ordinariness of this man,
his heart failing and nothing to say?
Awaking, snappish, resentful, confused;
sitting with knife and fork at noon
in judgment on himself;
aching toward dinner, poor boy, newsboy,
fatherless boy, cut clean through,
dying for affection—yet proudly declining
to present his bill to his Maker
(however prudently refusing
to tear it up). One almost smiles
to read of it, although one has,
to tell the truth, sometimes
been a shit, however inexplicitly
complicit, *n'est-ce pas?*

.   .   .

Dying in earnest—as he was earnestly
doing—we are led to ask about
the Maker of the lion and bear,
the infinite night-shining stars,
O bright and brighter than before!
and creatures who go here and there
entangling well their various ways
on this our simple shining star.
Who is He? and by what right made us
not as we are not but as we are?
or loses us and then are neither?
And must we leave these ways, this shining,
such creatures, and the lion and bear
to His bad accounting and His inconstant care?

Humiliated, his ambitions broken,
and never, certainly, a lion at heart,
he sweetens what little he can,
tramping the low domestic earth,
hero of the hearth, the garden's guardian,
carrying the groceries in,
setting them down, brewing his own, pleased
in the pleasure of daughter and son, turning
the TV on, turning it off,
turning it back on,
punctual and solvent and undecided,
meaning none of it,
or standing dazed among the peaceful summer
greens, almost in the distance seeming
an ad's beatitude: idiot-consumer,
aging, awestruck, meek, and grateful
for the profuse and profound rightness
of all this wrongness.
                              Beyond pain,
pessimism; beyond
that, his heart cuts back
—the vise's blank ferocious fix:
fear, bewilderment, betrayal,
enmity, despotism, whatever

he swallowed or spat, all of it,
he bends and crushes together
in a powerful shrug—savagely suppressed.

I will tell you a story, it goes like this.
With waistcoat and a watch (the enormous one
that ticks so heavy, wound down
as ever and running slow), he hurries
into darkness (oh, too late! too late!)
toward a party by now long over,
the garden cleared of cakes and tables,
the little celebrants packed off to sleep
or sent out sleepily to wander
in gloomy lanes, or under hills
that slope away among stones,
led forward, poor dears! by a fictive light.
Tender and round, busy, abstracted,
everything on his mind and his mind
on nothing, quickly pleased, easily affrighted,
he hastens after, unable now
to catch that small courageous band,
hurrying badly and reeling forward,
tired, it is true, yet not disheartened
on his forsaken way where no star shines
and their laughing chatter long since faded,
faded then and reappeared, roaring in lanes
and on the hills, then reappeared, then faded.

The pain of it does not ease; this is
too much, we say, let him have known
before the end his glittering scene:
himself poised with shotgun, two yelping
beagles in a snowy field, a rabbit
never too soon forthcoming from brake
or burrow, the sky total and unexpended.

The Heir

He is a surgeon resectioning the heart.
Confessedly dead, yet the corpse
sits up and shouts at him, "You idiot,
do you know how to do anything right?"
And tries to grab the knife or the dream itself.
It seems to him they are struggling over
the very nature of reality.

On the bed awaking, he who was the doctor
is now the patient. So short the life, so long
the convalescence! Sad, square, and aching,
he accepts his father's dead heart, commonplace,
appalling, and the old man's misery and maiming
return in the son's chest to their brutal beating.
Devoted and good, his normality resurrects
in dull parody that bitterness and failure.

Unloaded, held to his head,
the catastrophic life clicks repeatedly
in the empty chambers.

                              Sitting in our room now
and carried away for a moment, he says, as if
repeating an important lesson, earnestly,
with yearning and with pride, "Actually,
Dad and I have the same sense of humor."

Reredos Showing the Assumption
into Heaven of Frank O'Hara

Farewell, sweet Pinocchio,
Human, all-too-human child,
Dead on Fire Island
Where the bad boys go
On making asses of themselves.
Death ought never have made you good
By altering your flesh to wood.

. . .

Thrust from our theater of cruelty
By a happening of fate,
The mad butch-taxi
That drove you into a state
Alien though near, too like us though far:
O supernumerary and star,
In the bright with-it summer air,
Your impromptu on surreality
Is worthy of our universal flair.
Garbed in death's sticky drag,
Out flat like a *déjeuner sur l'herbe,*
Your body's nakedness will not be late
For its brazenly touching date
With a corner of the Hamptons' turf,

While talents of the *Tout-New-York,*
Catered by a mournful museum,
Entertain eternity before
Your blue eyes' novel tedium,
And ascend from breadlines to headlines
To mumble to your catafalque
Heartfelt idiocies.
Toward cosmic in-jokes like this,
Your attitude is perfectly correct:
Flat on your back looking flat up.
You would have disapproved
Our solemn squish, but

Your spirit now, caught
In a sharp, ascending draft
And crowned with the lyric hair
Of Saint Apollinaire,
Sweeps off to Dada-glory
Amid *sons et lumières,*
Musée of Infinite Inventory
Where all pigments are a sweet
Supplice-délice,
And the lovely paintings leaning
Gaze down at our inferior world.

Lounging in open corridors,
The statues loiter to discourse
In alexandrines that beguile
The covert Muses in the peristyle.
You will write, at last, in French,
And with endless lovely women,
Fleeing their heavy husbands' exigence,
Play duets upon the piano.
Your Curatorship will be
The *Catalogue raisonné des derniers cris.*
Assemble, collate, file, remit to us,
Via pneumatiques of heaven-sent confetti,
Your final views of our sad Cosmopolis.

Seeing Red

I

Twice a week, fantastic and compelled,
Bette Davis in her latest film,
beyond the half-drawn window shade, voice
ablaze, she yanked a suitcase off the bed,
unloosed the death ray of a drop-dead stare,
the parting gusts of her furious red head.
"You'll see!" she screamed and slammed the door.
So?
    So nothing. She crept back in
and cried and fell asleep and slept.
A lion was on the landing,
a mouse was in the marrow inching.
Cornered, she poked at the burning eyes,
she spat at them, she hissed.
Fury and Misery.
The lion leaped and tore her thighs,
mice were gnawing in her feet.
A restless girl, a rotten period.

"Feh! She talks like a mocky."

                So, my sisters

while we lie and peep across the airshaft.
Then I, like the summer dawn's ambitious sun
—eager to shine and burning to please, pink
with preference—ignite my gift for scorn
in the absence of understanding.
(Let them be praised! these red-haired sisters,
they taught my senses' prosperous bride
the famine arts of transcendence:
bitching, snobbery, condescension.
Their smell, the pale juvenile nighties,
the bloodlettings of their reddened fingernails
on passionate mornings—damp and idleness
and tempers and kicking in the tangled sheet
—brought me to a woman's country
of warmth, disorder, and cruelty,
biting envies and a smoldering shame,
so that I don't know yet if my mockery
is defending a privilege or a pain.)
My act is idiot approval that stings
her sleep. I am the little devil spurred
to spank those cheeks and roust her from bed,
nerves afire with sarcasm and applause.

    2

One day, I think, driven as always,
she got to the door and didn't stop,
set off with her squat delirious suitcase
to wow America, or marry
—like an absentminded salesman,
his dirty wash in the sample case,
and they want it! they buy!
Who needs talent, with such despair?
What else is America for!
Bad news, bad breath, bad manners,
the grievous suitcase marches on,
prophesying from every corner.
"Betrayal!" it screams
and snaps itself shut.
What a start in life!

those scraps of rumpled underwear and clothes,
sloppy habits, bad teeth, a roaring tongue,
a crummy job and worse marriage.

   3
Straddling your freckled shoulders,
riding high and sly in 'sixty-nine,
smiling (no less!) and sentimental,
each time I shift gears, underfoot
I feel your wronged hysteria
revving in the block. What
have they done to your gut?
                              Cracked
moon, homeless ginger cat,
I want to take off on you,
pilgrims to nowhere,
streaking toward Skid Row
and failure like the vast frontier.
My young heels drum
excitedly on your tits.
At midnight you awake and cry,
My pride is injured,
my soul is empty,
my heart is broken,
my womb has died.
O my brother,
avenge me!

Rising beyond the pane,
red and pale, feverish, gaunt,
burnt crust but raw dough,
you grip your satchel
and leap through the window into
the middle of the Great Depression,
your eyes endowed with total misunderstanding.

   4
Would it be too fatuous of me
and too late, too squeamish, too phony,

too perfectly American,
touching three small fingers to my brim,
to say across thirty feet of foul airshaft,
thirty years of life, "Help you with your bags, Red?"

The Warriors and the Idiots

Our themes were three: defying dangers,
triumph over dangers, respite
from danger. And weapons, four: knife
and light, blood and the burning maxims:
Stain a breast before you foul your pants.
Pay twice the price, if you pay at all.
Defend father and mother, kith and kind.
These others were not warriors: ninnies
and nuts, the palsied pencil vendor,
Mongolians, morons, the dwarf. Strewn about
like pumpkins, squash, or stumps grown over
with moss, they lay quietly beyond
the law, observed no imperative,
enacted no command, these children
too cruelly punished in the womb
to endure a second forfeit. Stultified
by darkness of the forty days, they had,
as if tumbled from a broken crate
or shivered constellation, rolled to a stop
in the sun, like damp oranges, like fallen moons.
Wherever we went, their grunts admonished us:
There is no victory, there is survival.
No, there is only recollection.
You think you have survived because
you can remember when you were
at once both swimming and drowning.

Even Messiah of dogs and cats
will overlook them on his final errands
through the streets, and Paradise take place
without their spoiled hosannah, they content

to remain at any angle whatever
in the sun for all eternity.

Night and the Maiden

The children run away, they hide,
teasing the twilight on the leaves,
they scatter under shadows, their eyes
blink out, their voices vanish.
She follows and calls them in to sleep,
her cry impatient, but hears itself,
astonished, flirts alone, succumbs, desires
labor, desires a companion solitude,
and rises to compel the listening stars.

Toward her the stars send forth their night
—prince, husband, stranger, death—
bearer of the dark illustrious names.
He overtakes her in the wood.
She is startled by the dark pursuit,
a brilliance fallen too close.
Having come so far tonight,
leaping over all the ways,
dropping toward sleep, he draws
his darkness from the sky to light
within the empty heavens of her flesh
the lost inviolable stars.

Elegy for a Suicide

I

Behold, these flowers of the field,
how deft they are at their windy games!
Unjustifiable, unjustified,
they are not weeping,
while you stand apart, growing thin

among the prattle of the flowers, their tidy,
childish sentences:
                    Naughty! cries the daisy.
Yes, you pumpkin! the other replies.
Will you give me one? asks the rose,
for me and Linda?
And bend together gossiping, telling
the sweet things they have eaten.

            2

Feeding the children, we overcome chaos;
their eating blesses the food, blesses
the monotonous manna of our lives, feeds
our hunger for meanings. It is our commonest
form of prayer, naming the bread-word in the bread.
The blessing, too, they eat; the blessing's blessed;
eternity emerges at its growing point.

            3

Tyrants, these girls convict their lives;
ruthless, humiliated beyond endurance,
will not be appeased, they want
nothing! abhor the common food,
push it away imperiously, command
a better thing, then get it themselves
from the box; their frustrated wills conjoin
with a guilt—that is a frenzy! Now
unbearable to think two thoughts at once.

            4

Who is the child who will not eat?
Who knows her name? Can't she be found?
She is a secret, breakfast and dinner
preferring death; turning away,
saying nothing, unhappy child.

            5

The little girls are calling the big girls
about them, for instruction, to play house
and teach them to behave—out in the backyard.

Why do you linger in a corner and won't play,
your black hair curling, eyes sullen, trembling,
thin? Ghost already? Your breath so bitter?
They want you for mother, calling in flat voices
stiff with light, Play with us! Play with *us*!
So shy of the light, you stoop to tie something
with a sudden erratic energy, hiding
your face, your fingers tighten, you drift away.
Excited, the children rush forward
shouting, Here's the baby bird again!

6

Hungry for destinies, if only
to find a crust, I follow.
Starving, if I demand of you,
will I be fed?
Past the broken ring of children
jumping in place, calling; concealed,
you lean your head on the tree,
stepmother to yourself, waif, and groom.
Gathered to bless the emptiness,
you impersonate a family,
giving, taking, in the perpetual
moment, impossible wine.
Faltering, jarred, reaching,
what do you see? Quick,
your secret, is it a destiny?
Is something fulfilled?
Louder! What are you saying?
That you're urgently, mortally *hungry*?

7

A sparrow hops to the plate.
The past is a crumb to him.
He flies away. He comes back.
He eats it, miraculous food!
Children totter at him, exploding their hands.
He flies off. A circle is completed.
They put out a second morsel.
Eternity is this crumb to him.

He possesses and divides it,
fulfilling the law.
Accursed, all parents cry
that all they have done is useless,
the unjustifiable bread unblessed!
You have cast a profaneness everywhere
but on these children, sacred for your sake.

To Waken You with Your Name

Almost at dawn, she babbles
the names of her childhood,
precious dolls dressed up
because they have to please:
Let go! Don't touch! Stop it!
Well, they guard her too,
though spiteful at times and nasty
and wanting always to have
their toes kissed. Tumbled hair
has touched her sleep. It is such
a little way to go . . . if the dolls
do not mislead. A breeze
feathers her hair. Hush it! Oh why
is the soul sent on errands
in the dark? with its list
of names, its fist of pennies,
its beating heart? Why, to buy
an egg, of course. See,
hen hides her egg under
the sycamore tree—smart girl!
The meadownight smiles and
rolls over in sleep. Startled,
in flight, all ears, she stares
from its edge at the old ladies
under parasols dragging
the morass of their legs.
Their smiles are tranquil and tiny,
solicit her to come

over to them. Heartbroken,
she bolts from the death-wall,
outspeeds her reckless body
that runs on its flittering shadow.
Arrow, what do you desire?
Nothing Everything Nothing
—I was born on the empty air,
cloud tops were my cradle,
and I am two, and one, and two.
To have been a child is such
responsibility—to keep
those old people from dying
you may have to stay child forever.
Who-am-I? is pretending she's
asleep, the lazy thing!
Who-was-I? makes herself
useful and carries the names
for her in a special box.
And whom will the child marry?
for marry she must. If ever
I marry, it will be
no one named in any book
ever written or read. *Who-will-
I-be?* is someone else's
doll, displeases her, she will
say a bad word to it,
and throw it down, and refuse
to look back.

To waken you, Carmen
Fidela, with your name,
I linger at your sleep's side, but
can I be gentle enough
touching you with these beams?
the day asks. And it *is*
day, called so by every chance.
Then happily the arrow climbs
to the height and sees that all
is there abiding faithfully
in the light with open eyes.

Awake, my dawn, my daughter,
sings the day, I have no
tenderness that is not you,
no distance untouched by you
idling and singing here,
for whose sake I have
abandoned the night.
I am no longer dreaming,
she says, but have I done
what I set out to do?
Both now and never,
it is you, says the day,
you and none other
entirely in this light.
Day, touch me, call me again!
she cries a second time,
for I wish to awake.

From *Lost Originals*

As Fast as You Can

Loosed from the shaping hand, who lay
at the window, face to the open sky,
the fever of birth now cooling, cooling?
I! said the gingerbread man leaping
upright laughing; the first faint dawn
of breath roared in his lungs and toes; down
he jumped running.

Sweet was the dream
of speed that sped the ground under, sweet
the ease of this breathing, which ran
in his body as he now ran in the wind,
leaf in the world's breathing; sweeter still
the risk he was running: of boundaries first
and then the unbounded, a murderous
roadway that ended nowhere in trees,
a cat at creamspill looking up, mysterious
schoolboys grabbing.

(Certainly they saw him,
a plump figure hurrying, garbed in three
white buttons, edible boots, his head a hat
in two dimensions.)

Powerfully then
his rhythmic running overtook the dream
of his flight: he was only his breathing.
He said, entering his body, *Like this
I can go on forever.*

Loping and leaping
the fox kept pace, hinted, feinting, over
and under wherever, licking his chops
and grinning to the hilt of his healthy gums.
Breathing to his toes the man ran faster,
free in a world that was suddenly growing
a bushy tail and a way of its own.
No less his joy for the darkening race!

Brilliant thought had dawned to his lips;
he understood it: Thrilling absolute
of original breath! and said, *The world
desires me! Somebody wants to eat me up!*
That stride transported flying him off
earth and mystic into the fox's maw
blazing. One with the world's danger
that now is nothingness and now a tooth,
he transcended the matter of bread.
His speed between the clickers was infinite.

Tell them this, that life is sweet!
eagerly he told the happy fox
whose pink tongue assenting glibly
assuaged the pure delirious crumbs.
(Others fable otherwise, of course:
having outsped our sight, he dazzles
the spinning heavens, that fox our senses'
starved pretention. How else explain
the world's ubiquitous odor
of sweetness burning and the absence of ash?)

Shimmering and redolent, his spirit
tempts our subtlest appetite—there he runs!
freely on the wind. We sniff a sharp
intelligence, lunge and snap our teeth
at the breathable body of air
and murmur while it is flying by,
Life is unhappy, life is sweet!

The Titanic

Secret in a woman's coat, her hat,
his face hidden by a veil, crazy
with fear and shame there among women
and children shivering in the boat,
he escaped huddled over an oar
on the cold and coldly misted sea.

His last sight was the deck awash and screaming.
Sick to the depths of his stomach,
he retched on the gray Newfoundland shore
and drowned in the bitter syncope.
Under a hovel roof, he woke
naked in a woman's arms and could
remember nothing, having become
what henceforth he would call *himself.*

One hundred fathoms down, withdrawn
from every future and larger than life,
with nothing left to lose or wish, the Titans
sit in their eternal afterglow
and with glorious instruments—
curving, belled, and fluted, the fruits
of a golden age—blow upward,
in vast unison and bubbling serenity,
toward the solemn void, the dizzying precipice,
Nearer My God to Thee!

My Olson Elegy

> *I set out now*
> *in a box upon the sea.*
> —MAXIMUS VI

Three weeks, and now I hear!
What a headstart for the other elegists!
I say, No matter! by any route and manner
we shall arrive beside you together.
Envy, Triumph, Pride, Derision:
such passionate oarsmen drive my harpooneer,
he hurls himself through your side.
You lie and wait to be overtaken.
You absent yourself at every touch.

It was an adolescent, a poetboy,
who told me—one of that species, spoiled,
self-showing, noisy, conceited, *épatants*—

voice breaking from the ego-distance like
a telephone's, not a voice indeed
but one in facsimile, recon-
stituted static, a locust voice,
exhumed, resurrected, chirring
in its seventeenth year, contentedly
saying, "And I've just completed
section fifteen of my Olson elegy."

Landscape on legs, old Niagara!—all
the unique force, the common vacancy,
the silence and seaward tumultuous gorge
slowly clogging with your own *disjecta,*
tourists, trivia, history,
disciples, picnickers in hell;
oh great Derivative in quest
of your own unknown author, the source,
a flying bit of the beginning blast,
sky-shard where early thunder slumbers:
the first syllabic grunt, a danger,
a nameless name, heaven's tap on the head;
you, Olson! whale, thrasher, bard of bigthink,
your cargo of ambergris and pain,
your steamy stupendous sputtering
—all apocalypse and no end:
precocious larvae have begun to try
the collected works beneath your battered sides.

See them now! dazzling elegists
sitting on their silvery kites on air
like symbols in flight: swooping daredevils
jockey for position, mount a hasty breeze
and come careering at your vastness
to read among the gulls and plover
—but the natural cries of birds do not
console us for our gift of speech.
Embarrassed before the sea and silence,
we do not rise or sing
—wherefore this choir of eternal boys

strut and sigh and puff their chests and stare
outward from the foundering beach.

King of the flowering deathboat, falls,
island, leviathan, starship night,
you plunge to the primitive deep
where satire's puny dreadful monsters,
its Follies and its Vices, cannot reach,
and swim among their lost originals
—free, forgotten, powerful, moving
wholly in a universe of rhythm—
and re-enter your own first Fool,
inventing happiness out of nothing.
You are the legend death and the sea have seized
in order to become explicable.

—Smell of salt is everywhere,
speed and space burn monstrousness
away, exaltation blooms in the clear:
fair weather, great bonanza, the high!
—swelling treasure, blue catch of heaven.
The swimmer like the sea reaches every shore.
Superlative song levitates from lips
of the glowing memorialists,
their selves flash upward in the sun.

Now you are heavier than earth, everything
has become lighter than the air.

Hump

Arriving at last, he threw down the burden from
his back, his hump, the mailpouch his father.
Well, he thought, straightening, *these* letters
will never be delivered, unless themselves they go.
As if in answer, glittering and quick,
as white as milk, the ancient promises dove

into the pores of the ground.
                              Hump stayed put,
fuddle-fardel changed and changing.
It made him laugh and weep to see
his heap: marvelous callosity
of passed possibles and plenty's
opalescent horn, the little fluxflocks,
oh made him weep and cheer to hear
love's lithe youngtongue's shaping song

mouthoozemuse
titwitwoostalk
stablebabelburble
mamadrama
murmur-butt
plum plump lump bump
mud-udder
underhump of moo-maid
clod of milkmud, of claycud
tongue of muddlemodeler spoon and spade
babyshape
so tender to touch: smother sup
sleeperslupper
bloomballoomboom
sayseedsomescatterthing
thunder lung
a ling a ling am
goat goad 'em scrotum
god prod in pod
rosey ring
hole hilly high light
skyskullscald
and down fall all!
humpty-thump in sulph-muddlepuddle
                in self-meddlepedal
                in silt-middlepiddle
dauphin-coffin
tumblestone and rubblebone
apocalumps
all out! all off!

and all groan up!
                    Last leaped forth
leathery, wizened-wise, he, Humpback self,
and stood curved, panting before him as if
from long labor, then stoopingly strutted,
confronted, while himself tender touching
and frotting a bald spot frayed on his back.
He saw the Hunch was tiny as a child,
aged as a sire, cackling as a goose, crackling
as fire, tricky as trouble is was he,
manjock grizzled, fizzled, fiercer-farcer,
stick stuck in earth, bent body C,
and held a bag of pennies, held a key.

So that is what you look like, he addressed
the humped one. Who are you? My father are you?

You who are, impostor?
What have done with son,
child of dreams, child I would have been?

Father, he I am, that very child!

Then I'll eat you up, you worstwurst, you father
-fodder, huffed the gnome, puffing and swelling
and showing the sharkshead that grew from his back.
For I am thy father-farter, thy thunder-thudder!

Eh? Say again! I dare.

                    I am die fudder
-flooder, die dunder-dudder, die blooder!

And my sputter spitter! How could runt you
eat me giant? he asked his father.

If no respect, no, oh pity then me
who need a thousand years to straighten back,
so long have bent at dismal diking,
abandoned, alone, and none relieves,

bitter nights bright days, wanting wee,
waters within, without, withholding.

Not shamed you seen such bad posture?
Now tears he could not withhold.
Many they were, obedient to gravity.
O better I had never been born!
bitter I niver bin bone, 'lone and muvverless on erf!
His numbed lips could scarcely make the sounds.

If father curses life, what shall son say?
Nothing. So said he never and never.
But hunchback held not his peace:
Pursuing future, dreaming self,
half of you has been desire,
other half, conceit,
but desire does not savor always,
sweet conceit sours in its season.
Bitter bastard, do not deny me, do not
refuse my legacy! I am your father
and your father's fathers. I am your key,
crouch on my here heap, this hump
of refuse, wreckage, scurf. Pisgah my.
Sinai. Moriah my. My Ararat.
Foresee I promised earth, son and city. Way
is narrow, is hard, passage difficult,
wince will you going through. Go, too, I
may not, help shall, save you maybe,
am key.

He touched the hunchback's back and found it ridged
like the frozen sea. Indeed, he was the key.
Quickly he turned him in the lock then.
Key melted, and hump broke
and stone broke, the river ran by.
Briefly he saw blue eyes bubbled, floating
on the water, their gaze of pain, puzzlement,
eternal shyness too too much to say goodbye.
And wild water's mouth sucking itself down, drowning,

shouted, Save yourself, you sonofabitch,
but save me too, save our family, our history!

Stooping he drank the knowledge that flowed
at his feet like a mountain stream, so cold,
so strong, so pure it humbled and broke his mouth,
stung his ears and stopped his heart
like sentence of death: the taste
beyond spitting out, extenuation,
of his unmitigable mediocrity.

He knew then he was not free,
but of what he was not knew not,
nor to what end or why.

The Jumping Children

The field is lively with children. Although it is night and sleep is
commanded, they are awake, linked perhaps in secret to the
antipodes, the day. Dressed in the styles of forty years ago, like
discontinued angels, they do not move forward or back, they are
jumping, crying as they rise, I want to be, I bet myself! singing
as they sink, I am my point of repose, no other.

These, who have just begun to master the simultaneous leaping and
wing-beating, repeat their abrupt impromptu floppings like
dancers warming up who take off without apparent cues,
collapse before completing the arc; while others, as if testing the
ground underfoot, hop a bare bit, never exceed the measure,
come down with patient zeal.
Some jump higher and higher, bounding up in great leaps, their
little throats swell like gulls', they soar and sing. The joy in
descent is no less than the leaping, their concentration is
absolute, their fall is flying. Afoot, they lift their knees like
runners after a race, half-bend from the waist, and windily
shake their dusty cloth wings on the clattering wire frames.
The cripples with withered legs, with powerful crutch-wielding

shoulders, who—if they were actual children—would have scuttled after the crowd of racers, one side dragging, the other leaping forward, jump now in eager hobbled verticals, balancing on useless legs until their arms take hold and lift them from deformity.

The children with the largest pinions leap lowest, endure longest, appear in their endless hovering hardly to move at all, comets whose flight so far exceeds a lifetime they seem never to absent the sky, as though they attended an unending revelation.

These others flex knees and drone until their heads reverberate with the sound of motor flight, suddenly their chests' marvelous din lifts them before their legs can spring.

Unaware of the power of fragility, little hunchbacks, with their mysterious conformity to invisible circumstances, crouch and hop on one leg only.

Jumping is a pleasure, a mystery. And it is exciting to be among so many. Breathing the space, they refine themselves, each becomes his single substance. Straining, he leaps, his leap overtakes him, jumping lightly onto his shoulders.

Now they are bounding in the beautiful dark interim, eager to jump from the embrace of your fantasy, to be actual children who press bright bobbing faces against the high windows and peer into the darkened room, where you lie in bed imagining their ebullient society. Even now, they crowd the street at your door, call you out with irresistible greetings.

Morton's Dream

Dying, Morton saw a child who was
the child he'd been, who would become
the man he is, now almost no longer
is—already the boy's shoulder had
huddled subtly forward as if it cradled
a heart attack, some incurable effort
at perhaps an impossible freedom;
he seemed, bright against the subtracted

dark, to have banished every background.
Then Morton understood the missing world,
the hidden heart attack were one.

Could he have stopped him, crying out,
"You, go back! for out of every
possibility, you alone will die"?
His throat was glued shut. The child
no less pursued him, loomed forward, soon
would be as large as he, soon be him.
Or would have waved him off . . . but the boy,
helpless or too resolved, made no sign,
did not stop. Then Morton touched crushed hand
to broken mouth and sucked the pain it held,
and huddled in mourning for the child—
father, son, himself, his heart, which?
—missing forever from Paradise.
Culpable, the bitterness of his shame
united with the mystery of death
in something he could only call hell.

Behind a high overshadowing wall, dark,
barred, forbidding—surely that is
Eden, he thought—he heard the creatures
he had refused to be, harelip, crocochild,
calf's head, lung, shy imperfect beasts,
carouse, thump, groan, mutter coarse
unwordable noises, strangled gutturals
that shuddered in him as if, deep within,
a giant hand was slamming doors.
He thought, If I could see them once again
I might not die. So great his yearning,
one door stayed open a crack, a slit . . .
quickly all of him slipped through.

The Marvel Was Disaster

1

Aboard the wreck, passengers crowded
the windows, peered out. And saw
a band of children struggling in the surge
of a purely green and sunlit field.
How amazing the field's swift flow
forward, and that children had appeared
plunging toward them at its farthest border!
And they, happy to forget their obvious
wounds, were thinking, So, we are wrecked
relative only to all the rest, with which
we no longer keep pace, no longer desire!
Forgive their error, they desired so much
—how else could they be dying?—and yes,
they heard far off the children courageously
singing Courage! to their reviving hearts.
See there! see there! they shouted inwardly,
each gesturing in his throat to a child
overwhelmed and farther off than ever
but pressing toward them with all its might.
Nonetheless, in thought at least and blindly,
they were leaping forward for the rope
the distant hands held out . . . leaping
for a point a world at last
without direction.

2

The children who came across the field
to gawk at the fabulous disaster
found it toppled in a dry ravine,
its forwardness collapsed, its body
smashed open, rusted out, gutted;
inside it nothing, stale emptiness,
the smell of old air in a tire—unless
the little babble they thought they heard
was cries of children crying out, or beating
of something, a heart, hidden, marvelous.
Swiftly the marvel was disaster.

Within the wreck, a whirlwind
blew up their lungs,
and looking out they saw the pasture:
a garden of cut gestures, blown away,
crushed in the sudden distance
—little bridge, bright morning, themselves
standing there, dwindling
in the infinitesimal splendor,
a pinhole blazing lost light.
No star can bring it back!
At this speed, in this darkness, they know
they won't get out again, ever.

X

am I speaking to you
    yes

are you listening to me
    yes

what time is it
    it is too early to say

how early is that
    before the bird,
    before dawn

is it dark
    yes

what is that
    your breathing

and that silence
    that is silence

where was I
    with darkness, death
    far away

. . .

and how did I come here
    breathing,
    asking questions

is it still too early
    yes,
    I cannot say yet

why can't you say
    I must listen

ought I to be frightened
    no,
    you must not be frightened

shall I go on asking questions
    I cling to your voice

will that be very long
    yes,
    not longer than you can endure

and then what will happen
    I shall say you are my child,
    the dead will arise

at dawn
    at dawn

and will I have my things back
    I don't know

will I want them still
    I don't know

what were they
    your toys,
    your tribe

. . .

why did you give them away
    you were dying,
    I thought so

was that right of you
    wrong,
    bitterly wrong

did I cry
    I don't know

why do you say I don't know
    I don't know

are you being honest
    I don't know,
    no

what time is it now
    dark

and will I have children of my own
    they will be numberless,
    they will name you in their prayers

will I hear their prayers
    you will hear them
    listening for you

is that what you are doing now
    yes,
    I am praying

will you be my child
    yes,
    if I can

what is my name
    you will know it

        .   .   .

will I remember that I was dead
    as in a dream
    only

where am I now
    near me,
    near my ear

am I as close as that
    yes,
    closer

but why am I dead
    I cannot say that

won't you tell
    I am afraid

did you kill me
    yes

were you alone
    yes,
    there were others

why don't you speak louder
    I am afraid

who were they
    very many

and am I alone
    no,
    you are many

who
    father
    fathers
    son
    sons

brother
brothers

why should I be born again
    I cannot live without you

are you also dead
    yes,
    I am dead

will you be born again
    I think so

are you me
    yes,
    also

will I have to stay a child
    I don't know,
    I don't think so

will I have a body then
    yes

where is my body now
    lying
    in a field
    on a hill
    near a tree

will I forgive you
    yes,
    I am unforgivable

why
    you will hear my prayer

and then I will assent
    I don't know
    I think so

. . .

why will I assent
    I don't know

and am I messiah
    yes

and messiah is a dead child
    yes,
    from the dead kingdom,
    hunting his children

and will I find them
    I don't know

and will I come to you at dawn
    promptly

and you will be here
    yes

and you will assent to my return
    I will try

and will you succeed
    if I hear the words

what are they
    I don't know,
    my words

what is assent
    my heart overflows

will my heart overflow
    with light,
    yes

may I sleep now until it is time
    I cannot endure
    not to hear you

. . .

will you continue to listen
    yes,
    that is my prayer

and you will hear
    breathing,
    you,
    I think

can you say more clearly
    no

will you wake me in time

Birth Day

And arrives where all are strangers, all
are kind. He thinks, We are familiar, surely,
since they are kind, and yet seem strangers
—or I am someone other than I think,
myself the only stranger.
                         They come close
now with smiles and offerings, with large
sounds, with faces luminous and vague,
with gestures inviting one to sit down,
to dine, to take one's ease, to stay
among them or, if one chooses, to leave
in peace, but later, later on. He thinks it
endlessly, teasingly perplexing; he asks,
Whom do they find so lovable? Someone
they are awaiting? Am I that person?
And believes himself an impostor
imposing, a grabber of gifts intended
for others, but senses afterward
how impersonal their kindness, how
profound their courtesy, that they should
have greeted him as brightly had he been
any other.

This is reposeful, a final
kindness, a tact, not to require response
and answers. If there was another life,
he hardly remembers it now, or if
he came this way on a particular
errand, and cannot declare for certain
this is the place he started for.
His gestures mean to say, *No matter,*
I will not oppose your kindness or stay
estranged or go away from you ever.

The Party

In the flat cosmic suburbs
beyond Altair, there
too they decant and sip, space
is a continuous seething
of lively chatter that is
very much our lively chatter.
And in the suburbs beyond
beyond-Altair, beyond
everywhere, in fact, the same
tinkling and telephones, the same
closing of frigidaires,
a generous hubbub of voices
like our voices,
the same odor and press of persons.

The last last vacancy
has been filled, and far off
the grains of space tip
and drift toward us, bumping
into others not unlike,
and now there is someone
who arrives at the party
just a little late,
garbling apologies,
glass in hand, a trifle high,

to be sure, looking
like the neighbor next door
and saying that "out there"
is "in here," that
really nothing is beyond,
nothing that is not ourselves,
since the universe is us.

Space leaks through the floor,
and goes on to other
parties on other stars
that are, of course,
the same parties,
the same stars.
In the spacelessness where we are
as we are,
oh, beautifully immanent,
buzzing, swarming, completely
in touch with everything,
we raise glasses and voices
and rapidly say all
the names of which we can
think, to toast
whatever it is
is missing our lives.

Rue Gît-le-Coeur

Come look at the girls, said Edward
from the window, rue Gît-le-Coeur.
We ran to look.
Stories down, some black queens
stood shrieking in the street. Then
the burble of Paul's tolerant chuckle
accompanied their disfigured joy; then
two Arab boys drifting through the flat
as through remembered desert, it was
as dry almost, as dusty as that.

At noon another—ex-student of
the medical fac—could be seen
waking in a farther room: some
swarthy figurine washed up among
the dingy rivulets of a sheet,
rubbing sleep-sand from his eyes
with fragile dirty fists.
Half old pasha, half mamma,
Edward pottered in a tattery robe,
emptied ashtrays, vaguely dishragged
a table, childlike handed 'round
bits of Dada curios in polyglot,
clippings, photos, collages of
outmoded monsters, broken, twisted limbs.
Someone said it made him think
of shreds of Greeks hanging, heaped
in the cyclops' cloaca-eye-and-maw,
the roaring cave's dark doorway. Speaking
of Greeks, Paul, tamping his pipe
with a scorched thumb and puffing, explained
about the war between the gods of earth,
the gods of air, the former smoldering,
blasphemous, full of spite, the latter
quick, arrogant, deceitful, thundering.
Was this place a pinnacle or hell?
Babel, perhaps. Hell on high.
Now we could smell the darkness in our light.
At two, the psychoanalyst from Łódź
came in, years and years out of Auschwitz,
a neo-nihilist loaded with matches
from the Holocaust. Little flames
leaped from his coat, from everywhere
about him, his eyes gleamed, his forest hands
rubbed cracklingly together and he laughed,
certain that nothingness would be
preceded by fire, and every brilliant
horror have its utterly dark sabbath.
In that faith, he glanced around the room
and rested.

The Tenor

The tones are pure,
                               but in his mouth, too much
too long in use, you hear the surging gangs
of children at their grimy murderous game.
They kick up dirt with their heels; they shout, defy,
accuse, drop to a knee and take deadly aim
while their stuttering throats slam bullets out;
when they win, joy careens and smashes through them
like a speeding car out of control; defeated,
they bluster and brood, deflate, droop; they cheat
too often; caught, they jut their jaws, grab for more;
they moralize, they give the raspberry, the finger,
they whisper, mutter, backbite, consume, secrete,
they swear and forswear and bear false witness;
their bickering and deliberate quarrels
wreck the game; furiously, they begin over,
hurl themselves into play with the abandon
of bursting pods; they scatter; they change sides
with swift and passionate righteousness.

Meanwhile, he is singing away
as if there's no such thing as history.
His eyes roll up for the high notes in little
mimicries, he stands on his toes.
The butterfly blue heavens escape
the mile-high nets, something
flickers on the heights, something
not itself not anything else
disappears.
                  Down
in the mouth, wanting
to shove the kids aside,
his tongue flops fuzzily,
caterpillar from the green leaf blown.
It's all *bel canto* and mucky shoes.
You can taste every lozenge he ever sucked.
Gallons in the salons.
Mouthwash carbona cologne beer steam starch.

The fraying vocal apparatus in the closet
is an old waiter's black suit:
stiff with habit, stands at attention, knees
bent, hand held out, pockets distended;
one cuff in the soup, one foot in the gravy;
worm wants it; dog
daunts it; cat kittens on it.
Song?
He mourns mewfully.

If only the world had one unadvertised pleasure!
—and one unmentionable terror!
and one note free of every melody!
he could spit those children out and shut the shop
and live happily humming till millennium comes,
should anything be worth the saving.

After the Flight from Rockaway

They hurry, they take
their utensils, their little
gods with them;
now light
throngs the empty sill,
this purity being
looked through by sunny
lane, by sand, by
unmeaning chop and lilt
of waters.
In the carts
the potted cactus, the
geraniums, the broken
drum and frying pan
and little creaking
chair jolt forward
into exile in
the usual ecstasy
of self-perception.

No one any longer
looks back, and burning,
quick to restore
the empty realm,
leaps to the window dancing.

Our Leaders

No longer troubling to charm, curt,
without cadence, they bark their lies,
impatient of our credulity,
like teachers who repeat the lesson
for idiots stuck on the first page.
They pity themselves, complain
our stupidity forces them to lie,
and say, *Why can't we do as we please?*

Their guile, complaints, their greediness.
Capable of nurture only, we
are like mothers, we nourish them,
believe what they say and repeat it
for one another, knowing the while
credulity isn't enough
and something not easy is required,
a pretense of intelligence,
a sacrifice, a faith they could believe
worthy of their treachery, worth
betraying. It is adversaries they crave,
and what lies we think we hear are
higher truths we have overheard.
                              But nights,
the children sitting in a ring, we take up
the papers, speak aloud the pathos
and mystery of our leaders' lives.
Alone, in dark chambers, in ordinary-
seeming chairs, at the innermost recession
of a thousand thoughts, they reach decisions,
while wives bring warmth and grace and wit

(we venerate their warmth and grace and wit)
when they are tired or under the weather,
servants trot softly in the hallways
with urgent whispers, vehement faces,
and only with the utmost diffidence
their dogs roll over—lips in rictus,
eyes alert, little paws held up like sticks
—begging to have their bellies scratched.
To know this is a constant pleasure!
Then, to move our coarse fingers along the lines,
over the inscrutable words, to murmur their names,
to feel ourselves becoming more human,
to draw close about the fire!
                              At such moments,
overcome by shame for our clamorous natures,
we look down, our eyes seek out the children,
we see their small heads, unimaginably
like ours, bent above the pages, the furious
concentration that grips their innocent,
unblemished faces, their minds that leap ahead
to seize the ending before the tale is done.
This generation, we say to ourselves,
they will be different, *they* will be better!
Powerfully, they bend our eyebeams to themselves
—we see, we *feel* them bending within
our unbreakable domestic circle.
This is awesome, this is more than sweet.
And what would life be without affection!
—it is our solace, our achievement,
it is the language we speak.
It says that everything is true.
And truly, as we disbelieve less, the world
becomes miraculous beyond believing,
though less a place requiring us, less, at last,
our own.
              The thought of our nonentity,
the world without us, this large bare ball
flying empty into the empty day,
is stunning, takes our breath, like something

intimate and alien, like a knife
in the lungs.
        Our leaders chide us,
for sentimental, for living in others,
but can they guess our helplessness?
We break another stick from the ramparts
and thrust it on the fire set blazing
by all the power of our affection
—and another necessary lie comes
quiet from the matterless night, settles
panting beside us, warms a bloody muzzle
between paws, snuggles down toward sleep.
So everything ends, like this, near a fire
in silence and wonder, our fingers idly
soothing a murderer's nape, and somewhere
out there, a last bitter scream doesn't stop.
They don't bother stifling it,
even with a lie.

Meeting in Lyon

The winter night gives birth before me; it is you
hurrying from the mists of Lyon
between the New Hotel and Place Carnot:
shock of dullish hair, widow's peak,
dead uncle's baggy suit, dead nephew's
bursting coat, dirty collar, varicose tie,
suitcase so torn you've webbed it with cord.
In broken French you ask for the bus to Bordeaux.
In broken French I answer, crying out,
That way, sir! with confident misdirection,
never dreaming you'll go, yet off you rush,
limping grandly, swinging your free elbow.
What business could *you* ever have in Bordeaux?
Might as well ask for the bus to Budapest,
the bus to Chicago! Oslo! Maracaibo!
Why kid me, a stranger in the street, asking

for outlandish places, pretending
a life to live and all that says,
history, property, people, god,
that whole landscape of the arbitrary
to give you breath, to call you darling!

And so you go,
country on your back, selves in a satchel,
a cipher becoming the century.
Powerless, you do nothing, recur,
like a myth, echoing around the corner,
stepping off boldly on the wrong foot
toward the empty provinces of rain.

A Balcony in Barcelona

For Madeleine Morati-Schmitt

I

Space abstracts the body, and the eye,
more avid, reaches toward some clinging point
way way off. But it is the twilight,
gentle and victorious as an undertaker . . .
O there are weeping mysteries here, something
I knew that I've forgot, some creature-thought
yawning its drowsy, dim way to the lap
of a little cave. At times like these one feels
suddenly one has misplaced the whole sky.
Now hill and sea are asleep in caves,
and far away the ancient port lights up
and little roads on the slope are lit and go
floating off in the dark immensity.
More, more lights! cries the eye demanding only
the impossible. Grand burial in the air,
the stars in procession—is it my body there,
my eye following it aloft over the city
and over all and on and out of the world?

With so much sky there's so much weather. It's
like being at sea, where the day's wind or sun
are a destiny filling all the time till sleep.
"Looks like rain today," which won't be the same
as yesterday's. Today's weather is today's.
There is no other news on the balcony
but what comes drifting down from above, rain
today, tomorrow sun. We're that close to the gods,
who speak in elements and have no other
business but leisurely conversing, charming
the sky with bolts, with clouds, with subtle
pituitary whispers and large vascular
digressions. Our bodies listen, brought always
to the same postures at the railing to gaze
with the same powerful vague intent. Rain
it is today! A rainy day in Barcelona
is all the rainy days the world will ever need.

Six Sailors

To Pete Foss, God give him good berth!

Shipped deckhand June of 'fifty-one
aboard the *Willis Van Devanter,*
chartered to Union Sulphur and Oil
(stack colors dull ochre, black)
and carrying coal from Norfolk out
to Dunkerque, France, on the Marshall Plan
—old *Liberty* de-mothballed in Baltimore,
shaken down, painted over, and papered
with a pickup crew, scourings of the seven
saloons of Hoboken, Mobile, Camden, Pedro.

Here we are, bosun, carpenter, watches. Jake,
Cox, Wally, Slim, Chips, the Finn, myself,
Ole, Moe, Chris the Dane, Pete Foss, bosun,
average sorts of monster, more or less:
brawler or bragger, wino, nut, nag,

bully, slob, simpleton, thief,
this carp of leaden contempt,
this john aspiring to mackerel,
these sponge, crab, clam,
bottom-feeders almost to a man,
lungless on land, finless afloat,
sifting the margin of muck
with sodden sense and cramping gut.
Adrift in wide iron belly
amid tall waves always at world edge,
sailors are liable to misadventure
into monstrosity, forgotten
elsewhere, lost to themselves.
                                        Near
mutiny, storms at sea, quarreling
drunks, fistfights, a broken screw, two
stowaways, a crewman's fiddle stolen, heaved
overboard or hocked, kangaroo court and Moe
condemned to dine alone for dirtiness,
Wally of the middle watch busting open
lockers, out three days slugging hair tonic,
shaving lotion, as if the stuff were scotch,
Lulu and a second whore clambering
over the barges and hustled below
before the ship had ever touched a dock.
These the adventures, nothing legendary,
just "adventures," nothing more, anecdotes
from someone else's less-than-war.
                                        Otherwise,
our common peaceable humanity's
old routine: chipping gunwale rust,
soogeeing the wheelhouse down, bow watch
under the stars, the coffee pot perking
day and night, the binnacle's hypnotic
click-click-click, meals and meals, cards
in the mess, Pete Foss's lined face pokered
around his pipe, sunning out on the hatches,
winch work, fire drill, boat drill,
endless talk of sex, endless trivial
housekeeping chores of homeless householders

wandering on the wide wide sea, sleep
in the throbbing, rolling, roaring, yawing, shivering tub.

Each from his isolation, each
from transmogrification,
his little pleasure
or lengthy sleep,
a sudden gracing woke;
the mast, our common labor,
a confluence of task and wave,
of waves blown into wind,
the one, the pure transparent day
brought us there together.
At the infinitesimal inter-
section of these historic enterprises,
commercial, national, imperial
within an indefinable cosmic
context, six of us climbed the mainmast
with beak-nosed hammers, buckets of paint
to scrape it clean, to make it new.
Gulls dove, dolphins rolled,
sun swam ahead on the sea,
and we wind-jockeys on bosun chairs
in our thrilled community
let lines go and flew, out around
the dancing lodgepole of the turning sky
that first and dazzling morning of the world.

Bembú a su amada

A María Luisa Pedrosa de Alexandrino y Zaira Elisa Del Olmo

She says, "Bembú" (my cognomen, surname,
Panache, alas!), "poet named too well for lies,
Get out! I will not look at you again!"
She climbs the haughty tower of her wrath
And with a final imprecation casts

Herself naked on the roaring wind.
Dido reigning amid the raging populace

Of her pyre was not half so glorious
As you are stamping your foot on the floor.
My anger fizzles, admiration flares.

By the sainted mother who bore you,
Your worthy uncles and lamented father,
Solid men of esteemed position,
Merchants all of Iberian delicacies
And local products of the highest caliber

Sold in two suburban branches
And in the main store off the Plaza,
O redolent heiress of Park Provisions,
Pensive or busy at the counter
In the cool green depths among the jars

Of saffron, cinnamon, and chili peppers,
The monster cheeses, the Asturian *cidra*,
The pickled parts of *toros de lidia*,
And tins with scrollworked, gilded labels,
Fine testimonia of kings (kings in exile

Or dead long since from natural causes,
Whose fluttering spirits haunt, blue ribbon
In a bluer hand, the fairs of a fairer day)
—Reflect on those dusty, lightless monarchs,
Their proper queens alongside thinking hard

Of dignity and their estates, with skirts
Of stone on stony knees, their consorts,
Loyal in death, loveless and unappealing!
And do not suffer your lovely ear's abuse
By what those whisperers impute to me!

As I respect your blessèd mother,
Your uncles and the family business,
The lace that hems your bourgeois slip,
The droplets gleaming on your tender lids
While you complete the inventory

.   .   .

Or verify a bill of lading, know,
If I could tell you in my voice itself
And not in this impersonation,
I would say I love you all
Beyond approach or approximation.

That I am Bembú, bohemian, poet,
Posturing vainly in the public face,
Have given all my sighs for publication
And your heavenly tears to the dreadful cheeks
Of poetry readers—forgive me, *nena!,*

For I cannot, yet cannot change my purposes.
And what is any other but a pale
And seeable moon burning with the beauty
Of your almond eyes so fierce and sweet
I am blinded if I look one minute!

Too timid to be Homer, for all my mad
Ambition, brightening his night with song
Singing *that* denied his eyes' possession,
I glance aside. The meager sights
Starve my eyes' continual craving.

That flaming day they took you from me
In their shiny, flatulent car, the gloomy
Folk of your family crammed among,
You continued smiling with exceeding
Joy, my heart has not altered to this day.

Wait for me at noon before the store
And I shall escort you in the streets
Of gossips who joylessly contest with tongues,
Those files of envy scraping harmlessly
As cricket legs on the gates of heaven.

We will go the long way 'round, and by
The roundest way return. You shall be seen
To take my arm, I to incline my head.
By these signs we shall be known
Those unknowable noons when the star

. . .

Is burning and stillness both
And both in our sufficing shade.

Translated from the Spanish of Juan Díaz Bembú,
born in Corozal, Puerto Rico, in 1933

To S., Underground

Conceit is not news,
vanity not news,
nor the jaunty cripples of a season,
impresarios to their famous
lyrical humps.
                    And yet
these thoughts keep me awake, or I
awake to keep such thoughts,
insomnia striving
between shame and envy, saved
by neither from neither, between
nihilism and indignation,
beleaguered by both.

But there you are
with a mailing list and three forgotten volumes,
your toe in the door of forty,
faithful to failure—childhood's eternal
province—hard times' new hero
in a last corner of the old place,
sniffing the ancient culture of spilt milk,
living lean in a fat time,

my friend,
of indefinite gestures
that wave the light away,
of smiles of stymied gentleness,
of patient carbons,
your black virgins going gray
but keeping in touch,

and puns that go nowhere punctually,
obsolete timetables
of your misery,
your autumn anthologies
shuffling the loose leaves,
your little flame,
your sadness,
your embarrassed tongue,
old porter fumbling bags,
all unspeakably too much to bear.
You gaze out, and nothing there
dissuades you from your privacy.

S.,
it tempers my mind to think of you,
your tiny vortex, its peaceful dwelling
like water on a drain, dauntless
and quiet, spinning, creative, stooping
to scan the humblest darkness
with diffident clarity;
you are gentle and do not weary
and persist for failure, carrying
your small debris around
and around—the lightest things
the deluge left—and you drop
toward its deeper issue, imagining
the earth's unenunciated
still there where your paradise drowned,
the tribe of lost aboriginals,
thick, buried deep, dumb roots
in a place of restoration.

And so you put children together,
wittily, out of whatever: scraps
you find or rummage in the street,
recollecting these neglected,
the tiniest leavings—bits of stone,
bits of metal, glass, and wood.
And topplingly you pile up your solemn
statuary, these little emigrés

from your childhood's orphanage.
They stand there waiting,
each two-inch child alone in space,
hundreds and hundreds, a millennium
of foundlings in a falling world,

you down there
barely breathing in Brooklyn,
buried live and flinging up
your daily bucket.
The coprophages of success
in the poses of pride, corruption, and wrath
caper on the earth.
You grope in darkness, they grovel in light.

Waking Words

The evening sleeps that stars
may be conceived—see,
they shine, the infant worlds!
How simple that was,
to sleep to the naming
of stars! You slept,
and speech was born in light,
the infant words,
how simple then was!

Come, says happiness,
that anachronism, naming
you and taking your hand
to follow to its early
country. What pleasure now
to see yourself by glow
and fulguration, to be
the star that is here
and star that is there,
the leap and light
—dawn, transparent star!

From *Leaping Clear*

The Handball Players at Brighton Beach

To David Ritz

And then the blue world daring onward
discovers them, the indigenes, aging,
oiled, and bronzing sons of immigrants,
the handball players of the new world
on Brooklyn's bright eroding shore
who yawp, who quarrel, who shove,
who shout themselves hoarse, don't
get out of the way, grab for odds,
hustle a handicap, all crust,
all bluster, all con and gusto all
on show, tumultuous, blaring,
grunting as they lunge. True,
their manners lack grandeur, and
yes, elsewhere under the sun legs
are less bowed, bellies are less
potted, pates less bald or blanched,
backs less burned, less hairy.
                              So?
So what! the sun does not snub,
does not overlook them, shines,

and the fair day flares,
the blue universe booms and blooms,
the sea-space, the summer high, focuses
its great unclouded scope in ecstatic
perspection—and you see it, too,
at the edge of the crowd, edge of the sea,
between multitudes and immensity:
from gray cement ball courts under
the borough's sycamores' golden boughs,
against the odds in pure speculation
Brighton's handball heroes leap up half
a step toward heaven in burgundy, blue,
or buttercup bathing trunks, in black
sneakers still stylish after forty years,
in pigskin gloves buckled at the wrist,
to keep the ball alive, the sun up,

the eye open, the air ardent,
festive, clear, crowded with delight.

Was. Weasel. Isn't. Is

WAS

Was dark things bleeding away beyond
their outlines, was walls roaring, closing in,
or subsiding in bruised, unaccountable
oblivions. Suddenly, the lights came on:
growing, he was learning, was learning that
bodies and things at ease in their auras
must not be touched until they consent,
can not touch until you say they can.

And everywhere the sun, the early light.
And they, with large features, with large limbs,
benevolent giants in bright colors
on the streets of Brooklyn, moving always
in relation, by courtesy and pleasure,
separate, with a glowing separation,
defined and with a glance of recognition
courting the other's sunlit advancing
definition, the other's passing wish.
Me first! deferred to *After you!*
—with a tip of the hat or a nod
or an arm waving one gallantly on.
There was nothing their enormous bodies,
their gentle manners had not simplified.
Here and there, around a subtle, a consen-
suous point, their purposes, their speeding
maneuvers and high, heady murmurs met
and turned in a dance, a steady pacing:
their salutations smile, *Dear Sir Madam Child!*
their partings are signed with open gestures,
Sincerely Truly Cordially yours.
Distance itself consented, itself was touch.

A constellation swarming in the sun
in a common, a communing vibration.

And drifting at night, going to sleep,
he wished, with what little of his will
was left, no longer to uphold
the gravity of everything. He said
they could, and saw them fall and flow
together, droplets with little lights
starlike, drinking one another mouth
to mouth, conjoining and clarified.
Under the coiling fluency, on the stones:
the body of transparence lying still.
Eyes open, lips to its boundlessness,
he saw this, too, he saw it through and through.

WEASEL

Later, something else: sense
of secrets, choice, couplings, bias,
a broken consensus; sudden
nodes and surging, flares
over a field of crevasses.
Yearning incomplete tender
excited implicated in
the murder of communal majesty
reckless desperate pronged—he feel-
eeleels.
        Blackout.
And reappears: triumph
of skepticism in the guise of sex
—or the other way around—
a weasel in a wolf skin, appetite
probing forward, anguish biting back;
acrid awl-toothed ferrets, first
profaning mammal, his notions run
among the old identities,
grand immobile eggs of great saurians,
stave them in with a paw,
dabble sharp noses in the golden yolk

after the hidden copula, the payoff,
tit-for-tat, gobbet of muck on the palm.
What the hell is it all for?
run fast
consume and void
shake a paw at the shit.
Sudden turning, quick shying
of his snout in revulsion.
Despair composed this snob?
Airs blown
from distant bodies.
Digging down, flings dirt backward.
For great cravings small gravings.
And a muddy mouthful.
Screw my fellow man,
my putz is my brother!
Shame shunts him off.
Cross to the other side of the street.
Cover your tracks, move on.
Bestrides the ruined positions.
To live this caricature?
To *live* it.
Prong stiff into the March wind.

ISN'T

Except for reassembled curiosities,
inarticulate vast bone-stacks visited
by dank schoolchildren in dull museums
(half gawk, the others scrawl initials),
or thunder walking upstate in a low
rainless sky over miserable hamlets
where the dead cars brooding in dooryards
outnumber the starving inbred villagers,
scarcely anything survives from that epoch.

Things as they are.
The even voice
weighs them together and says,
Such *and* such, on *both* hands
—*see,* clod here and *here* cloud,
as they happen to be,
their tactful balance.

The clod in the hand is heavy,
damp, dumb, grainy, old, cold, odd,
composite, shapeless, neutral, small,
sifted through the cleansing worm.
Well, so be it.
                    And so be it.
The sun comes over the cloud,
cloud comes over the clod
—the light, the light-of-hand—
and grass comes up,
singulars out of the earth
lifting their spears and shouting, *Ahhhh!*

Stanzas: The Master's Voice

Piddling small derivations with large
enthusiasm, taking his puddles for seas,
paddling in a sea of stimuli, to which,
playfully, he over-responded:
imagining perils and then the wave
that lifted him to safety while he struck
vainly at its steep and frightening flank,
then tumbled down bump on the waiting shore.
These were the pleasures of his setting out.

Of his arrival the pleasure was the sounds:
whistles, piping, voices, tall hooting in
the trees, among empty places, out

of high rocks uplifted like organ pipes,
clear calls in wells and holes and hollows and halls.
The world had voices, or was itself a voice,
a garrulous race that spoke all at once,
at random and loudly to no one he could see.

What did manners bid him do? Stay silent,
as one too young, as one not spoken to?
Or greet these breathings with his own replies?
He did them both, soundlessly opening his mouth
in tune and time to the calls that sang about,
that rang more faintly now with his grimàcing.
And now beneath he heard the constant scratching sound,

like claws that scrabbled habitations in the stone.
That crackled in his ear as well—his own desire.
Silence then—and then a peeping repeated, like
a small occasional star, was all of sound grown pure.
To father voices, become my father! he swore.
Death had given him a master and vocation.

How easily his competence exceeds the song!
What the master could do once only and then
arduously, he achieves over and over
on the ample pages of his copybook.
He need not strive to compose. Does not. He writes.

The words enclose their own intention.
His art is writing, pure and simple.
He is the completed world's unfailing scribe.
What he writes repeatedly is simply perfection.

Diligence and stillness and peace, his lowered head
and pursed lips, are the little pastime of a large
distraction—he is listening to something else.

From the black shore behind the words, a small child,
a last master, is saying something he can't quite hear.

There is no time, this line has not been written.

Beethoven's Bust

To Richard Howard

The zero year, the dark eel body,
rushes forward, pours over itself
and disappears under the sky's black rock.
Suburban streets and rain in Buffalo
this Thursday night in harsh November.
City an instant above its falls.
The torrent smashes the lip and thunders
into a brief abyss; hither each guest,
trapped by his mediocre buoyancy,
floats on the swift affluence of conceit,
the sweet influence of wine and chatter,
of laughter, food, electric light.
And music now, a phonograph floods
the scene, a warming clatter of song
includes and moves whatever moves within
—and lends these particles a seemly
magnitude, these dissonants a structure;
so music rehears and rehearses, recalls
and recalls the irrevocable until
what cannot be revoked can almost be
desired, and the dumb fact is fate speaking.

In dry sufficient middle age
they come to on this nether shore,
gathered in bright rooms to toast
a *quartetto* on tour, four famous fiddlers
in turtlenecks and tuxes
who, beaming after Beethoven,
paddle the flux and artfully
snack up compliments like ducks.
Now Fortune wakes, now sits up
and rubs her eyes, presides
at the world's first levee.
These happy few, and if fewer
happier, are happy too to feel
their *angoisse provinciale* warming
to provincial self-complacence.

Glances are exchanged:
the continents and capitals
drift into range.
Passwords pass:
the universe is middle-class.
Whoever piqued themselves on making do
with second best, discover now they do not
know one another, have never met, maneuver
by delicate mutual repulsions,
veering to avoid the other's wake as if
it were a wine of desuetude that could make
them ponderous, bristling, and obsolete
—battleships among the swans.
                              Indeed,
they strive to see beyond each other, vie
to see beyond each other's seeing, beyond
even the visiting stars, into
a place never seen, too transparent to be
a place, timeless, too bright. As far
as any eye can see all outside is
a belated guest running for the door,
then nothing more, the dark incivility,
the rain, more darkness, nothing more.
                              Meanwhile,
the successes perfect their extraversion;
their glance when they look at others is bold
and gleams with pleasure and incredulity
—"What, you here? you lucky stiff!"

Whatever his luck, he too is here,
in from the rain to blunder for comfort,
the pleasure of standing in a crowd,
has brought his antique precocity,
his style the changeling prince—unknown
to himself and yet suspecting greatness—
his air startled, indignant, sniffish,
as if he'd caught the devil cheating at cards
or, simply, defecating on the deck.

          .   .   .

Somebody's poet, he is introduced
to somebody's mother. It is poetry
they speak of, not motherhood,
though not at first, for first she recalls
her history, Junker girlhood, husband
—precocious martyr—murdered in a camp
in the thirties; then half casually,
almost a throwaway, "He was not even
a Jew. *Ach,* go read about it
in Shirer, if you like!"—gratuitous
infidelity from which she has not
recovered, will not, forty years after,
forgive.

        Recalling the irrevocable?
Well, music of a sort, someone gagging
on a spine. *This* horror doesn't go down
for all her swallowing, won't come up
for all her saying it out.

                And has *he,*
he wonders, been accused, impertinent Jew
who didn't die? He almost hears the slap,
death repeating its insult on her face,
sees the face stunned white with failure
before it stings red with shame.
So it is better to speak of poetry
—their theme, aptly, Death and the maiden—
while the dark eavesdropper, the final
husband, sidles closer with the shadows,
a mock martini chilling in his hand.
Hair poked out like stuffing from a dollhead
tatter, face scored and delicate and white
—old shell or shipwrecked moon in daylight—
she calls for silence with yellowed fingers
and searching for words stoops and peers,
lady at the oven door who drags out
piping in their pie after fifty years
the verses of her German youth.

        · · ·

Hölderlin, Rilke, Mörike, Schiller . . .
the names of great dead poets drop.
O matinee idols of Eternity,
great brows and noses glimmering to
the farthest rows, the highest balcony,
their oversized Orphic heads now float
along the carpet's lotuses and sing
on death's Parnassus all the endless
artificial noon.
              Just now, tonight,
they are praising loveliness of women
who know that poetry's a caress,
language purified to sweetnothingness,
showers of seed on a shadowy Eve.
Ruhe, Ruhe, she croons aloud. Remembrance
and reverie, release and rest,
engender in a vowel, *Ruhe, Ruhe:*
lulled, tumescent, gravid with
an endless, gray, and even sea,
its Baltic strand where, royal maiden,
she galloped brown horses in the foam.
And who can save her in the swart sea?
Follow me! Follow me! the hooves plash away.
Poor bedeviled prince who cannot rest,
into the sea's little profundity
he whips his marvelous mount, out toward
the water charm, the voices, and the voice
within the voices revealing his name.

Only the swell wrinkling under a wind,
a wake too wide to be a wake,
a world too wide to be the world,
nothing there, no one to save,
no maid, no martyr, no people,
and the prince himself gone far under,
weighed down by armor, waterlogged.
Only a child's kingdom under the wave,
the first light darkening, the faintest babble
from above, a muted sociable flutter
of tunings, teasing, footsteps, puffing

that blows out the candles on the cake,
a fading cheer!—music too awkward
and small, too homely and young to leave
its little orchestra, spoons shovels beds
(domestic murmur and tinkle and tears),
too brief to recall time from other places
or send it spiraling in long eddies.
A crone like a cork bobbing in time!
A generation whirled beyond his senses!
He braces to take it all on his back,
to uphold the flood, if flood is all there is.
Lungs scorched with salt, about to burst,
he sees the silver burble of his cry
gaily ascend the silent deep.
The chain of light fishes him out.

Surfaces and kicks for shore, escapes it all
—with what alacrity! Swallows sweet heavens.

So we are born, in our instant of greatest
terror. The mighty stay long until
they leap screaming for the world; others
patter in as lightly as the rain.
From nameless dying he could not bear,
he is born naming the horror, choking
on the name.
        Dawn.
             And now
you hear a first intelligent croak
sounding in the littoral grass
—human, almost; suddenly you
imagine the eyes, *if* you can bear it!—
then farther off and going fast, as though
toward its dismal lair, the patter perhaps
of light *faux pas,* then
a little sigh at last.

So, *voilà!* here they are after all,
high and dry in the corner
of a darkened parlor, on a sofa

tilting off toward the end of time,
mediocre muse, poor poet—he
doesn't please, she can't inspire—
cast away from the party together,
almost like maiden and boy
their matchmaking families marooned
and already seem hardly to miss
—while elsewhere in other rooms
the party sorts itself through chances
and changes, deferences and differences,
makes a sense of sorts circling around
its empty center, the dead one, the lost
martyr, the silence riddling the structure.

Let us step back now, as the lamplight
seems to, and permit them, semi-
strangers abashed and silent, to sit
forgotten where time's plunging
has flung them for a moment half-
unaware in puzzled abstraction.
Each, absorbed by his divergent dreaming,
dreams alone, but in our departing view
disposed as if they occurred
on a picture's visionary plane,
neutral, full, abstract, eternal
—she a princess at seventy
shaking off death's importunate arm
around her shoulder, he
a frog of forty
sitting on Beethoven's bust,
trying to understand.

Leaping Clear

> *Circumambulate the city of a dreamy Sabbath afternoon. Go from Corlears Hook to Coenties Slip, and from thence, by Whitehall, northward. What do you see?—Posted like silent sentinels all around the town, stand thousands upon thousands of mortal men fixed in ocean reveries.*
>
> —HERMAN MELVILLE

1

Excrescence, excrement, earth
belched in buildings—the city
is the underworld in the world.
They wall space in or drag it down,
lock it underground in holes and subways,
fetid, blackened, choking.
                        Shriveled, small,
grimed with coal and ash, shovel in hand,
his dust-sputting putz in the other,
like death's demiurge come up to look
around, to smudge the evening air,
the old Polack janitor on Clinton Street,
turd squat in the tenement anus,
stands half-underground in darkness
of the cellar steps and propositions
passing children in a broken tongue.
Quickly, they crowd, they age, they plunge
into holes, and are set to work.

2

Encountered at estuary
end across beaches and dunes,
or opening out of the breakwater's
armlock, a last magnitude
of bay, or beyond the crazywork
of masts and rigging down a street
suddenly, the sea stuns,
moving into itself, gray over
green over gray, with salt smell
and harbor smells, tar, flotsam,

fish smell, froth, its sentient
immense transparent space.

Walking in Coney Island, bicycling
in Bay Ridge on the crumbling water-level
promenade under the Verrazano,
walking the heights above the Narrows, driving
on Brooklyn Heights, then slowly at night
under the East River Drive past the empty
fish market, past Battery Park, and then
northward driving along the rotting piers,
or looking downriver from Washington Heights
into the harbor's distant opening,
I recovered one summer in New York
the magical leisure of the lost sea-space.
Breathing, I entered, I became
the open doorway to the empty marvel,
the first Atlantis of light.

Windy sun below the Narrows,
Gravesend scud and whitecaps,
coal garbage gravel
scows bucking off Bensonhurst,
Richmond blueblurred
westward, and high
into the blue
supreme clarity,
it gleams aloft, alert
at the zenith
of leaping, speed
all blown to the wind
—what, standing in air,
what does it say
looking out out out?

And the light
              (everywhere,
off ridge, rock, window, deep,
drop) says,
              I leap clear.

3

Recalled from the labor of creation,
it was glancing as it flew, and saw
looking out to it the shimmering
of the million points of view. To see
Brooklyn so on a sabbath afternoon
from the heights, to be there beyond
the six days, the chronicle of labors,
to stand in the indestructible space,
encompass the world into whose center
you fly, and be the light looking!

The demiurge of an age of bronze
sees his handiwork and says it is good,
laying down his tools forever.
To see Brooklyn so in the spacious ease
of sabbath afternoon above the Narrows
is to say over and over what our speechless eyes
behold, that it is good, it is good, the first
Brooklyn of the senses, ardent and complete
as it was in the setting out of the sabbath.

An Era of Laughter

At the onset of an era of laughter, it was thought to restore the
integrity of the temple with satire. How proficient everyone became
(and how delighted to discover this universal talent)! Even the
dullest were soon masters of ridicule and could satirize satire itself,
while the few who could not grew expert in the modes of laughter.
There was nothing but laughter—laughter and integrity.

When the blind dwarf (manacled, unkempt) was led in, the
temple, as if not to be outdone, tittered and roared, cast itself down
and rolled on the ground in a devastating parody of collapse. Nor
were they spared who kept aloof—you, for example, who read this
text smirking amid smithereens. Private smiles blend nicely enough
into the general shambles of idiocy.

The Prodigal

Fifty years and not a nickel to his name,
the fat lines of his credit expunged,
his heritage the milt-clouded muck,
he dreams he is a victim, dog-bitten,
flea-chancred—The Disinherited One
he calls himself, plunking down three last words.
And so he runs with the runts and weird,
the world's culls and thwarts, a desert wrath
slavering for the succulent towns.
His cohort, his conquering dolts, crowds
an outlying village street. *We have
come back!* they shout, but their joyous
mutilated cries summon no faces
to the horrified windows, bring salt
foaming out of the broken roadways.
Dire under the stars, they know it now:
earth detests them. They buzz about
in confusion, dismay, terror, rubbing
their snub noses over long stupid cheeks
and turn their simple sullen faces
here and there, casting for a way back
into the wilderness—the founding fathers
of the second republic.

The Good Life

After the dioramas, the *Refugees Fleeing
on a Road,* the *Burn Ward,* the *Bomb Crater,*
and other such vivid scenes of war,
and live families of little Chinks
handing tea things 'round in a sewer pipe
—and oh as they stood there in awe at how
the lesser art of art could imitate
the greater art of war, that bulldozing,
those vivisections, oh stood naked almost
in awe before their awe, they felt that day,

one family among many, they felt
the force that surged along their linking hands
strike the dumb resistant wonder and slow
to a simple warm domestic glow:
they were happy to be there together—
and then the big blowups: world leaders
taking it easy at home, looking somehow
like family and sad like your old man
—all of it marketing the point about
war is h_ll in sharp, telling images—
well, when you pressed this certain button,
well, all of a sudden light and sound
started in, everything was all mixed up,
so confused you didn't know who you were
—it was like the world was going to blow!—
noise of armies clashing invaded
their ears, and terrible dark except,
behind red celluloid, rockets madly glared.
They crouched down and closed their eyes and were scared.

The light at the end of the tunnel proved
to be the orange roof of a restaurant,
a cockcrow of Early Colonial dawns.
There—under a mock-up of the Park,
oh it had everything, right down to crowds
of really tiny figures, themselves maybe,
each with a tinier dot of shadow like
a period lying painted at its feet,
it was, you would say, like heaven, seen
from far away, of course, and at the same time
you were in it—that was funny—and there
they sat down with other families
to portions of what turned out to be warm
shit.
      Well, then they knew the war was over
and which side won, which didn't much matter,
and bent their heads and said, Thank you, lords,
for taking reality out of our hands
and giving us the good life instead.

March 1974

Nervous and vital, he, too, danced forward to heave his flaming javelin at the band of elders who barred his way to the secret and the treasure. And yet, although he clamored and raged in the forefront, the attackers were so many, he found himself too far off to tell if he had dented that fussy reticence and dull certitude, that infuriating self-complacence. And if now and again one of them fell, it seemed, filtered through that distance, the result of invisible blows.

But when, long after, he had struggled to the top of the little eminence where they stood, his sword out to skewer the old bastards once and for all, they said, spreading their arms (and neither weakness nor fear could perturb their sluggish pentameters),

We thought you'd never reach us with relief,
you've been so long. Now come and stand where we
have stood, hold up the standard we've upheld!

Their standard (as he saw for the first time) of shame (as he thought almost for the last) was a bit of bloodied bed sheet, the elders feeble beyond belief, and their secret, their treasure, there below them on the plain, a city of graves. Now he understood they were in fact death's brightest, bravest face, turned not to guard but to hide—with overweening pity or else in shame they could offer no better—their horrid town from the eyes of the thronging young.

No longer a will and its blindness but a fatality and its intelligence (such as it was)—and no less embattled than he'd always been—he, too, with a senile passion for repetition, tirelessly joined in the carping antiphon, barking out his odious part at the horde pressing toward them,

Stay where you are!
          So it has always been.
So must it always be.
               I told you so.

Antonio, Botones

Para *Aguirre*

Tourist, traveler, consider this child:
Antonio, *botones* of the Ida Hotel,
of every hierarchy the base,
the bottom of every heap. Oh, too clearly
one sees it: vainly God flexes and waxes
His most apparent effulgence, wanly
He wanes in the lens of the soul of
Antonio the dull, the unperceiving.
And a little lower only, the Caudillo
(who dreams he is a boy pillaging apples)
has thrown an aged leg on the high hedge
of heaven and tottering atop the backs
of his Ministries (not excluding *Hacienda,*
not forgetting *Información y Turismo*)
tries to hoist himself up and clamber over.
Push, push, push me higher! his order flies
down from the apex of effort, along the chain
of command, by way of the Ida's owner,
its "maiter dee," desk clerk, barman, straight down
to Antonio in the lobby. And there
the little bell is pinging wildly, Oh please,
Antonio, for the love of heaven, just
a tiny bit higher!
                    And he on whom so much
depends, his jacket spattered, one button
dangling, ears clotted with cotton, his eyes
glazing, his nose just about to be picked,
Antonio the absentminded, the empty-headed,
sleeps on his feet, hears nothing, fails to grab
this client's valise, to open the outer door,
or pick up an unspeakable butt
disgracing the lobby and the noble carpet
—and witless, unwitting, spares the Caudillo
ultimate vulgarity: success in heaven.

Lowest of the low, Antonio, *botones*
of the Ida Hotel (two stars twinkle

on its lintel), Antonio, lowlier still
than the hem of the little chambermaid's skirt:
he's like earth and like the feet of turtles
—he bears all slowly, himself stays hidden.
The traffic flow of orders down the pure,
the crystalline pyramid terminates here
in a puddle, a cipher, a fourteen-year-old failure.
Others glimpse the summit, hear a faint cacophony,
the Leader's stertorous cries, and they respond,
they go higher, come closer, see clearer—but not he.
Then who will clean the lens of Antonio's soul,
so smutted and smutched, so foggy and gray?
Not the Caudillo and his ministers; not
the technocrats, their meager darlings; or
the middle-class poets of Mao who chant
the pompless despots of the magic capitals;
not the saints in their cells, or cadres in theirs.
True, each one wants Antonio for his army
(maybe he's a muse? he seems to inspire them all,
for his sake they pray, profess, or rule—they say)
—but something in this world has to be gray.
Then let it be the soul of Antonio,
unsalvageably so!
                    See,
wipe the slate clean, the slate stays gray!
—and makes the more brilliant those brilliancies
that great men scrawl . . . all over Antonio, who else?
. . . before they pass on (and, naturally, don't think
to tip). Never mind! humble beneath humility,
he asks for nothing—it makes the ages weep.
Never mind! so faint, so fine the line between
acceptance of everything and consent
to injustice, the saints, the very saints
in bliss, even San Anónimo in his,
eyes blinded with their souls' radiance,
drag chains across it continually.
Never mind!
—Shall shade shine, or earth be lustrous?
—Oh, surely not until the fiery blast
of God's breath pronounces final judgment!

But brilliance justifies itself, you say, and I
agree, I agree to all this glory
                              —and yet,
tourist, traveler, set down your suitcase here awhile,
consider Antonio, how his father comes
and beats him, how he takes his money, how
the Caudillo, impaled on the hedge of heaven,
cries aloud in his agony, If only
this innocent would try a little harder!
and urges him on for the glory of Spain
and its rightful place in the Common Market
—useless, of course, but what can you do?—
and how his boss, fed up to here, throws him out
and two days later can't remember his name
—while prancing ably in his place you note
his junior *confrère,* the former incumbent of
the Suiza y Niza (one star) down the street.
Consider Antonio, this simpleton,
this put-upon unresentful child, who can't smell
the carrot (yet feels the stick), who elicits
your sympathy as he thwarts your interest,
who tempts you to tamper with injustice
—only to drop your luggage on your feet:
                                        cram
your pride of life in his lens, see the world
as he must see it—then your eyes are stiffed,
then spasm cramps your brains, then effulgence
stains and shining shames and brilliance blemishes.
—Oh impossible to live there, awful to visit!
Nothing to do but take off on a trip
—and leave Antonio, incorrigibly
unpathetic, unorganizable as dirt,
creatively screwing up still another job.

But who is this leaping for your valise?
Well, it's not the local clod, it's not
Antonio, thank God! What a relief! Someone
a centimeter taller, some blue-eyed go-getter,
leaps from the desk, leaps for the door, his buttons
blinking out your warmest welcome, Francisco

by name. Now here's a boy who doesn't appall
the clientele or his bosses. Efficiency's
transparency, looking at is seeing through;
it's like the swallowing of a good gullet;
no glum opacity, no crap in your craw,
nothing retrograde: indeed, the future
personified beside a revolving door.
One sees beyond him to the world as one
has always wished to see it—sunny Mallorca!
under the international sun: white furnace
of a furious polyglot declaring
in simultaneous Swedish, English, French,
I too am a tourist rushing here and there,
although, truthfully, nothing new is under me,
a man of my time until I'm pensioned off
and relocated semi-permanently
—among damp shadows of the cheaper season
on a tideless island, with no tongue of my own.

August 1974

The Secret Work

Nadezhda Mandelstam has told the story. In Strunino, after her husband's arrest, working the night shift in a textile factory, she runs, sleepless and distraught, among the machines, chanting his forbidden poems to herself to preserve them. And so for twenty-five years in Perm, in Moscow, in Voronezh, Leningrad, Ulyanovsk, Samatikha...

A man with chills hugs himself,
rejoicing in his fever. She,
the frozen century's daughter, rejoices
in her secret, hugs to herself
the prophet hiding in her breath,
the infant she keeps close, safe, swaddled,
speaking.
          She covers over, makes him
smaller, safer, no bigger than

a seed, a spark—search where they will,
they will not find him here, yet here
he is, a little voice praying,
an enormous voice prophesying,
this live coal held on her tongue
burning behind clenched teeth.

To herself, in herself, over
and over, what must not
be said aloud, not written down,
not whispered in corners or left
to be smelled out clotting
at the ends of broken phrases
. . . the poems of Mandelstam
going out in Siberia's night.

Egg

I

Not
this mind,
these puns, a periplus
around a cosmion,
not mind widening this egg
to whiteness, a
universal, an o-
void in an omega, mind's
timeless waste:
poor
farm
pure
form;
not its dance of staggers, lame
capering caliper tacking
pegleg to legleg,
a moving mutiny around
a mute unity

. . .

that curves from salience
to silence, minding the store
with round redounding, O
mumly peepless!
its white the neutralest
effulgence;
                no, not
mind, blind in the blank,
feeling a way by longings,
shortcomings, listing at large
a topography of stumble,
ego type-tapping, *Eggo*
eggo echo eccomi!
replicating aspects of egg
as ectoplasm, a ghostly
difference,
                while going
about egg's beaued belly, belled
back—O, mothering curve
of contemplation!—mind
muttering, mumming;
                        not
this oaf of I'lls and ills, pale
aleph, cipher, white blighter
on its dancing chip over the dark
deep: not this mind in terror
of time, bringing its white treasure
on the wild tangents, yawning farther
into itself, its lurid, its phantom
sea;
        not this, not
these.

        2

O
-word, the
bird's cry, the o-
vum comes
in a cluck, in a clackle

of slime and lime:
this
egg
is
fresh,
minty and sage,
a wight right in greenward weeds
beside the green sea
at dawn,
this egg is all
for the day's throne,
the sun's slide up the sky.
Inside, a joke, a son
in a see, an I
in an eye in an *Ei:* these puns
are fatal are
fertile,
duplicating with a difference
a various redundancy,
the gold conflagrance
that differs into a dupling heart,
an oeufre,
orfèvre of *or*-feathers
-fingers -feeders -features -fecker!
An incubus.
An imp-unity.

Time crows over the crackling and over
the rising sun, The difference lives!
The chickling cheeps, I am the difference!

    3

Madam, Sir, abashed and saddened before
your own, your particular fates
—to differ, double, die:
Smile, idiots, look
at the birdie!

Father and Son

Set against each other, ready to butt
and struggle, with the same glaring look
of the eye and fiercely vivid anger,
son and father, isolated together
in daily deadlock, their form of murder.

Not sacrifice: murder. For it matters
that no command has brought together
the proud and loving father, the eager son,
mercurial and defiant, his image,
or ordered the day and brushwood for the fire.
This is no test, but plainly real,
this Moriah where, unsanctioned, unblessed,
unpunished, sons and fathers pause and wait,
and nothing is revealed.

Will no miraculous ram now come
bleating, trotting, wagging his head
like a slow wisdom on an antique page,
misleading death for the future's sake
and calling back the pair in pity
of the boy's innocence, the father's love?

No ram. None. Wildly, the father casts
about the rocky field, and grapples for
imagined horns to wrestle out a ram
from nothingness, as if to drag a god
into the stunned impenetrable world
and feel the rough material horn,
the rank fur, the uncomprehending staring eye,
and behind it the startled air's commotions
where invisible hooves are bracing—while,
almost glowering, the pitiless son looks on.

Piercing the frozen scene,
is it his own? or his son's?
or an ancient cry deafening his ear?
—the shriek this faithless toiling father hears

and one moment thinks a hesitant bleat
before he mingles death with his generations.

The Thief of Poetry

1

Girls he took from friends at seventeen
he lost in months and never found again.
Not so the books he stole that year:
face à face with his pounding heart,
the *Dirty Bloomers* of Baudelaire
translated into fact beneath
the null persona of his coat;
and closer still, like a blade slipped
through the dark intercostal spaces,
Eliot's *Poems* spirited from Macy's
in a folded X-ray of his lungs.

When he read "Prufrock" in the subway home
that afternoon, he was a cat crouched
before a saucer of milk: nothing moved
in all that train that illicit hour
but the pink tip of his tongue
and the white pages turning.

2

He waited all that year where three
roads meet—love, art, thievery—
in a wilderness of rumbling stone
while the great caravans went by
surging with goods and grief, waited
for lightning to point the way.
Lightning struck.
Was it defect of intelligence
or excessive timidity, a curse
that made vapid the family seed,
or simply an instant's inattention,
the tiniest mothhole bitten clear

through the universe? what made him take
words for the lightning that lit them,
bowls of milk for ah, bright breasts?

3   *Oedipus or Sophocles: The Road Not Taken*
He has been telling it with a sigh
—for sure!—ages and ages since.
Who might have gone limping toward Thebes
came tattling to Athens.

Avenue of the Americas

1

Check-grabbing in the neon effluvium,
the big spenders hustle from the table.
I'm fresh outta singles. I'll getcha
later, Joey," they yell the waiter,
or "Here, kid, keep the change."
The change the change the change divides
and redivides, fermenting in the chamber
of the unbroken floatable twenty,
lifeboat tilting on a depth of measureless
green, where you and you and you
and the waiter yaw in the wake
of the 40-long with sharp lapels
who swaggerdashes out, lifting an arm
that shows two inches of white-on-white,
a watchband glinting, a ring with red stone.

2

The bigshots bang down their phones
like guillotines. Buy Marvin!
Sell Harvey!
Headless Harvey!
Paraplegic Marvin!
Gas presses on the stomach.
God, let me belch Harvey, let me

evict Marvin!
The office girls hurry. "Mr. Sam,
Mr. Sam, you didn't take your pill
this morning. You'll *kill* yourself!"
He sighs. All over the world
the cigars go out again. And a good
man, among mother-daughter
mistress-wife, reaches the end
of his bicarb.

The City and Its Own

Among the absolute graffiti which
—stenciled, stark, ambiguous—command
from empty walls and vacant lots,
POST NO BILLS, NO TRESPASSING HERE:
age and youth—Diogenes, say,
and Alexander, dog-philosophy
and half-divine, too-human imperium—
colliding, linger to exchange ideas
about proprietorship of the turf.
Hey, mister, you don't own the sidewalk!
Oh yeah?
Yeah! the *city* owns the sidewalk—*mister!*
Oh yeah! says *who?*
Thus power's rude *ad hominem* walks all over
the civil reasoner, the civic reason.

Everyone has something.
Everything is someone's.

The city is the realm of selves in rut
and delirium of ownership, is property,
objects made marvelous by prohibition
whereby mere things of earth become ideas,
thinkable beings in a thought-of world
possessed by men themselves possessed by gods.

. . .

So I understood at twelve and thirteen,
among the throngs of Manhattan,
that I dodged within a crowd of gods
on the streets of what might be heaven.
And streets, stores, stairs, squares, all
that glory of forbidden goods, pantheon
of properties open to the air,
gave poor boys lots to think about!
And then splendor of tall walkers
striding wide ways, aloof and thoughtful
in their nimbuses of occupation,
advancing with bright assurance as if
setting foot to say, *This is mine, I
am it*—and passing on to add,
Now yield it to you, it is there.
Powers in self-possession, their thinking
themselves was a whirling as they went,
progressing beyond my vista to possess
unthought-of worlds, the wilderness.

These definitions, too, have meant to draw
a line around, to post and so prohibit,
and make our vacant lot a sacred ground.
Here then I civilize an empty page
with lines and letters, streets and citizens,
making its space a place of marvels now
seized and possessed in thought alone.
You *may* gaze in, you *must* walk around.
—Aha (you say), conceit stakes out its clay!
—*That* is a cynic's interpretation,
pulling the ground out from under my feet;
I fall, I fear, within your definition
which, rising and dusting off my knees,
civilly I here proclaim our real estate,
ours in common, the common ground
of self, a mud maddened to marvel
and mingle, generously, in generation.

A Player's Notes

To Hashim Khan

1 There is impatience in many disguises—weariness, reluctance, zeal, the desire to win, the fear of losing.

2 What is not impatience is the game, pure and simple.

3 Properly presented, with patient attentiveness, the ball is a surprise his opponent would not wish to refuse, will, with appropriate care, wish to return in kind.

4 Failing to attend to his opponent, he is doomed to try to exceed himself, is doomed further to succeed in defeating himself.

5 Playing for self-transcendence, he wastes and destroys himself, lags behind in order to fly forward too fast at the last instant.

6 Always the phoenix, unhappy bird who appears only on the threshold of the calcined house.

7 The game is not intended to flourish on the wreckage of reality.

8 Truly, reluctance (weariness, failure to attend) causes him to arrive late for the ball. Just as truly, his desire to fly, his dream that he can fly, that he is flying, cause him to arrive late for the ball.

9 The daydream of flight spreads its phantom pinions in the lost instant of his failure to attend.

10 Dropped onto the treadmill of his daydream, one ball will never reach him, while the other in the freedom of the game rushes past with a savage whirring of wings.

11 Gasping for breath, he asks, Is it possible to survive here without being reborn?

12 Rebirth—if that is the issue—comes from renewed contact with the eternal, as in its momentary flight on the court. Therefore, these are forbidden, these are enjoined.

· · ·

13 Forbidden: hairsplitting, pessimism, fantasy.

14 Enjoined: knowledge, good humor, the exchanging of gifts.

A Tale of a Needler and a Nailer

When everyone was going out
to brilliant day, to vivid night,
something had to be given up,
years ago when the world began,
something had to be left behind:
a token to darkness
a prize to the past
a nod to night
a nickel to mortality at the gate.
Let it be me! they said,
me, me, *I'll* stay.
I sew the world to sleep!
I hammer the world awake!

Who were they? you ask.
The tiniest old men
who never were born,
twins, in fact,
and bent together
like halves of an O
but back to back,
a thousand years they'd need
just to straighten up
—what stubbornness, such loyalty
to the shape of a room!
And such doom
—like two little children
trapped in old age,
who can't grow up, who can't grow back.
A nailer, a tailor,
the one and the other.

. . .

And here today, right now,
at the top of the stairs,
with bent-up nail
and beat-up chair
on a broken floor
with a hammer only

and all of his might,
the nailer hammers, he hums
aloud to himself,
"Hey, watch out,
stand back there,
don't crowd me!
Dummy, can't you see?
this hammer's no toy,
the thing itself!
a hammer for real,
wood handle, iron head,
just see it flash
its sky's-worth of arc,
it drives home
in a single blow!
—the whole of heaven
on the head of a nail.

"Now who would have thought
you could get so much
on the head of a nail?
A nail? a nail? who said a nail?
Children, did *I* say a nail?
Now you've got my goat.
I don't *need* a nail.
See, I throw it out
and I hammer away."

True, true, he hammers away.

And back to his back,
his brother stoops,

too patient, too still
to stitch in time,
with one little needle
and one bit of thread
and one ray of light
where dust specks blaze,
where filaments float:

"Cloth is waiting,
the button waits.
I squeeze my eye
to needle's eye.
By smaller degrees
and more and more quietly
and last so you can't even see,
I bring the thread near."
Then they glow in the trap
and they answer each other:
I pound the world apart.
I sew the world to stay.
Here's a knap on your noodle.
Here's thread in your eye.
I speak louder.
But *I've* the last say.

Bang! says one.
Shhh, says the other.

The Golden Schlemiel

So there's a cabbie in Cairo named Deif.
So he found 5000 bucks in the backseat.
So meanwhile his daughter was very sick.
So he needed the money for medicine bad.
So never mind.
So he looked for the fare and gave it back.
So then the kid died.
So they fired him for doing good deeds on company time.

So the President heard it on the radio.
So he gave him a locally built Fiat.
So I read it in the papers.
So you read it here.

A poor man has less than weight, has negative gravity, his life a slow
    explosion. Barely he makes the days meet. Like doors they burst
    open. Money, job, daughter fly away from him. Irony, injustice,
    bits of horror come close, cohere.

They are with us, the poor, like the inner life which is wantless, too;
    our souls' white globes float somehow in the blue, levitating and
    bobbing gently at middle height over the bubbling fleshpots.

Our effort to remake the found world as the lost reverie is desire.

So, little Yasmin was sick, sick to the point of dying.
She was like a garden coughing and drying.
And suddenly her salvation was there, a sheepskin, yes,
a satchel of money meekly baaing from the rear.
A miracle in the offing?
That famous retired philanthropist named God
was back in business? was starting to take a hand?
Directing things maybe from the backseat?
Maybe.

Restored to its rich owner (he tipped a fig and a fart, a raspberry of
    plump nil), lying safely on his lap, the money was mute again,
    was superfluity, and root and sum and symbol, both lettuce and
    lump, of all evil.
She too approaching that state,
Yasmin, a flower, meantime, dying.

For the locally assembled daughter a locally assembled Fiat.

Too wantless to imagine the money his?
Spurned the miracle and thwarted the grace?
So loved the law he gave it his only begotten daughter?
Effed and offed his own kid?
Saint and monster, poor man and fool,

slowly exploding—Deif all this.
Yes, one melts at his meekness,
scoffs at the folly, trembles
for his stupor of bliss of obedience,
gasps at his pride, weeps
for his wantlessness,
grunts when irony that twists the mouth jabs the gut.
Then horror—the dark miracle—roaring, leaps
into the front seat, grabs the wheel and runs you down in the
     street
—while you sit on a café terrace innocently reading the paper
or, bent above a radio, feel the news waves break against your
     teeth.

Deif in grief. Deif in mourning. Deif bereaved.
Deif in the driver's seat. Deif without a beef.

And daily in four editions and every hour on
the hour, the media heap your dish with images
of sorrows and suffering, cruelty, maiming, death.
(Our real griefs in their imaginary jargons.)
And you cannot touch a single sufferer, comfort
one victim, or stay any murderous hand.
Consumer of woes, the news confirms you
in guilt, your guilt becomes complicity,
your complicity paralysis, paralysis
your guilt; elsewhere always, your life becomes
an alibi, your best innocence a shrug,
your shrug an unacknowledged rage, your rage
is for reality, nothing less. Yes,
you feel, murder would be better than hanging around;
if only your fist could penetrate the print,
you too might enter the reality of news. . . .
You switch the radio on, hungrily turn the page
of sorrows and suffering, cruelty, maiming, death.

Pasha, President, playboy swing masterfully
above our heads—what style! what heroes!—fling themselves
over the headlines into the empyrean
beyond our lowly weather—ah, *there* all the news

is blue and blank, those soarings, those mock descents,
they are writing their own tickets in heaven.
Fortune, true, is spiteful and fickle, and glamour
itself must stalk them—but cannot shoot so high
as impotence dreams, as resentment wishes.
Gorgeous, limber, and free, like our consciences,
a law unto themselves, a darker law to us
—in their suntans our shadow.

And where they fly, the lines of force accompany,
the patterns of deference continue to comfort,
a maggotism distracting irony.
Their rods flatten others, their staffs flatter *them*
—you and I pay for the lies we get,
but heroes get the lies they pay for.
So here's the President's ear on the radio's belly
—if there are rumbles in Egypt, he'll know it,
he'll proclaim, Fix this! *(Fixed!)*, Do this! *(Done!)*.
And here is Deif's story beating at his eardrum.
Tremble, mock, shrug, or writhe, you and I
cannot write the ending, cannot snatch glory
of authorship from anonymity of events.
The President can. The President does.
His literature is lives, is Deif smiling:
golden, seraphic and sappy, sheepish, sweet;
is Deif not understanding a thing and grateful
and happy like a puppy given to a child.
He speaks: his fiat is a Fiat,
assembled locally and worth five grand
(out of the President's pocket? Pal, guess again!)
—which cancels Deif's deed down to the penny.
Deif has no claim on the moral law, no dignity,
no destiny, no daughter; his suffering
won't embarrass, his monstrousness appall;
injustice is removed, and nothing left in its place,
the spot swept clear, blood expunged, crowd dispersed,
and Deif himself sent to park around the corner,
a bystander to his life, a pure schlemiel.
Deif never did anything, nothing ever happened
—all for the greater glory of the State.

. . .

Exit Deif with his dead daughter in his arms.
Re-enter Deif in a Fiat meekly beeping,
and overhead, Yasmin, the locally dis-
assembled, the wingèd, pointing down and proudly beaming.

Upon such sacrifices the gods themselves shy clods.

Riffling the pages of sorrow and suffering,
the President carefully lowers his hydrocephalous head onto the
     news he made.

Besides, the State abhors the inner life, finds its rich wantlessness,
     its invisible reverie uninteresting because unmanageable, damned
     because unusable. Incapable of inactivity, the State cannot
     submit to stillness and seeks precisely to create the desire it will
     manage. It requires neither pensive persons nor upright citizens
     but a smiling multitude. The State is a Midas. Every absence
     and invisibility it would make bright material, for what is
     invisible—Deif's resolve to return the money or patient grief
     recollecting the spilt petals of his lost jasmine—what is invisible
     the State believes deplorable, knows to be dangerous. Such is
     the anxiety that caused the President to lift a finger, to touch
     Deif.

To reconstitute the found Fiat as the lost daughter.

Wheeled, powerful, in progress; altar and throne
and golden veal, leviathan and juggernaut;
and nearby, one Reda Deif—once slowly
exploding, once a spirit darkening
all earthly glory—observes the State
adoring itself as its image.

Easy to amend injustice. Hard to be just.

Deif attending the vehicle.
His *air de chauffeur,* a man
who defers to a car, infers
his value from his deference.

He bows, approaching the door,
bows to the aura and glory
around, behind, beyond, within
this scrap of State, this scrim
of status before the reeling stars;
he bows to be bowing. Air
now of one waiting for
its owner to appear. Deif knows
it can't be Deif, must be another:
grand, glowing, ponderous, a meteor,
breathtaker and heartstealer, mover and shaker,
who merely presuming possesses,
imposes, distresses between his flashing
attraction, his haughty don't-touch!
Let poorman-Deif dare show his face,
guarddog-Deif will show him the door!
He shifts from foot to foot
beside himself beside the car.
Embarrassment? Well,
ecstasy.

Seepage of eternity we call the sea, the sky.
Such spacious summer nights come also to Deif,
the sky enormous, intimate, Deif too brief, too dusky.
The universe invites him to fly—if only he *could* fly!
It snatches his heart and throws it into the blue.
The cosmic wafting blows it away.
Must I? Must I follow?
he asks the whirlwind's roar.
His heart will shatter to encompass all
or, lightless coal, plummet through the dark and azure!
Lies down again, throbbing, where he was. Schlemiel
and saint and monster are cradled and tucked in.

However theatrically laid on thick by fate, how did this tiny whisper
    of injustice exceed the general and deafening static of woe?
Do you think Deif's boss called a press conference to announce the
    shafting?
Or that his neighbors issued a news release?
Do you think Deif himself told the story?

Really? him? that schlemiel? And to whom in that Calcutta on the
   Nile?
Maybe you think it doesn't flatter the President a little too neatly?
Think it isn't the least bit imaginary?
No poets of Presidency in Egypt?
No P.R. men in Cairo?
Do you think there really is a man named Deif?

I think I prefer to think that Deif exists,
yes, and even little Yasmin dead dead dead
indeed, dead for a fact.
I think I prefer this horror
which tells me it is possible to feel
if not to believe.
Only horror survives our raging irony
and we survive by horror.

So one delves a death and turns . . . a pretty penny,
some moral quid for all that mortal quo (O wit
for woe!)—O "think" and "feel," increments
of spirit that transfuse, that elevate! Erect
atop her grave, oh, how a great heart gushes, floods
the frame with gladdening news: One *has* come through!
—which makes one, after all, complicit, one's spade
a spade, Yasmin, Deif one's victims, one's life
vicarious, vacant, oneself a fiction
held up to a Fate, shattered by a Fury.
Pluck out your radio, rend your paper!
Savage death demands a savage discipline.
Down your head, roll in the dirt, mourn!

As to bad before, so now to better fortune:
Deif submits. Incorrigible schlemiel,
he doesn't grab it with both hands,
one on each tit. See him!
insulated from earth by rubber,
two fingers gingerly on the wheel,
his other arm out to catch the breeze
as he drives into the sunset of the real,
his position false but increasingly familiar.

Fortune sits on him like a ton of shit
—a raven of another choler—and smiles.
Sociably, he returns the smile.

Farewell, Dcif! Farewell, brother!

This Way to the Egress

Impatient to be under way, he boarded early; still the boat delayed at quayside, then floated off into the house of spooks. What a disappointment that was! Where are the real terrors, he demanded, for which he'd spent his life preparing? Oh, but the eulogy of terror—*any* eulogy—would have stultified his dying, kept him as he was, an aging man becalmed in the luminous still sea of his transcendence. Instead, these too obvious frights, all burlap and cotton batting and sprung wires, an old mattress dump, unbelievable!—it wouldn't fool, much less terrify, a child—and revolting! the stink swaddled his head, he would have vomited—and then the wine- and urine-stewed supers who manned its machinery, headsmen and skeletons, murderous crones and farting trumps that made a pass at troubling the dark—couldn't the universe do any better than that! What a sendoff, who'd *want* to come back! So he kibitzed his dying, feeling mocked and cheated, it was so unworthy, so demeaning.

Of course, something kibitzed him back. That was the ordeal of laughter. (It could have been better.) Storms of hooting and heckling drove him backward, each affronting buffet pushily took a bit of his life. Swept away, unable not to be where he'd been before, how much he should have liked to join in the party, draw power from the chorus of wise guys and with it howl out the last laugh, be *named* Laughter—mockery's own mascot—and claw his way back to himself, to anywhere! But the laugh machine really *was* laughing—to itself and yet at him, as if it were his own râling breath, mocking and sustaining, or this little boat of wires and tubes that bore him so poorly. Mad, mechanical, unreal, still the laughter was appropriate and, therefore, genuine, had to possess *some* understanding. He saw that. He *was* ridiculous, not heroic at all, a little boy, and maybe less than that, a baby, probably, who couldn't

wipe his own behind. And all his rage a huffing grotesquerie, as if
to give death a scare—it was right to boot him out of the world
like this. Absurd to be so helpless! Ridiculous to be so absurd!
Nevertheless, the ritual of derision did not fail him, secured his
passage and kept him company all the way.

Sons et Lumières

Even in the first instant of its fiat, the voice of God seemed
badly dubbed, the words a curb in the mouth that outran sound.
Nevertheless, at the end of time as at its beginning, cracked,
clouded, flickering, thin, the light that responded touched
everything with its original clarity, its first glory.

The Gift of Life

In memory of Lionel Trilling

The age's principled ingratitude,
a viscous cant of self-begetting,
as if we *realized, fulfilled* a *self,*
who are indeed fictive and empty,
transparencies where eyebeams cross:
the points of intersection blaze
into sight, a sudden glory, light
looks back at light, star sees star,
and together are the shining of heaven.
And now and now and now an eye blinks off.
Unseen, I feel invisible, destroyed.
And every eye will shut away the luster,
and we and all will be again
the volatile nothing, and clear clear dark.

From *New and Selected Poems*

The Thousand Nights and the One Night

King Shahryar was a dream of omnipotence distracted into bloody existence by his wife's infidelity.

Abandoned by maternal night, her faithfulness in which, innocent and whole, he'd slept, finding himself mortal, he became lethal, and each morning ordered time destroyed, whatever womb carried his seed—until Shahrazade, charming him with the spectacle of his helplessness, of a world he couldn't command, made him into a story and shut him up tight between the covers of a book.

Suspended in the mothering flow of her voice and jostled by the friendly turbulence of its flux of destinies, hearing himself told and retold, at one with his dreamer, King Shahryar sleeps happily.

And blue banners unfurling are all his days.

The Ecstasies

che fè Nettuno ammirar l'ombra d'Argo.—DANTE

He swam, but swam in place, the place was his,
the whole of it, all the sea, and he its self
and sway, storming or still—and never still,
ecstatic platitude of the sea dazzle
and reaches, the dark reverie downward,
dreaming itself toward a fluent point
dispersed in a thousand silvery centers,
bubbles lofting and kissing themselves
into nothingness, the spray lifted and blown,
expatiating in broken syllables
—and he held close by the dream of the sea,
a wonder of water where he moved and touched
the light, saw the transparency, always
light moving, the clear ecstasy.
And splashed but couldn't speak, having no words
in the imageless sea. Then startled, started.
The little blindness of the marvelous
Argo's opacity pierced Neptune's brow,
and wavered into sound—the image sang,

and sang inside his coursing bones the in-
conceivable commonplaces, Sky, fire, star,
and offered him to all the openness.

Three Tales

To Sanford Friedman

Why is there something and not nothing?
Because we have been spared.

CREATION

Out of himself matter and shining.
And now she smiles and swells.
Sky is mother, clear and cheering.
Sea is mother, strewn face upward
to heaven—blue, pellucid, fragrant,
a petal. She is pleased, she is pleasure,
gathering his light together.
On the seventh day I opened my eyes
and was good: looking, I lit;
seen, I shined—a spark
in space, space in a spark,
world in a world of worlds.
He lets the worlds go and goes away:

father hides in clarity
—how clear the endless seventh day!—
everywhere at rest, at play, calling: Children,
knock on my door!—But no one answered,
no one was there, the house was empty,
all of it open and ours entirely.
Teasing, he said: Look, here I am, I'm here!
We couldn't find him in the clarity,
and where we looked window, wall, and door
all were namelessly bright, all
were water, sky, and shore.
We flamed and flew in the ecstasy.

. . . The land is his, his hunger the law.
What he gets he eats. I cannot endure . . .
Blood in the streets, the very streams
seem butchered, the sky a piece of meat . . .
A *friendly* horror (the mouth emits
a smile, the eyes just *show* their teeth)
takes them in hand, terrified, sick.
Armies of tots flogged toward his maw . . .
the nimble, the quick, the tender, the sweet . . .
gibberish of shrieks, then drivel of limbs.
I *saw* this, hidden in a heap of knuckles.
The little hands were still reaching . . .
I'm smeared with it. I feel nothing . . .
Later on I heard him explaining
(I scratch these words with splintered bone),
"Because, after all, I'm your father.
What else do you think I made you for?
You owe me everything, your food, your drink,
your being, the ruddy flesh off your backs . . ."
This was no figure of speech . . .
And then, "Ungrateful, where are you hiding?"
(The shark, too, complains of his prey,
Why aren't they more *forthcoming*?) . . .
Still later he was at his bookkeeping,
counting off on his fingers, muttering,
"Six days to get, fetter, fatten—that's
six days of fasting. On the seventh day
I eat." The monster! . . . *Moloch! Fiend!*
Leads each moppet up to the dish
and pointing all around he whispers,
"This is the world. You will die. Sorry, nipper."
. . . I caught him afterward asleep.
Still slobbering gore. Nothing fancy: I shoved
his jaw down his throat, sent the head flying . . .
This feeling of freedom, this joy . . .
Strange, for all the absence of ogres,
existence has proven no less fatal . . .

and every death marked Final.
The sky is gone, just swallowed up . . .
I think I'm dead, too. Look at him,
his chine stripped, his jaws still clacking . . .
I coolly fought to save my life . . .
no longer rage to keep my innocence.
I know who is my father's son.
Look at how they look at me,
push close with hunger, or run in horror.
Can't a man eat in peace anymore!
My kids still think they'll live forever.
I don't have immortality in my guts,
only a clot of frozen terror.
I'm hungry, too.
I'll poke down deep in theirs.
If there's any heaven in numbles,
I'll find it, I'll eat it all.
I'll teach them! *I'll* stop their staring . . .

SABBATH

Whose children are these advancing in me
to greet the little boat bearing the wide bliss
and lead it lamb-like ashore by its painter?
Mouths, limbs bathed in a clarity not theirs,
where have I known them all before if not here,
pushing and dragging the sabbath dawn
up the beach with shouts and laughter,
scrambling for places and rowing the air?
There *was* no other world, *is* no other day!
Where are these flowers rushing in place
all the sunny afternoon?
The perfect speed of the daffodil
is the daffodil perfectly still.
Who are they, overturning it with dusk
and crawling under the hull to sleep,
lustrous voices, selves invisible?
Whom are they begging for stories now?
I *know* a story, it is their own:
These children have been, they will be, spared!

—Of all the worlds I made, this world alone
I did not destroy, but died instead.
Who am I, clear and dark over the sea,
dark and clear above the stars, the open
embrace, at once the greeting and goodbye?
Who will tell me while I understand?
What are they whispering snug all night
under the lulling rain, little and great?
Patter and pleasure of their sleepy conversing.
They name me *sacrifice*—their old man
is snoring; call me *sabbath* and *ending*
—the death consumed in clarity
—the clarity that makes the birth clear;
call me *distance*—and I depart;
the universe—I disappear
and am immortal and forget.

Family History

GENEALOGY

My family tree is mist and darkness.
Century after century,
one lay upon the other begetting me.
Then my millennium in marshes
and wandering obscurity
revealed my heritage:
monster, I lack immortality,
my race is superfluous on earth.
The last, the final generation
—after me no other, or someone else—
I lay down on top of death.
We keep our appointments with fate,
even if fate does not;
though no one came to kill me, I died.
I the ghost that I begot.
My tree is night and fog.

.　.　.

The pink clue of Mama's tongue,
the tip of it between her lips
when she concentrates, picking
at knots or threading a needle.
So she must have sat as a child,
a bit of sewing in her lap,
the tip of her tongue out showing
in imitation of her mother
or mother's mother—but I cannot
follow the clue any farther
and have nothing else to follow
into the lost domestic dark
of some small corner of the Pale.
Now she is patient but quick:
no false move, no motion wasted,
nothing that needs doing over,
nothing overdone or stinted,
everything measured *so,*
sized up by eye and no
anxiety, no pedantry.
Only now have I understood
I have no better measure for
the fitness of things than her gesture,
dreamy and alert and left-handed,
of pulling a thread to length
while the spool runs 'round in her hand.
She is proud of herself as a worker,
tireless, versatile, strong,
both craftsman and laborer.
When she aims her thread at the needle,
her wide gray eyes intensify
—in them no want, no waste, no withering—
and it pleases her to say,
"Arbet macht dem leben ziess."
Oh, if it does, if it did
—though smeared in iron on the gate to hell—
then of hers the overflowing sweetness,

like a sugar tit touched to battered lips,
has made something of the darkness sweet.

IN THE EYE OF THE NEEDLE

Up on chairs as if they were floating
toward the kitchen ceiling, two sisters
are having hems set to the season's height,
to the middle of the knee, and no higher,
though they beg for half an inch, a quarter.
Robust and red-haired, they are two angels
beaming and grinning so they could never blow
the marvelous clarions their cheeks imply
—and I, fang still tender, venom milky,
small serpent smitten, witless with pleasure,
idling, moving my length along, spying,
summoned to Paradise by giggling
and chatter.
            I saw this all
in the needle's eye—before time put it out—
compressed to two girls' gazes, hazel-eyed
and blue-eyed, one gentle, one imperious,
the soul at focus in its instant of sight,
expressive, shining there, revealed;
the seed of light flew down, a spark, two bits
of human seeing, and lay upon my heap
of gazes, bliss inexhaustibly blazing.

THE SINGER'S SINGER

"Vos zol ton a Yid? Epes a shneider."

David at his harp, humming and clanking.
Fifty years of this have rounded his back,
and bending forward *looks* like prayer.
His rocking feet speed the iron treadle,
the needle fangs down faster and faster,
under the little foot, little teeth,
rising up, feed the cloth forward, male

and female together. Allegories
everywhere! A holy era for sure!
With rags, with crazy remnants he saved
—hoods and motley and mops and stars—
he pieces a garment together, cut
to no pattern, sizeless, mad, its unity
a oneness of confusion. "Old fool,"
I say, "what living man would wear your suit?
You sew for monsters, or sew for no one."
He glances up, blue eyes still squinting:
"The stone wall of terror on which you break
your head: nothing can be thought, nothing
can be done—and so, to do something,
to think nothing, you break your head.
You don't break down. You won't break through.
I, too. I sew an endless suit
to clothe the mist and keep it warm
and give it any shape I can.
My son, my son, here, please put it on."

Cloud of Brightness

Who stood in cloud and made it shine?
Stupidity, confusion—in these, yes—
then faltering, refusal, feigning;
hiding in these, I returned
toward your presence, cheeks burning,
bold eyes aflame in the hooded places
—yes, I denied you in these.
I would not go forward,
swerved, balked, evaded;
at every forking chose
the farther way, savoring
everything I put, in secret, between
—the world my mask, my teasing.
And where you stood, distant, the cloud
thickened and glowed up brighter.

No matter, I would go away farther.
A world off still, I stood
before you, guilty, contrite
(these, too, disguises), and dared not
look away and dared not see
the being, brightness in the cloud.
Nonetheless, in his sanctuary
of punishment a child dares everything.
I greeted blindness, terror
of total dark, the cloud of myself
—only so, malingerer
in midst of glory, can I
recover my good will
from black mineral.
I cannot spy who sees me,
shut eyes or look aside.
I am seen completely.
So must I wish to be seen,
since law is: of you can we know
in measure as we are revealed.
No other darkness intervenes,
no light bright enough to see.
I know your bashfulness.
Shine now to the blind
your shy epiphany.

Rowing on the Acheron

These two sitting across a table
suddenly were seated side by side
out rowing on the Acheron.
She'd asked, "How often have you died?"

Could one embrace so close to hell,
he might have caught her emptiness
against his empty breast and made,
perhaps, a shade or two the less.

"How often have you *failed* to die?"
He mocked at her? and with his pain?
The prisoner of dialectics
can never cease rattling his chain.

So, two moving solitudes—so oar
and oar to either side—kept pace,
the stream so small, so shallow
they might have left it any place.

It seemed now not to matter if
the immortality in reach,
the universe aching to speak,
should never choose them for its speech.

The river they rode on moved in them.
She craved its flowing identities,
he to pass beyond remembering.
Failure, too, has voluptuaries.

Each saw as each was: she, on her side,
a savior take her death and die;
on his, Pluto, scavenging for lives,
was tossing back the lesser fry.

Her vivid bones a jetting flame;
he a crystal nothing could consume.
But here came the waiter with the check,
the busboy sweeping past with a broom.

Delicate, swift, their waking glance
exchanged the vision each had seen,
their next was blank, the last returned
their smiles, and set the table between.

The Human Circle

At a *vernissage* and then next day again
at the poetry reading—the same faces.
No, other faces had undergone a like
refiguration, a leveling estrangement:
Picasso persons, each with paired visages
(and a third queasily both and neither),
a crowd of aunts, uncles, cousins by aging,
as if a common gene of caricature
was unmasking itself in them; and yet
their furious tippling and chatter before
the gilded driftwood on the walls—chilling with
the tomb's disparagement of speech—or mutual
hailings next day while I shuffled my pages
did not persuade me their recognitions
were welcome, their reunions joyful.
Gaunt or puckered, with tanned-over wrinkles,
hair thinned to floating white wisps, enfeebled
—oh, I knew they all were strangers, yet seemed
deformed familiars from another world
or perfections there degraded in this,
say, lords and ladies of Byzantium
gone to ground one summer in South- and East Hampton.
They, of course, were looking back with glances
saying they almost remembered my feather
—whatever kind of bird I thought myself—
their puzzling eyes all but squinted the words,
What, you, too? How you have changed—nephew!
It's true, I was the youngest there of all the old.

I remember that I sat waiting, to one side
on a metal chair, in the state of someone
about to perform, intense, and removed farther
by intensity, not nervous, but like
a racehorse in the gate: I was mad to go
—without knowing where to or what I'd say
or whether hired to please or to harrow,
or entertain or prophesy or confess

—or all of these, and out of my entrails,
inoffensively of course, charmingly
if I could, with a slight bending of the neck,
a certain exposure of the throat.
Or knew to whom I was to read my stuff,
or what they wanted, coming as they did
—as I supposed—week after week all summer long
to hear unremarkable actors, in ordinary
clothes, without sets or music, and poorly lit,
intone their mostly lackluster scenarios.
Perhaps I'd been invited to tarnish quietly
for an hour—in the dampish basement of
a dreadful cult of mediocrity.
They knew me? Bards of a feather? Welcome, *nephew*!
Well, and who *did* I think I was writing for?
Beautiful illiterates wholly alive?
Too arrogant to look down, abashed
to raise my eyes, I stared straight ahead—then stood,
hearing myself introduced. Nobody,
at least, was chewing gum or taking notes.

And they all fell silent,
as the dead do,
who lock themselves away
and not for anything
will ever come out.
The silence of the dead
is a lifetime's silences,
speech subtracted and withheld
from the living circle,
a sum of immortality
stored up in powerful jaws.
Therefore, the stories of the dead
are also the living speech
of the human circle.

Once there was a little village—so went the story I told them—once
        there was a little village, a human circle that filled its world
        completely.
From nowhere, a stranger came, stateless, exile or wanderer. Of him,

they knew, they could know, nothing—he was entirely a secret, was secrecy become visible, seeming, in silence, to stand closer to each than any did in speaking.

Now they perceived *their* secrecy, the unstated power each held against every other—not particular, paltry secrets but a powerful will to secrecy, in which everyone shared: a shadow and substitute village, not the human circle but its opposite and enemy.

He understood, darkly, that it was given to him to reveal the secret and renew the circle; so *he* would stand revealed, be instated.

Someone dies; he, too, dresses in death, puts on the pelt of silence, the dog's head and paws, and, feigning death, lies down beside the dead one. With furtive claws he tears at the hypocritical death, he drives his muzzle into it. Now he woos the dead one with silence more powerful than the silence of death, singing, *I know you live, and will lead you back to the place of the living. Arise, and come forth!* Snatches its silence and runs. A glance—the bones fall back.

In his mouth the secret is raging as if, possessed, it were his secret. He speaks it, but out of nowhere it howls aloud to the human circle: *I am alive! I live!*

Its cry is the power coursing from each to each.

It roars in the applause rising against the silence to celebrate the immortal covenant of the living. And welcomes back the scavenger.

"We are alive!" they all cried out.

Noises roused me from the story I was telling
the dying. Not fifty yards away,
higher than our heads, invisible
in the chill summer fog, Atlantic combers
were booming through the late afternoon.
Apparently, I had been reborn here,
in a museum cellar, where some new power
announced itself in their quickening hands:
they were applauding themselves with full hearts,
me with faltering confidence
—I could see their mouths and eyes,
the good humor of one, in the other
the horror.

But each at last to his own house.
So, the circle broke, each one
not less secretive but going
with his secret lightly,
like readers of stories who, silent themselves,
stand revealed to a world of revelation
—while I remained a moment among the chairs,
grinning, and bowing my head.

From *Elegies*

FIRST

As the life goes on it starts to double
and loop over; acquaintances, chance meetings,
poems, places recur tumbling in the backflow,
grinding together to indifferent likeness
or pounded bare of old senses but senselessly
inscrutable now: what *could* they have been?
were they ever themselves and not their substitutes?
were we ourselves and not our make-believe?
did we touch then and speak, touch as we spoke?
And our stories were truer for touching?
our contact more generous for our phrases,
the human circle larger, more hospitable?
That is past mentioning, past believing,
bubble now, or gravel clattering.
And others move in our manner, speak our mouthings?
This mimicry doesn't flatter,
mockery where not a curse
—a stale folly feeds a fresh disgust.
Time palpable and conscious in us.
Not ourselves; said nothing; these things never were;
muddle of grit and figments:
                                    the juvenile
poet, death's blabbing messenger boy
in one elegy I wrote, four years later

was the message other couriers spoke;
the young Spaniard to whom I translated "X,"
in three weeks himself a dead child
—indentured both to the same bully;
this poem, begun before a death, may yet
endure to include others: I feel at times
I am writing in a race with horror
—dregs of anecdote I can bear no longer,
smoothing in my swell, in meditation;
I will crash, and course at random,
myself confounded in myself;
can the breaker say what
is what? tell what from what?
I drink my drowning.
Shameful if one takes the bully's part.
Your corpse, now, is your true impostor.
And each of us comes lugging one home,
a griping in the wave's bowel.
Grief or grievance? mourning or self-pity?
A thousand-mouthed turbulence is roaring
for eternity.
          Time breaks the bubbles of stone,
drowns the sparks in the cunning baubles.
I have kept nothing entire, clear, alive,
having broken my words, quenched my vow
—how will I authorize reality?
Seeing these things, one sees
one has lived too long, outlived too many.
Pastiche of being, duplicitous, demeaning.
Your impostor is your posterity.
Some other is seizing my I, my speech. I repeat myself.
I am myself repeated.
The surf's tooth snags on sand, worries, gnawing
one spot, roars; it will go no farther;
too ample to be intelligible,
the thunderous echo engulfs the glittering original,
yet is powerless to tell the story, move these words upward.

SECOND

We wake to poetry from a deeper dream,
a purer meditation—expanse of light
in water pressing unquenched on our eyes;
we swam in seeing, our bodies saw. . . .
Voices distracted me and I awoke
. . . and after the voices died remain
wakeful at midnight near children,
telling them stories, what the voices spoke.
Our tales evoke a living circle,
chime among presences, possess the sound
of being heard; we hear them so, resonant
with listeners, who come close in the dark;
our tales are such late echoes of loss,
but a promise of recovery,
the deeper dream come back as the common place.
And so we shape our stories to acknowledge
company present, include them, name
and feature, in the tale, narrow to their span
the girth of powers telling calls up out
of the turbulent nothing: and they rouse,
they come ashore glistening, plunge
toward being, while their riders, swift
in the stillness of the tale, crouch
whispering into the ears of the dark
—it is darkness the children are riding,
our words in their newborn voices
rich nonsense free of our perplexity,
our rage, of living, too trivial,
too precious to mean anything ever,
and the darkness listens as it runs—
Yes, go, *Beauty! Wind! Time!*

I am those words
alive in their mouths
while they speak me;
I am their breath,
the missing companion
who comes again

and again to the lips;
and air that lives
in their telling;
the evocation alive
in the air.
And laugh to live on,
so pure and senseless
a spell
     —if only I
do not survive
my posterity.

How quick the horses ran,
how quiet under the earth.
Was it a waking dream?
inside a dream of sleep?
They rode and whispered too well.
I have been telling to the air
this story the children will never tell.

THIRD

Voices roused him and he woke.

Or say he stumbled into wakefulness, found himself on all fours peering over a doorsill. In the dark, bignesses—bulk or shadow— blocked his way to the light and out.

And say they rumbled and hissed in every part and movement, and this was their speech, outlandish gabble that made *him* the stranger, not the denizen he'd thought. And that they hid nothing meant he was no guest either, but someone extra, of no account, in fact, no one at all.

Say their number was indeterminate: two, or several, many more, one; in every form dangerous. So he called all the same: bully— and kept his vigil.

Say, latecomer, squatter; then bully could dispose of him as bully wished; his being here, his very existence were scurf, the skin of nothingness. Cleverness might keep him alive (bully was strong, bully was dumb), it could do nothing to clarify his status, or the status of anything. He crouched down better.

Say he might hope someday to become mascot to a team of gods.

Forget it! Or say benevolent despot—and show bully how bully ought to be. Fat chance!

Say, seeing little, he heard much, overheard, rather, since bully addressed only itself or muttered back and forth to themselves. Just as well; he would not have believed anything bully said to him directly. Always with an ear out while seemingly dawdling, hanging around; always on the ball of one foot pivoting, veering with the voices—no blast of bully's might catch him broadside; at last, little more than an ear, overgrown, overhearing.

Say bully was unworthy of such delicacy; he was too considerate, really, he should have torn the words from bully's throat.

Say the voices turned for worse—the rude banter louder, the hissing ominous. Most miserably: in his fear he had nothing to cling to but the very thing he feared. So he hung there by his ear, hearing.

Say this moment of his conception filled his ear to overflowing; now he conceived of himself; he was the other, the third person of the bully's discourse, the *he,* as it were, of bully's brutish hee-hawing.

Say outrageous to discuss him *in absentia;* still, he dared not by any peep signify his presence; discovered, he would be hurled down and made to vanish, the subject of a sentencing he would never hear or know ever was being carried out. Thus, unassuageable his terror of absence.

Say, unable to bear more, he made of the murderous din a phrase to mumble over and over, rocking himself in his arms where he crouched and crooned to his failing heart.

Say it saved him—this sentence of death that became his charm, his talisman, the anthem of his being and secret motto of self-denomination.

Say, long after, he understood all that racket, *this bully bully bully* he was forever mumbling; in that moment, also, he forgot it; and, forgetting, uttered it as his own. Now he was in the other room, his shadow no longer, solid. Amnesia would do as innocence. He suspected nothing. He had arrived.

Say a small figure, a mere curlicue of being—himself or another—crouches at the doorsill, peering over.

Say this story he overhears him telling.

FOURTH

Three selves of me set out together.
Stooped and strident, I did worship power
and take the bully's part—the side of death—
against me, stooped, defiant: I cast me out
and left me to die raging among stones.
Two of me went on together. At Three Roads,
I rose up and, striking back, struck me down.
Stooped and white now, I, the third of three,
surviving both, fare onward alone,
telling my bloody story with one hand out.
That is all I know how: suffer, sup, survive,
perform for the world world's scandal of self
—See *me*! clamor I; squeal out, Why *me*?
if pinch squeeze in, yet quick, given
the respite of a single breath, to wink
and sneak a grab for crust or crotch.
In secret, I am proud—whoever
this I is, who, surrounded by death
on every side, crows here and now.

FIFTH

To move forward with the world, to be
in time with time . . . is innocence.
For a thousand miles the wave keeps pace,
strokes smoothly on in phase with force,
at one with the festive crowd
and one of its joyous more and more;
it buoys itself and drives ahead,
renews in the trough the power it
expends at the crest, shape it then
surpasses and leaves to lapse behind.
I love my innocence, it chants,
see my transparence, I have nothing to hide,
therefore, I cannot ever die;
my existence is benign, the air
I breathe is borrowed from no one;
the drowning see my breath, and smile

—except the evil, whose badness starves them,
monsters, they merit their bulging eyes.
I bask and sing, am smooth and shine.

The figure in the wave, kneeling, half dazed,
half drowned, battering its head on the ground,
lifted and pushed forward inches, chokes
and blusters into the water running down. . . .
Out of time, sea-sick, sucking
the slack scum between wave and wave, here
is when you discover in the reflux
the theme of age: the falsity of innocence
—your every breath an act of power,
you live to injure, survive by murder;
while you were lethal, you were innocent;
floundering in the raging slop,
powerless now, you grasp the fact of power.
Your lung half bitter broth, you blurt:
Existence is my enemy, my life
attacks me; my past, maimed and vengeful,
returns in a wave, is heaving inside me;
my retching rises to possess me—the dead,
large with my past power, overpower me.
Grievance is death usurping my throat,
is death already speaking out as me.
—And you struggle to spit it all out,
you struggle not to go under, struggle
to assent to indeed go under as
an equal who negotiates with death.

SIXTH

I want to tell my story to the ground
I want to whisper my trouble to the earth
I want to lie down and ease my heart
I want to put my mouth to the ear of earth
I want to fill my mouth with dirt
I want to fill my eyes with darkness
—let earth be my sight! the fallen earth
poor old lady earth, poor queen, poor body

I want to feel each grain against me
I want to be clay and marry with clay
Let my words be stifled! there is no story
it has all been told, I have nothing to say
I want to unloose and subside, and seep away
I want to follow the sparks below gravity
I want to quench my glory, shining offends me
I want to be November in the clay
The cold slime will not frighten me
I want to vanish, why should I stay
—exile is my homeland
I want to know nothing I want to see nothing
say nothing be nothing never again
I want to tell my sorrow to the ground

EIGHTH

Death is mindless, like gossip
—these dregs of anecdote we cast
hopefully at our glass houses,
or cast toward one another simply
to be rid of, passing on what
can't be thought, what bears only
the interest of iteration,
fool's gold, chunks of pugnacious fact,
or fiction stupefied as fact.
Fools, of course, we are avid for them,
as hens are for hard baubles
with which to grind the daily fare.
So our dead return to figure in
the stories we tell—not to remain
unthinkable, not to be cast off
as odd, inert, mere facts of matter.
And that they keep returning is
the tale that clearly becomes them,
the one that keeps us at our telling,
keeps us gossiping across the grave
about every imaginable thing.
They are emissaries to absence,
who bear our tales beyond our voices,

and speak for us—of us—to all the dead
in their past and vanished country,
repeating our tales of sun and cloud,
what we murmur into their eternal blink
to tell them how it is today with light,
with dark, such weathers of consciousness
as we, moment by moment, wander in.
And they return with news of nothingness,
their quietness of someone listening,
in which, finally, we hear ourselves
speaking and heard, absent and here,
in passage and lingering as we step off,
ourselves and other—these revenants
who press to our own their missing faces.
Without this, we would—when all is told—
be poor indeed in a well-lit dead end,
the bright misery of a shadeless world.

Ever After

To Noemi

The beginning was all a puzzlement:
the small mouth in the sand, its dark trickle,
pain she wanted to run from and couldn't,
then a fiery thistle of fingers
pointed or waggled or beckoned or prodded
or said, Pay attention! Her eyes, bright-new,
were coin for that: she kept still and looked
—however hard to know what was a sign
or just a self idling beside the road
and did it mean her, whoever she was.
Still, she went on, getting the knack of it,
and little by large everything opened up,
the signs leading onward to other signs,
the riddles rearing in her path like stiles,
too high to jump but easy to slip under;
and misplaced whatever had to be found
again, and followed every misdirection

until it came true, and ran needless errands
so whatever else had to happen could,
so the white horse who came to her in the wood
would come to her saddled and carrying
a king, and believed unbelievable witches
and little wizards her body sensed were kin,
and by subtle experiment and profound
meditation discovered her powers
and the power of her prince-making kiss,
too extraordinary almost to use.
And so it was so, after all—and all
that often-diverting foolery had led
somehow to a state figured in the stars:
every night she saw a kingdom go to sleep,
and, gleaming shoe buckle to sparkling
diadem, rose and possessed the heavens.

And saw, from the height of her life, she had lived
a story, had, as though enchanted, obeyed
the dumb talk gesturing in her limbs, while she
—her passionate hunger for mysteries
nothing that merely happened could sate—
had wagered herself against everything,
demanding always, "And now? What happens now?"
And now? And now she was telling the story,
an old woman talking to children.
Words came to her, so perfectly at the pace
of things they seemed not to move at all—and now
the odd details of her journey grew lucid,
the wilderness, at home in itself, made sense.
And telling it again made the same sense
again, made it deeper, gave it pleasure,
the water came up in the bucket clearer,
from a cooler, stiller depth of the well,
and where the bucket knocked the wellcurb
the wood buffed itself clean on the stone,
until her life lay clear in the grain.
She touched it, beautiful, neutral, itself.
"Ever after" was really the afterlife
where she would be telling her life over.

No longer checked, exhorted, driven
in an agony of forwardness,
the fierce horse walks over the tranquil plain,
bobbing its nose in an oaken pail.
The children reach down to pat its flanks.
She is happy. So.

          And once again
let herself drop until no bigger than
a pale thimble in the deep, but bountiful
and great when she brought the darkness up
on her lips, potable and clear and filling,
and touched them so to the children's lips;
and, gleaming shoe buckle to sparkling
diadem, rose and by all ways at once
kicked free and scattered across the heavens.

The Tortoise

Surely he deemed himself swiftness personified, muttering as he went, My name is Diligence, I am Alacrity: I leap to serve. Yet while one or another blazing messenger came and left a thousand times, the tortoise on the vestibule floor—at each flitting shadow, at the trembling of flagstones under the skimming feet, at the little buffets of air—paused a thousand times to rehearse his ancient repertoire of discretions. As if all this coming and going were aimed against him, or against the word he bore most carefully within.

Comic or pathetic he may seem to those of us who measure his miles as inches, who at every stride hurdle a hundred diapasons— yet the throne room shall greet the tortoise with unstinted glory and the new message entrusted him shall be no less urgent, no less momentous.

Then see the majesty of his slow turning, his smile of wisdom too wise to smile. Oh, see how high his foot is lifted!

From *Teach Me, Dear Sister*

Millions of Strange Shadows

Courtesy came before joy.
The greeting preceded the recognition.
I thought it would pass me by, the great crowd
that came singing itself home from the feast
(where I was heading—too late! I thought),
and raised my arm as passersby do
in the street, nodding vaguely as if to say,
Yes, that *is* you—whoever you are.
(And thought, But they left the party too soon.)

Whoever they were: all those forgotten,
those still to arrive, faceless, familiar,
singing, and flowing after their song,
millions of strange shadows, strange lights,
that rose from darkness, that now came close,
gleamed in salutation, spoke my name.
The voices made it new and the same,
not mine only—theirs to call me by.
And though I alone was flesh there,
shadow and light and song pressed around,
escorted me wholly among them
—they the true body in which I walked,
the words that made my throat veridical,
and here the feast that roamed the roads
and sang in the streets from dawn to dawn.

The Bathers

Can there be women alone and no serpent near?

The haze conceals a hint, the hint a presence . . .

Student of opportunities, he licks the air . . .
"Who are these, flittering swift perfumes,
this pair of pairs,
in two-piece swimsuits,

two black, two blood-red,
in taut and ruffled satin,
waves of their hair waves of the sea?"

Touch one anywhere and you are touched by all
—so every raindrop holds the whole sea.

"Who are these strangers,
with sharp little teeth and little pink tongues,
deftly clicking bobby pins apart
or running a thumb along a halter strap
—strangers but as if intended?"

He moves by mere percipience,
his senses draw near.

"Who lifts an arm, who shakes her curls,
flirting with the universe
—just to show the others she *can*,
just to let it know who's there?"

Sways elaborate kinks aloft,
preens his keen head.
"But who are they, after all?"

Oiling their arms and fiddling with their hair,
making it behave, not be such a bother,
sprawled or sitting one to a blanket corner,
all combed alike, all made up alike, all
dressed in the uniform of loveliness,
and each the queen of her brilliant parlor,
what can North Star be telling South Wind,
blond Sunrise express to West's brunette
with eyebrows arching, with shrugging shoulder?
"I love cerise!" "I can't stand chartreuse!"
"Me, I'm just crazy about egg-clairs!"
"Kessler's napoleons . . . they're much too sweet!"
"My sister's new jumper is really cute!"
—precious tastes by which they mean to say
that not all raindrops are the same,

as if they could make themselves crystalline,
as if they were not constantly flowing away,
waves of their hair waves of the sea . . .

The beach's whole ear, he would listen forever . . .

Too innocent to sense the serpent there?
that certain air of consciousness
in the air? Not letting on,
excited, they talk louder—to civilize
the creature, to tame the bold fella, whisper
to coax him closer . . . teach him this
is how you treat a girl, this is what
a lady likes, this is how he must say,
how run her errands like any common
kid brother (no harm if he thinks himself
her pet), how stand there charming not
scary, now lay his head harmless halfway up
on her milky thigh . . . till devil himself
would hold still to have his toenails painted
and beg favor to rest on her the sunlamp
of his exclusive attending, be her own,
her private, particular sun . . . so great
her neediness is, so great must be
his services—his servitude for her distress,
drowning in beingness—as constant
and changing, as endless as the sea . . .

"The wind's coquetting hem,
wave's dark underneath and white release
—brightness too brief!"
His single name for the glittering
of opportunity is woman.

Every girl has a dream, every woman a story.

If she makes excuse, saying, *"It'll mess my hair!"*
"It's too cold today!" "Really, I'm still full!"
"Oh, I just finished putting my lotion on!"
if she doesn't walk out into the whole

embrace and flowing—then has nothing to say
when she goes among other women
telling their fibs fibs fibs, and must sit there
like a dummy without two cents to chip in.
If she doesn't, the little pitcher
of her lap pours nothing out,
no stain will darken down her skirt
its uncontrollable sap of sorrows and time
while she looks at herself unbelieving
—betrayed betrayed! If she doesn't,
there's no gathering her womb's wet spillage,
and never will learn she has nothing, is
nothing herself, no domain, no house, no land,
servant to everyone's hunger, discarded
afterward, if not devoured during,
her one inheritance her own nerve
—oh, *must* have her way, since she has nothing else.
And later, no laying out the dead,
no lamentation, submission, surviving,
no letting the lid down gently,
and letting drop the tiny hidden trump:
denied the first, oh sweetness always of
the last word and taking off the last trick
and leaving the table utterly bare,
and sitting on before the dark waves opening
and closing their jaws over the bare beach
while she says her story out to the sea,
"I *have* been bloody and I *will* be
a bellyache to the wave that takes me!"
—and always pleasure of the whole deck
snug and full in the palm of her hand
while everything else goes on and on
being nothing—unless she lets it be her:
even losses enlarge her, her secrets, lies
—a fate with the fortunes asleep in her fist—
so massive now that nothing escapes,
so great she hardly knows all she is,
but *feels* it whenever waves come
and do pretty please to her feet . . .

.   .   .

Day toward evening; discreetly,
the serpent recedes, seeming to bow and waving,
takes up a post among the shadows, waiting . . .
Who are these bright flecks carried along
on the tiding flank, still speaking?

"My mother needs me!"
"I promised my sister!"
"My father wants me to help!"
"My boyfriend's waiting!"
To be required, requested, rich
in society, in obligations, not
less or left behind, and belong
wholly to their time, as if they were not
flowing away . . . They pack up, go heavily
—the graces of dawn are donkeys at five
in service to what old discipline of bearing,
opportunity to others but such problems
to themselves, dull silhouettes lumped out
with comforting bundles, bulk and clutter
of being, cards, a shoe dangled, clothing . . .
a little while longer their radio's
portable rumba stays on dancing alone
above the sand it will not stir at this
late hour . . . looses its last little thunder . . .
No animal in sight, north or south, east
or west, no likely chance, no lively wager . . .

A serpent alone and no women near?

Waves have licked the beach clear.

"But who are these,
lightly daring forward,
who approach, who appear?"

They

Adam alone had been Adam
unknown, shadowless under
the sun, lost in shadow under
the moon, lost in thought that thought
all things and found their names, and yet
could not find Adam in its thought.

The thought beyond Adam's thinking
grew visible and saw:
Adam abandoned, unwitting.
In her regard he saw himself thought,
in her thought found himself, found
Adam. His lips parted. Adam.

Endeared to himself in a globe
of thought, now Adam thought
multitudes of Adam
vanishing toward purity
—himself, a column, line, a point,
then volumes of inanition.

Pity him! the serpent whispered,
placing the knowledge on her palm.
It was round and simple and shining:
You see how he consumes himself,
he is dying. She saw,
and offered the fruit, meaning:
of her might Adam eat
without himself falling to food
—of her, of Eve, he could eat.
Then Adam lay there, sated, sleeping.

Figures crowded his dream in glory
—while she, who desired only
the bright raiment of his gaze, now saw
her nakedness of food, food
he had dared and then possessed, then

surpassed, he, sealed as himself, as
Adam—ungrateful, starving.

What was she to herself in thought?
As little as thought could be to her?
She needed him bitterly
to raise her being to his lips,
cherish her lowliness by eating.
Descend into blindness, into
simplicity? be food again?
his food? less and less Eve?
sweeten herself all over?
despised again? devoured again?

Forgive him! the serpent hissed.

A Crone's Tale

To Françoise Krampf

Tell you of the witch? Well, so I will, child,
as well as ever I remember the story.
Now the witch was an ordinary girl
and not half so pretty as you, and like you
grew up to her life on an island's small place.
And seeing there the changeable wilderness
of water, that plashed and sparkled among rocks
and stroked the sand, then fussing and willful chased
the little boats from their paths, and later
was wide shining distance, indifferent to all
and different from everybody—seeing this,
why then, she set her heart on the mystery.
And so she stood and called out names to the sea,
every name that ever the girl could think.
Now you must take care, child, what names you say.
Your cry for help, your offer of kindness,
both sup together in the name you speak.
So you must take care to what name you answer.

Now I will tell you the ocean heard her.
As foreign sailormen it came ashore,
well, and every day more of them came and more,
strange hollering things that stood up in the foam
like waterfalls, or on hands and knees trickled
to the windy beach and lay about drying,
or came like spraywater by the stinging wind
blown there, beardy and rough and rimed with salt.
Well, as sailormen the sea came ashore,
as animals it stayed on there, listening
to nice syllables spelled clear in her breath,
they the wild element's soft embodiment,
they enchanted slowly to domestic ways.
Now, child, you have seen the salamander, how
it lies in the winter hearth sunning on coals
and laving off ash with licks of its tongue,
and you have heard the air's sprites in the wood,
and seen the grizzled field lift a green head
and dart the dainty tines of its silent tongue.
Just so in her stable were round strange backs
running like waves under the drover wind
and many snouts were leaping up together
and butty heads slapping the whitewash posts,
and rushes in fury and fright, and patience
nibbling along inside the green centuries.
Many were swine there, and never swine only,
but sheep they were, too, both mister and missus,
yes, hens and horses, geese and goats and cattle
—now let me see, who is it I have forgot?—
and whiteface rabbits and many mice as well,
all trampling up the one scatter of straw
and taking molasses, taking stews and slops,
good things to eat she fixed in the kitchen,
green things that in her garden sprouted up.
And came to her running ever she called them,
"You, Henry," "You, Alfred," "You, Charles," and such,
good names all, such names they were as your brothers
would have and kings of the happiest place.
Or came if ever they heard clump of her shoes
or kirtle whisper to the hay's shining raff.

Well she knew it was the sea in her stable
that came to glint there with thousand bright eyes
and pricked up ears and made eager noises, nudged
her hand with moist noses, sucked on her fingers,
that sat down guest at her floor's low table,
that warmed itself in itself in its sleep.
And ever we want, child, the creatures by,
to have the good of them, the milk and mildness,
so must we do with victuals and kind voices.
Oh, if that were enough! But there's more than it.
Here now, I've dropped my thimble, just wait a bit.
Run, sweet, and pick it up where it rolls away
under blue chair, I can just see its gleaming.
There, that's the good child . . .
Well, as I was saying, she kept the straw clean,
she freshened the water, she did not scant
the poor sailormen that came to her shore.
But one of them she would by no means feed,
by no means would she call him to her,
but left him to roam the shoreline all day
and wade the white streets of the broken wave.
Him alone she kept a stranger, until
the night long when beasts snugged down in their sleep
he only cried out "Circe, Circe" to her
as if the sea's self with a human voice
at last would single out, would summon her.
And ever all night she was held around,
but she bit back the word, by no means would speak.
She thought she drowned, and then she didn't drown.
I forget what happens next, but no matter.
Now the girl had what most her heart wanted.
She lived on an island, she married the sea.

It may be you shall think one day to marry.
It may be you shall walk beside the water,
hearing it keen the feeling it cannot say.
Then must you put fingers to ears, lock eyes shut
—or shall in pity cry out names to it,
shall hunt its far shine in every eye comes near.
Or it may be you shall never . . .

Here now lay your finger on this knot. Just so.
And from deeps may come to you a daughter.
Perhaps shall call the child for me . . .

So now your old grandmother, as fond as old,
gives you her blessing, and a kiss goes with it.
Remember her name in your prayer every night.
So out goes candle now—now you must go to sleep.

Eberheim

Eberheim, *je pense à vous*
—or try to, though unable
to bring you into any field
of vision: in Vladivostok
buried as another, the narrator
having followed the wrong cortege
one hundred pages after
your first appearance in the novel:
that "horrible groan" (they waited,
fruitlessly, for a second) from
an "adjoining room"—in Petersburg
where, coincident
to bloody skirmishing in the streets,
you were beginning
to begin your dying.
Your "life" two brief notices
of two phantom events,
and your obituary
three glances meeting to agree
you were better off so.
No showing forth here—even
an epiphany in a brown woolen suit
would have been brighter—rather,
a hiding away, a vanishing.
What *can* resolve your image?
—pity must blur the whole
in bloating the detail,

irony diminish all
for clarity's small sake.
"Elderly," "penniless," "exacting,"
shyest of all the entries in
the who's who in solitude
—how *is* one to place
an exemplary irrelevance?—
half-expunged, fugitive, yet familiar,
like the brother of a famous face,
and even less than ink on paper
—Eberheim, I think of you!

The Biographies of Solitude

Blue the hills, red the fields,
where the kisses and blows were dealt . . .
How eager they were, marching away,
enlistees in the horde of love.
Farewell the sweethearts
—they never came back.
Welcome, sisters of solitude.

And who will say these lives have been?

Solitude has no biographers.

Nonetheless, hands move across the pages.
Nonetheless, empty pages go from hand to hand.
Nonetheless, papers blow over the landscape
of magical names, the beautiful promises.

One is in snowy Idaho, raging.
One in California sits before her mirror,
considering death.
One takes hot baths in Tennessee,
to calm herself, calm herself down.
In Kansas one scribbles madly.
One walks in a daze in the crowds

on Forty-second Street, barefoot,
her feet bruised, day after day.
In the hospital of the wind.

What the flood has spared is given
into the keeping of the whirlwind.

Day after day the wind
numbering the losses . . .

"From now on I will love only myself."
"I no longer try to make sense to people."
"It's all a game anyway."
"Back then I still had my ideals.
No sacrifice was too much for me.
I was strong. I felt everything."
"I don't even pity myself anymore."

They bite their lips.
Shrug their shoulders.

"What is there left to protect?"
"Who can you trust?"

How America is immense and filled with solitudes!

In Old San Juan

I've come to visit Doña Trina,
to pay respects and receive my blessing.
At the kitchen table under the great clock
where an elegy is always ticking,
this is me sitting mute in the center of
her amphitheater of darkening photos:
children and their children, nieces, nephews,
while Doña Trina fussing to one side
plays the prompter with sherry and whispers

—So many successes, such lovely spouses.
Can age be the good thief who's carried off
every bitter word she may once have known?
Her small talk levitates a world of praise.
And I must say they are looking down at me
in the kindest way, as sweetly as the cakes
from the icebox, the *turrón* on the table,
or Doña Trina sugaring my ear.
For all the fan's dulcet stirring, it's hot
in here, I feel in danger of becoming
gingerbread in this nice lady's oven
—nothing can be *this* sweet!
                              Ay, Doña Trina,
your tales can't make good so much betrayal.
Who could believe the little show-offs
would go so far, and so far away, become
doctors, lawyers, *professionals*?—oh,
the shamelessness of all epiphanies!
Why do we insist on growing our faces,
when one might instead have been a sunny wall?
Such heartbreaking gleams leap from photographs
of youth's full cheeks or fresh little moustache,
Latin style, circa nineteen-fifty!
Somebody strike me blind before
I glimpse my own opacity
—obese with accomplishment, I obscure
as I impress, abashed when I think,
Who could ever dream over all this flesh?
Set me, Doña Trina, among your pride
of photos on the piano couchant,
or on your mantelpiece to keep the time
with two syllables only,
tick for things, *tock* for nothingness,
and let me hear you murmur, twittering, wise,
not how far I've come but how much I promise.

The Salon of Famous Babies

Of course, she knew he loved her, but how he did
nagged at her and pestered, refused to shut up.
No, she wouldn't mince the words in her mind:
it seemed just ordinary stupid love,
ignorant, or unaware, of itself, of her,
so unobservant, so lacking in detail
it was almost, *almost* an insult—she
would not have loved a puppy so!
                                  Well, here
was something that needed doing, and when
she loved now it wasn't that simple old love,
but serious, *teaching* love, love that would show him
what loving really was, working, taking pains,
thinking things out.
                         It put her in a rage
how little he saw even this, even now!
As well teach ducks to drown as teach him not
to take it all as owed the world's own son and heir.
Oh, *his* idea of love was feeling fine
and saying *Bless you* and *Okay* to everything,
and nodding *Hey* in her direction, where maybe
he sensed some pleasant thickening in the glow.
He thought love was checking in to count the house,
and his daydream of glory always the feature,
with maybe in the gawking crowds her face
repeated a thousand tiny times (at least that,
dear god!) in the last row under the rafters.
She saw it in his eyes sometimes—and it cut
to the quick to see him . . . so, so *limited*,
how in everything he did a little man
inclined lazily in a little bow.
                            No, no,
no, loving meant alertness, meant knowing her
bit by bit *and* (enthusiasm had added
had not prudence disallowed it) *through and through*!
What saved her patience was pitying him:
that trim, self-sufficient poverty of his,
which never even dreamt what worlds it missed

—a thousand vitalities ablaze each instant
around his head . . . that once a week some thunder struck.
Why, anyone with any wickedness in her
might truss and stuff him, and go her way whistling.
Lucky for him, *she* was no empty shell like those,
she had feeling still, had kept her soul intact
and always would—if only *he* were man enough
to stand up to her and fight back.

                                  Nonetheless,
she felt her powers come: she knew—it had to go
without saying—that she was his superior.
Let him elevate that noble brow of his
in the salon of the famous babies, *she* knew
—just didn't she—*who* was the lion's hairdresser!
Oh, it might have been restful there beside him
—so slow, so unwitting—she'd have napped a bit,
but the injustice kept picking into her heart,
and she muttered *How dare he! How dare he!*
a thousand times, until she thought it once
—the thought transformed her forever—*Why, he dares!*
Amazed, she understood something awful,
that he was careless, dull, unattending from
a vast strength he had in secret: he knew
he couldn't be hurt.

                              So, it *is* a man's world,
she thought. Grand and mysterious, the summit
of his self-confidence rose from her very feet.
Everything had been a preparation—this
would be her crowning work: to climb to its top
and look around—oh, she would blink at nothing—
and see whatever was out there to see.
She would take the world's measure and, if it came
to not much, infer the mountain didn't either.
She was prepared for that, prepared to render
objective and final judgment on it all,
and then say if the climb was worth it or not
(on the whole, she'd guess, not), but would decide later
whether to publish her report.

                              In any case
and certainly, she would *not* be defeated.

Beauty

Jewish Brooklyn's bit of Muscovite winter,
Christmas Eve of 'forty or 'forty-one,
I and Papa struggling in wind and snow
on a dark land's end of empty avenue.
Suddenly she was there—seen once before,
not ever since—staggering from a side street,
superb woman some s.o.b. had knocked around,
punched six steps up from a musty basement flat,
tall, black, battered, regal, coatless, drunk, beautiful.
She caught my breath, catches my breath again
—exiled queen of a scattered warrior people,
or Venus led in chains, who hurls her shivered spear
forty years flying into the afterworld.
Beauty not to be battered down, love defeated.

To What's-Her-Name

Being there together could be too hot
for comfort, but that density of life
in common made us zip and buzz, and sting.
We knew our flutterings mattered—the future
was us impatient to become itself,
and our chatter, all those nasty or tasty
predicates, mere excuses to revisit
the loud patch of our intoxicating names.
That rant of pollination fevered more
than anything, than any single passion could!
And now we're thinned out, all gone off to die
or be the scene's newest young hothead's
or hot young thing's dull, bumbling ancestor
—and even you are full of irrelevant
reminiscences, as if too deranged
to do more than hover, you whose beauty shows
in all these scarred, disreputable gashes.

. . .

Back when your gentle attentions were picking
my heart clean in plain sight of everyone,
did I ever dream that, in pity for
your crumpled lips, I'd regret your smile's faint
fume of vitriol, your sudden, awful,
gulped-down squeal when you inched in for the kill,
the ready, shameless, hot gush of your gossip,
always virulent, always victorious?

Albert Feinstein

I

No angel does this: thickens, goes white.
Then some are *born* old, perhaps?
Not so the stern juvenile of distance,
Apollo staring from the sun, confirming
or destroying in the light of day,
as if youth itself were a judgment.
But then these old, purblind ones, craning
and pressing close to us?—Whispers,
or less, our lips just beginning
to part, a thought unspoken, hardly owned,
lights in them a pure intelligence.
Nameless or never rightly named,
and yet their faces glow.
                              This one,
for example, hovering beside
two student actors like their guardian
(darkness, an empty theater, the trio there
on stage, whom I, a stranger killing time,
have come across by accident),
—someone's called him "Albert Feinstein."
Albert *Fein*stein? Albert Feinstein
coaching college theatricals?
But Albert was a young man
when I last saw him thirty years ago,
as young as the clod playing "Adam,"

as poor "Eve": pedantic wanting
to be winsome, coming out cute.
We were young poets together!
sleek littermates in the epoch's wallow,
nursed and farted side by side.
His style was drowsy and whimsical,
like one who's unprepared but unsurprised.
Oh I half remembered the elegant stoop
thickened here to tortoise plate,
but not the silver error flagrant on his brow.
Why, he could be my father now!
But look at his face, see—what can
have made the witty fool grow beautiful?

2

So many years some handfuls of sensitive earth,
such artless "Adam"s and silly "Eve"s, who can't
express the sense they have by heart—and yet
their pain of shortcoming is bliss in him.
See, he is looking from one to the other,
radiant and mute and keen, his face lit with
the good intention waylaid in their clay.
See, he sets them in his circle of patience,
this bit of the fullness of time, all the time
in the world in a little sphere—where they play.
It is the least precipitous, the gentlest joy
—patience that overgrows the deadlines instant
by instant, that ripens the intimate minute.
"If not this time, then another time
. . . it is all *one* time," his attending implies.
And they understand it is a joy to repeat,
however poorly, because joy to be here
with one another and with this third
who makes their love possible, *is* their love
made visible to them, a quiet angel
they place in the keeping of happiness.
See, he has been cast into his own life,
in a drama greater than he directs.
Here Adam and Eve say each other's name,
there Feinstein ages into innocence.

See, because of Feinstein we go on trying,
the clod heaves himself up and turns over,
the girl grows solemn and deep, the globe shines.

The Drowned Man

We open our eyes and the world is light,
a radiance that opens our eyes.
As each of us has dreamed it,
so it is now in the sight of all
—cordial and plain and total.
Why waken here if not in greeting
to the embassy of everything?
Dreaming, I knew it would be so, but not
how like my dream, how truly known, how glowing.

A consciousness gone, a radiance lost.
The world is diminished by a world.
The embassy has tarried on the way.
The common light appears, displaced and dazed,
verbless, unresponsive, a stranger
who has closed his eyes—and if he dreams
our sweet breath after swimming and then
our little sleep, will never say; and we,
like the light, enfeebled, cannot wake him or speak.

Teach Me, Dear Sister

Teacher, muse, sibyl.
Three times in three guises
she appeared to him.

✦

Her great eight to his five importunate years,
she sat him and they played at school.

Big steaming pots of sun, their kitchen classroom,
where he, the simplest Simon anywhere,
did this, did that, as she would tell him to.
Then, one morning, he saw the world take form:
outlined in simple rules, and for subtle hue
her sober intoning, her sage and tender frown.
Alert to please, before she could say,
he sat up straighter, he listened carefully,
he told his swinging legs to stop
—bright baby ape who deftly locked the cage
door shut, then proudly handed back the key.
Gladness was: to be his better self,
to make her happy eyes, her brow be smooth.
His body stilled, his mind raced forward.
Everything everywhere could be something known,
and precious suddenly for being knowledge,
though not truly known until made known to her.
Her eyes were dark and kind. To them he sped
the little love bullets of his replies,
tidbits of world he would set before her.
Of all arguing dumbbells everywhere,
he alone rang out true and clear, to rouse
the day and say, Rejoice in her laughter!
—mornings when the sun commenced its decalogue
and scrawled a large and silent golden *aleph*
on their table's white enamel top.

        ◆

Old masters and young mistresses
                              —young Huxley's crack,
who recommended museums for cruising snatch.
Yes, something made them giddy, got them wild. . . . And he,
reconnoitering the galleries, wanted to understand.
Were these mere paintings? The place was like a zoo,
a menagerie of bright and breathing angels
sunning happily on walls . . . gods on holiday among us,
great naked pelts and swatches of four elements and darkness . . .
among whom you sauntered, swam, kicked up sand, flirted, got
    tanned,

got laid, drank pop . . . opulent and gorgeous, indifferent
to eyes that lit them, stares they inflamed . . . anyone
could gawk forever . . . at these overheating geniuses
in their stalled flotilla . . . unmindful of each other,
large jubilant babes in a marble playpen, each one
the president of everything . . . not civic types at all . . .
stars . . . but how accommodating, in grandeur and pleasure,
willing to shove over—and go on shining! . . .
their pantheon always with room for one more . . .
and why not? in this anthology of exile where they
no longer mattered . . .
                      What brought him to the bronze head
was the girl eye to eye, even nose to nose, with it
—to read its secret or to ask, as perhaps she asked
of everything, her own powers . . . whether to heal
or hurt . . . Of her he thought to recall the bright wad
of coppery hair and tan raincoat's diving hem,
its line exactly that a ship makes going down . . .
in this sumptuous flotsam of angel-animals . . .
He recognized the type: bright, abrupt, ungainly, confused,
patronizing the men she knew . . . other men made her nervous.
Well, which was he? wimp? or wolf? She never looked back.
The master must be losing his touch—though not his feeling
of connection with whatever woman he came across . . .
And was she dragging a leg? In fact? Or mockery?
And if mocking him, what sort of devil was he? Little, of course.
Oh where, he asked, have all the junior muses gone
who used to waltz within this sacred grove?
                      The bronze
was beautiful, a girl of eighteen,
he guessed, mouth and cheek still
delicate, her steady gaze
as if she held a moving thing
in view, flame or wave, himself.
What moved in him—broken or restless—
grew well, was still.
               The stillness glowed.
Her hair, upswept in a budding wing,
poised for the lift of a lively word.
Like someone at the starting point

who asks both blessing and direction
she was waiting for him to speak.

✦

A moving trance within a crowd,
she lagged its pace but, ferried on
the powerful forward surge, stopped
at the light with it, then crossed when
the crowd crossed Fifth Avenue. How many
days like this? in a thin dark slip,
barefoot, her blond hair knotted, hands
empty, her slim legs streaked with urine
and dirt, hardly able to lift her feet.
—Disaster must appear so when it looms
incontinent and purseless in the doorway,
with nothing in mind but barren motion.
And he, having rushed ahead and then
turned back again to help her, met
the perfect blankness of her gaze.
Dazed. Out to lunch. Nobody there.
More communion from an insect's glare.
He felt the world had lost its eyes,
himself vanishing in their empty noon.
She seemed as if beaten in broad daylight
and when no one intervened to save her,
she, too, couldn't stop to care, agreed
that she was nothing, superfluous, dust.
And drifted—panic's slowest immigrant
blown here out of the exploded future
to be the specter in the crowd's bad dream,
the person missing in the middle of the street,
beneath the mercy of anything.
Wake up, dear sister, he was trying to say
to the sibyl in her trance, but the woman
would not respond, so deep the charm that held her.
And the spell she was under was the end of the world.

Just Another Smack

Schoolmaster Auden gave them full marks,
"the Old Masters," for having understood
"about suffering" its "human position."
The view from Mt. Lectern was clear. They were,
he noted, *"never wrong."*
                                          One is pleased to see
things put in place, grateful for instruction
—though words like his might well inspire Job
with ruddied fingernails once more to rasp
excruciating music from festers and boils.
Sir, respectfully, is it possible
ever to be *right* about "suffering"?
—suffering which, after all, is not
just lying around waiting to be mapped,
but has abundantly its awful life.
I mean, sir, our suffering is no
Nativity, is never legendary
like Innocents slaughtered, Icarus plunging.
We lack that consolation. *Our* suffering
is nameless (like us) and newly whelped
and dying just to claim us for itself.

Perhaps, sir, you never meant all that,
had merely called in Birch the Learned
to make the new-boy romantics smart:
Let them not think their feelings so damned
important, that sort of rubbish and rot!
And one does grant a classic wisdom here
that *could* help young masters get to be old.
I mean: When they pass out the suffering,
don't insist on getting yours—you make sure
you're the one "just walking dully along."
The other bloke's never hurts as much.

And let's suppose you've gotten off clean,
left that little problem to be brought up
by others, and yourself "sailed calmly on"
into Snug Harbor. Well, twenty years later,

and now your life's a lovely picture,
and you just settling down to enjoy it.
Looks pretty good from where you sit,
lots of bright colors smack in the center,
with some poor slob getting the shaft
off in a murky corner—*he* won't be missed.
Why, will it to a fine museum, that's
what you'll do!
                    And then wouldn't you know it.
Out cruising, say, for a little action,
or maybe looking to change its luck,
Suffering just happens to happen by,
big as leviathan and calling you son,
and clouts enormously your shoulder blade,
and dispatches a knee swift to the groin
—by now you haven't breath to shout
or to curse the day you were born—
and caves in your ear with a whisper
(the last words you're going to hear,
doubled over now, dropping fast),
"Listen close. It's me. Only *I* got away.
And my message is strictly for you
—Hey, old fella, you've been elected."

Fresh Air

Social Constructions of Reality at Coney Island

IDEAL DISORDERS

Miles of rows of orange trash cans
all ah-ing to the sky was somebody's
idea of order at Coney Island;
another guy thought up the morning crew's
ragged line and lowered eyes—the daily stalk
of Parks Department foragers in green
straggling on heavy shoes and dreamily
lancing gum wrappers into gunny sacks.

Neither was anybody's idea of fun
—which was more like *dis*order, more like
just dropping public verticality
for open lolling about and wallowing,
down at sea level, off-guard, up-ended;
more like everybody getting together
and making a sea of "all of us"
alive beside the sea, ourselves
earth's numberless sands outfacing
the mirror shattered below the whole sky,
the slow monster under the empty motion.
Our being there was beelines over bodies,
was shortcuts swarming toward pleasure,
and half the fun was keeping it short,
and more than fun our thatch and hubbub,
our pullulation, of crossing purposes
filling the silence on the waters—until,
from the groin of comings and goings,
at three, at half past three exactly,
we hurled off a blanket to the day's height
the flying youth and cheering crowd—the sun!—
and peopled space with celebration.

A NEW WORLD

Torn maps, pages in spume
Crashing furniture of the shore
The nimble students leaping off,
who always from farther out
come riding toward us,
straddling desktops of the waves
—the water's glittering people,
the little pilgrims of light.

For these wavelets' chancing greenhorns,
our parents as they were, our future kids,
we the children of immigrants
walk in greeting at water's edge
and sing out the primer of fresh air:

Sky, president of thunder and smiles,
many-headed senates of the sea,
the jetties' bearded dripping courts,
and bully spanked home to his bad castle,
old death voted down the cellar stairs.
Everything, set free, arrives and shines.
All is a globe of recognitions.
Every creature of the place
—Utah, Kentucky, Idaho—
lit with intelligence,
glows as if about to speak;
wherever we look is looking back
with our gazes' own intensity,
the sun comes up, the waves
come up, asking our names.

And who *are* we, standing around
in bathing suits on the brink of everything?
We are Americans at the beach.

White confusions
Springs of the sea-winds' surging
—inland
toward mountains and prairies,
toward happiness.

THE GYMNASTS

Legs v-ed out from the groin's nugget
—the many figured as a single man.
Or the milling centipede of crossed purposes
pulling itself together and rising
from the ground up, in honor of itself.
And not to form the structures only, but
to be present in the flesh and confirmed
by others present equally to them
—leaving as early almost as the sun,
they come down from separate rooms, starting
from Elizabeth or Hoboken or the Bronx,

206

walking on their hands among us now
or spelling out with their spinning persons
leaping sentences of cartwheels and vaults.
Nearby, the bodybuilders are defining
their "pecs," biceps, "glutes"—glowing maps
of somber worlds in single display,
so distant that they sink slowly
into the background of every sky.
But here the gymnasts build themselves
together, embody what they illustrate:
serenity of power in action, strength
moving in matters of common concern;
and, by wall or mound or pyramid,
by honeycomb, womb, huddle, swarm
and tower—these sociable forms, forms
of habitation—in the middle of nowhere
bestow a sense to everything.

THE TOWER

A tower of men,
a tongue toward flaming heaven.
Now the last one goes up quick,
scaling fire to reach the baby
in the window of the burning tenement.
Everywhere, jealous angels look down.
The tower blazes up higher.
The faces puff in fury.
If we had breath to call him back . . .
His daring that makes the world come true.
—Arms uplifted,
he holds the whole sky open,
plucks the radiance from the fire,
the baby Now from the sky's *never*!
Oh, we gasp, Ah, we breathe out.
                              Just
as quick, the tower tumbles apart,
leaping every which way down.
Their yawp sends them crashing off,

shin and thigh, to slaughter waves.
And we, set free, have walked away
on the sand's radiant reaches.
                                    Now
the little kids go racing after
and smack up geysers, shouting.

The All-Stars

As when the fielders put down their gloves
and take up bats in their hands and pose
in a row on the dugout steps,
leaning forward, one foot on the field,
each in his own team's uniform,
each excelling at his specialty,
at the bunt or long ball or hit
and run or hitting where they ain't
or going with the pitch, each poised
within the flawless coincidence
of his competence and his name
—in token whereof his smile is grave,
leaving us to imagine the ball
stung on a line up the alley,
its mountain-making arc majestic
or tricky hop through a fielder crouching:

so it is we cave dwellers, rousing
to all that rumor in the stands,
stare from our own opposing dugout,
the heart's dark old colliery of awe,
and see—through the pure optic of fame—
daylight and then that pantheon
suddenly, like a burst of brilliants,
scatter across the great diamond
and take possession of the sunny air.

Read to the Animals, or Orpheus at the SPCA

> *A woman called and offered me a hundred dollars to
> read in San Francisco. I said, "Okay, but only for dogs
> and cats." "What?" she said. I said, "I charge five hun-
> dred dollars to read for people, but I'm interested in
> how pets respond to poetry. They hear humans speak-
> ing all the time, and I'm curious if they can tell the dif-
> ference between ordinary speech and poetry." "Can't a
> few people be there too?" "No," I said, "five hundred
> dollars for people, one hundred dollars for household
> pets. I can only give so many readings a year, and I
> want to earn the most from them." So she said, "I don't
> see the difference. You're reading anyway, whether to
> dogs and cats or to people." She's dead serious about
> this. I said, "Well, the dogs and cats don't tell anyone
> how long you read or how much you gave it."
> ... The last time I called [Adrienne Rich] I did so
> because a mutual friend said she was depressed and I
> might cheer her up. So I phoned her and got through
> her bodyguards, and she said, "Yes?" And I said,
> "Hello, Adrienne, this is Phil." She said, "Phil?" "Yeah,
> Phil Levine." "What do you want?" I should have
> said, "I want some pussy," because she was using a
> voice Mussolini would have used to a street cleaner.
> Instead I think I said, "Nice to talk to you."
>
> PHILIP LEVINE, interviewed
> in *Antaeus*, Summer 1980.

Dear Mr. Levine,
        You can call me Rex.
I am a two-year-old male dog—big, short-haired,
mostly shepherd—living the last six months
in this here shelter for wayward animals.

I read in a magazine how you looking
to adopt a cat. Me, too. Even if
I am canine, living with them day in
day out, I can say they totally cute.
Which probably is why they never seem
enough to go around. So flash on this:
our bitches really been getting the job done
—so maybe you adopt "some *puppy*" instead?

    I also seen how you looking to read
your poetry to us. We all were jumping.

We don't have budget for poetry reading,
so all of us guys been saving up for you.
Cool you cutting your fee. I pretty sure
we be able to hack the hundred bucks.
Supervisor say she be writing to you
on official paper, she say anyhow
after you seen our facility, you want
to turn it all back to our building fund.
But I say, Tell her to go stuff, yeah! I say,
Keep it—cost of cat *always* going up!

     Lot of poets starting to come around.
We animals got to be *in* thing now.
Bet you surprised how much poetry we dig.
Dickey, he read here couple a three times.
Ginsberg too. They charge humans thousands a pop,
but they wouldn't even take nothing from us.
I really dug Ginsberg's show—he got us
to sing along with him. *Om, om, om, om.*
Oh wow, us canines really turned on to that.

     Hey, they both great kids. And both of them say
they will come to live here when they retire.
I can dig. How often they meet up with
a group that groove on their stuff—and show it?
Fame have got to be a mean trip: get yourself
disappointed, misunderstood—a touch too much
idolizing here, a touch too little there.
Got to be why big shots get down on mankind.
Then mankind turn around, give them the bum rap,
yeah, mankind say they stuck up on theirself.
I say they got to lick theirself front and back
—in the right doses, at the right times and places.
Hell, they never brag, if we gots art to praise them right!

     Hey, bet you don't believe all the fans you got.
Every time *New Yorker* hit the catbox,
cats and dogs be fighting to read your poetry.
They really dig your deep humanity,
they dig your compassion for the underdogs.

They *know* you give them respect, feed them good,
never polish up your boot-tips on their bellies.
And be others here that get off on misery.
Pure breeds. Always be slumming. They kinky. They go,
"Oh, daddy, tell us what it like when you was poor!"
They *rub* their furs all *over* those fat pages.
Make me *sick* when they do that to your poetry.

      Mr. Levine,
I was born in the streets.
Never knew my dad.
Never been inside a house.
Never ate from a dish.
Never got to go on paper.
Yeah, I sniffed on the sidewalks,
I licked in the gutters
—I ain't shamed of that.
But now I want to make it to the top,
get to get 500 bucks a shot,
get to say anything I want to,
get to *go* on paper.
Get to beat the canine rap
—I be up there walking on two legs,
I be human, like god.

      Mr. Levine, you got to help me bad.
Hey, you adopt *me,* teach me to write poetry.
If they tell you no, then you sneak me out
after you read. Just wait till things quiet down,
then I tip you the high sign and we split.
But you watch out for Supervisor. Her bad.
Her Lady Cerberus. Her the Bitch Goddess.
Her never miss a trick. They's a whole bunch here
she caught already. Scottie and Papa,
Dylan, Delmore, Berries, Cal. She tell them,
You got to kiss my butt, 'cause this here the Hell of Fame.

      Mr. Levine, you lucky, you not famous,
but her *make* us famous, her make us household *pets.*
Give us fame-rabies just like them other cats.

I *seen* them on fire, raging and thrashing
to get theirself comfortable and couldn't
—their bodies all red with burning rashes,
like ten thousand hot tongues of wildfire rumor
was kissing them all over with their names,
telling them *who* they is. Pitiful how
they howl in pain, awful how they beg for more.
That fame, it's junk, and junk make you tame.
Best minds of my time foaming at the dentures!

      Got to cut out now. You remember what I wrote.
One way or other, I be busting this joint.
Hope this note don't smell too bad. Destroy it,
if you got to. Keep my secret.

Rex.
    7/20/81

Conversation on a Yam

    Fleas whose rag and beard I share,
whose body I inhabit barely
here on my backyard doxology
of four miserable yams
—Withered, Rotting, Frostbit, Green—
that I in a lifetime of effort
have dragged and huddled together;
today the easy fleas began
again, leaping up to see
this landscape of tumuli:
bare fields of bald personages,
each asquat his pile of yams
—inedible but good for building—
and about them gangs of hunched
and staggering smallish figures,
each of whom maneuvers in his arms
an offering larger than himself
toward one heap or other;

herniating with praise
and hardly acknowledged, he heaves
and hoists his pittance up
to the top of the daily tonnage.

Alighting, the leapers spoke to me.
The social commerce hereabouts
is heavy with homages.
Why this economy of praise?
"Because the delicate morale
of the high and the mighty
requires constant encomia
—else they get down in dumps,
too glum to banalize all others
to a vagueness of background, dim
screen for the flagrant cinema
of their own heroic figures.
Therefore each one clings to his hump."
But lively debates on culturing yams,
bracing acts of spiritual measurement,
wonderful questions of right and wrong
whose dextrous quibbling or quick evasion
keeps the suppliants supple . . .
                              "Are
beneath their masters' noses
delving the darkly measureless,
the mystery of themselves.
For this they need surpluses,
launchpads of panegyric
for hobnobbing with the stars,
hillocks of hymns and paeans
to reduce to a clear piddle
of personal essence."

The fleas leaped up—excellently
jet and joyous—and saw, and met
to meditate inside my rented ear.

. . . placatory gold hosannas they cram
under the high haunches of the great.

Because they like that moment at the top?
Hannibal's saddle *also crossed the Alps*
riding along under Hannibal's bum
—and even the humblest porter at rest
will clamber onto his burden and sit.
The mighty, the mighty themselves thunder
to astound the little yammerer
gawking blindly in their dark insides.
"Let the great one's faith in himself
falter an instant, and the world
fails, too, his hand then palsies on
the hard levers, and the machinery
of affliction clatters on, masterless,
anonymous . . ."
              How extraordinary
this awe you inflict on yourselves,
your craving for bosses and creation
of bullies, your hope to wreathe
the smeared harrow with the harrow's own
afflicted blooms!
                  "The hurtfulness
our mouths can name is the mordant
—and burns adoration into
the joyful animal throat,
inscribes a yam on the truthful tongue.
If there were no name to pray to, no name
to praise, how could we bear our pain?"

Bitter, bloodless, odorless, ocherous, cold
—among us the yam is not much esteemed.

Too bad. Remarkable creatures,
snoozing now in tune to my scratching,
I might have offered them a yam or two
for a song—sad short tally of praises
whose provenance I no longer recall
and that I ruminate and fuss,
boxing their compass too often,
into new and never less
unsatisfactory patterns.

Shall I climb off my yams?
Pull down my pile for good?
Take them out on the road?
Give them all away?
Unthinkable not to be in business.

But you, inching along in a furrow
under your burden, big or little, if
you hear my words and have a yam to give,
you know my name, you know where I live.

Elena

Because she did such terrible things to them
with her sexiness and long, sauntering stride
and how she smiled and didn't avoid their eyes
but came right back with remarks of her own,
because day and night she wronged and injured them
with her height and olive skin and heavy jugs
—*Madonna mia!*—and the creeps she walked
around with but never walked with one of them,
because anyone could see her innocence,
that having no women's tricks, what she had
to defend herself from all the guys who came
poking and pushing at her was craziness,
yelling out dirty words to hurt their hearing
and dressing herself up crazy *and dumb*
—because of this the hard guys from Cherry Street,
they were the ones who busted into her flat
and pulled her boyfriend off her, worked him over,
broke his nose and chipped two teeth.
                                    And then because,
naked, bronze, tall, she stood there and never tried
to cover up while she yelled to let him go,
because of that they crapped all over the place,
they threw her underwear around and stomped it
—to tell her how she had confused and hurt them—
then, at wits' end, beat themselves off and scrammed,

having laid the tribute of their tantrum at
the altar of her high and white and double bed.

The Memorable

The poem on the page was always indeed
the same text, which is to say, the same stranger
encountered each time as if for the first time.
And like a stranger, it was greeted with questions:
Who are you? Where do you come from? What do you want?
—and was, finally, because it lacked a voice,
accosted with shamans and other diviners
who were voluble in answering for it.

The poem in the mind and in the mouth,
the remembered poem, spoke itself again.
It was a friend as close as one's own breath.
For the space of its speech, all other words
lay down in its voice and became its words.
Spoken by the poem, harkening as they spoke it,
even soothsayers and interpreters
grew idle and happy in a charm of feeling.

The Epiphanies

Winter, the boardwalk,
the walkers moving into what,
neither visible nor unseen,
was clear sight, sheer immensity . . .
sun rinsing the stone fountains,
the bare herringbone old miles
of board . . . more mile and mile of sky
emptying toward Sandy Hook,
bright to pale, a whole openness
overhead, far out . . .
and the ocean composing gravely,

over and over, one verbiage,
fugitive, opulent, millions
of shadows, millions of lights
that rose and receded . . . rise and merge
in me as I write this out, now
as then are racing into being,
hold themselves out to shine
as I am stepping forward in the light.
Rare passersby who glance this way,
see, when we raise our arms and wave,
if light does not break on our lofty hands . . .
in one instant multitude walks the page,
in one gesture greeting and goodbye!
—we who nod and pass onward, each one
bearing brightness before him on his way.

Happiness

It is very difficult not to be happy about blobs.

A blob appears to be a modestly elevated puddle, a failed puddle, so to speak.

Unlike a tragic hero, no quantity of negated life, no yearning, discipline, suffering, sacrifice, can make a blob a larger or more authentic blob.

By the same token, one can't save up to make a blob.

The first time in my life I rose on two legs, I looked down on the space vacated by my blob and I laughed.

One knows all of a blob in knowing any bit of it, but the whole blob gives more pleasure.

Together with its contentment and unfuzzy outline, this makes a blob an excellent household thing.

. . .

Heaven by any other name would be boring. A blob neither knows nor wishes to know another name for heaven.

There are not two kinds of blob, or two ways to be a blob.

Nor is it possible to distinguish between real and ideal blobs.

If I say, "A blob," I do not thereby banish every present blob. Nor do I bring any absent blob to mind.

A blob is like a happy ending—it leaves you free to walk away.

I have walked away from many blobs, but no blob has ever walked away from me.

Decidedly, it is difficult not to be happy about blobs.

The Grand Magic Theater Finale

The curse was to claw the earth with their hands
in the dark until every cue was handed up.

And then the liberation of light blazing.
And here, out of their roles, the cast comes back
in costume still—how shy they seem of those rich
stigmata—marking time, shambling their steps.
See, the stars, too, have lined up with the chorus,
turning to meet our eyes and gaze frankly
at last, face to face. And look at the lot
bust loose, stomp and prance, shake that dyna-mite.
There's nothing they don't over-over-over-do.
And what life they must have to be so different
every time we look! Like half-molted metaphors
—at ease in two worlds at once—they ad-lib
and swank their old impersonations for us
as if to say, *All that was just kidding.*
This happiness is the serious stuff.

·   ·   ·

Their exuberance, their soaring
would break our hearts if they weren't making
everything larger, ourselves immortal,
with laughter. And surely they must know it,
singing out louder, reaching out their arms to us.
And who can say what they are begging and bringing?
Our cheering says, *Freedom! Feeling!*—from which
they wave, riding high, blowing both-handed kisses,
What wonderful people—you're all angels.
Not goodbye but hello, folks, welcome to heaven!

Talking to Fernando

to my son

Life is swell like this, life is great,
with everything going past all the time.
It's easy here—inside the speed,
just us sitting snug in the groove,
just us cruising on ahead.
Nothing's too fast, nothing too slow.
Hell, look, we've got no worries,
not when we're rolling like this.
We don't need anything else.
Things are smooth, right? things are fine,
nothing could be better than this.
Take the wheel whenever you like.
And when I drive, you don't have to talk,
you can sleep, you can look out the window
—that's cool, that's okay, everything's okay
as long as we keep on going this way.

I'll tell you what.
I want to give you something.
I want to give you a lot.
If I've got it, you can have it.
Want my Harley chopper? It's yours.
I'll throw in the windjammer fairing.
I'll throw in the slipstreamer 'shield.

I'll give you the stereo deck.
Really, I want you to have it.
Just name it, you've got it.

Meanwhile, it's so great this way.
Even when we get to New York
we don't have to stop—I mean it.
We can keep on going.
We can go all night like this,
we can go all year.
What the hell, we can go anywhere.
How does California sound?
I bet you we could make Peru.

Listen, I'll give you my golden helmet,
the one with the little decals you liked.
You see? I didn't forget.
I'll give you the silver jacket
I won shooting craps last year.
Remember my new green boots,
the ones with the fancy tooling?
I'll give you them, too.
I'll give you my honey gloves.

All of Us Here

All of Us Here

—OH, IT'S ALL SO

—*Oh, it's all so obvious!*

—*They say this show got some terrific reviews.*

—*I swear I did a double-take when I came in.*
Old SUBWAY SEATS, *used* TABLES, *metal* SCRAP!

—*These statues are plaster casts of* real *people?*

—*To me it's like a wax museum.*
—*Of* victims? *That's a new one.*

—*I think I'll just take a peek at the gallery register.*

—*Do you have any idea what plaster does to a rug?*

—*What's this guy got that I don't have?*
I'll tell you what. Connections, man, connections.

—*God, sometimes I feel* just *the* way *they* look.

—*I think he sympathizes with people.*
He must be a nice man.

—*I don't know what it is about these statues . . .*

—*Where are the café jokes of yesteryear?*
—*They're in the classroom, wagging gray beards!*

—*It's starting to get crowded in here.*
—*Who are all these people?*

OR THIS MIGHT BE OAFLAND

Or this might be Oafland, and these the local oaves
—Mr. and Mrs. and all the other Whites,

who are posing now in plaster clothes in a state
of cloddish wonderment, poor earth's brightest face
turned toward heaven by a random harrow tooth.
Oh, but these must be city folk stranded among
a derelict flotsam of ruptured contexts,
sticks and stones from gray, forgettable neighborhoods
that we ourselves escaped ages and ages ago:
KITCHEN SINK, BUS SEAT, PARK BENCH, DINER TABLE,
RESTAURANT WINDOW, CAR DOOR, LADDER, PHONE BOOTH,
         BAR . . .
And so we're quick to sense our advantage here
where *they* seem both out of place and stuck forever
in their bored borough of the 'thirties and 'forties,
while *we* are elegant and up-to-the-minute,
can come and go, preen our intelligence,
eye them boldly from all sides and up close,
and pass remarks about them in loud voices
—*because they can't forbid us anything.*
Nor are we either all alike or all one piece,
white clothing on a whited skin.

                    And yet, and yet
for all this contrasting vividness we feel
—never so alive, alert, ardent, bright as now,
this wonderful fuss of being human and young!—
their lumpish solitude admonishes our limber
volubility, from moment to moment makes
halt crimped stuttering abashed old moody poor
the smooth lavishings and lappings of our beings,
which, like water, would caress equally everywhere.
In time, they will all be carted off and dispersed
to hotel atriums and to motel lobbies,
to new museums, statehouse courtyards, bus depots
—today, however, we are compelled to grant
their massed redundancy the power of earth:
we acknowledge that Being (however poor) precedes
becoming (though swift, exuberant, fascinating, gorgeous).

Here at dawn light and by nighttime's neon, before
our rising greetings began to swell and after
our goodbyes' *diminuendo* on the stairwell down,

they—though lacking our stylishness, charm, fervor,
gallantry, spirit, fine clothing, wit—are silent,
they are motionless, they are mineral, and white.
And therefore, in reluctant recognition of
an order of immobility so old
that death itself must seem the junior partner,
our rich laughter turns to chalk and powder
in our mouths, and we yield this place to them.

OH, HERE AND THERE

Oh, here and there one seems poised between paces,
ready perhaps to push on, though not to step out.
But mostly they stand, sit about, or lie down
—in the averaged postures of average people
reproduced in a kind of stiffened pudding
we sense is harsh, cold, unpleasant to touch.
Surely our time is not stillborn and devoid
of vividness—*some* bright spirits walk the earth,
please the eye, impress and charge the memory.
But these, always a shy step out of focus,
how apologetic these lagging figures seem,
and how little they claim, as if the life-size
into which they've been cast is sizes too large,
the soft and friable plaster too enduring,
their bleak monochrome still one color too many.
It's true they loom like revenants in their scenes,
old blanks, cut-outs, massive absences who want
to climb back into the world which keeps on going,
misfits trying to get at least *something* right,
who mime with dogged, solemn single-mindedness
this one's lopsided frown, that one's wrinkled suit.
Is this why suddenly we feel it disloyal
of us if we smile, stretch, straighten our clothes?
—But it is only now we notice it.
They have no eyes or their eyes are closed.

If we were gifted at flight, lyrical, blessed
with clairvoyance, able to see our way past all
this obviousness to the possible impossible,

we'd mind less their collapsed spectrum of the human,
this mirror of literalness (which reflects,
which cannot see) that they hold up to our eyes
—recalling us too tiresomely to our too obtrusive
too tedious, too obvious, too mortal selves.

To be responded to is as close as one
can come in *this* life to immortality.
So we come and stand here and look at them
to make more answering life to answer us
—though it's like calling on the outcast next door,
like watching the hermit in the store window . . .
or whatever glimmer of kinship brings us back to
the eyes of animals at the zoo . . . If only
these figures seemed aware of one another . . .
If we could paint our faces on the vacant stares . . .
Some strangers scattered together among some stones,
what welcomes us here is only ourselves in
a sudden vision of ourselves, as if a first life
we were torn from should rise and recollect itself
and be embodied in us . . . when our eyes meet:
a crowd of powers in a single being,
the one, composite body of everybody
—original through all its generations,
part of, symbol of, everything ever alive—
whose burgeoning members wave affably and nod,
answering each one's silent question, *Yes, yes,* and *yes!*
—"We all shall die, but will none of us be reborn?"

But no, but no, they are creatures of paste,
too-large dolls left back in the solitude
of some local but permanent interim
—the terminal moraine where time ran out—
who hope no longer to be born at all.
Here they stay thumping their numb dumb humdrums
—where nothing is wrong except everything,
and what isn't grimed is broken, and what
is unbroken is unendurable,
and resurrection dips a dirty spade,
adding dust to dust, piling ashes up.

OF COURSE, WE WOULD WISH

Of course, we would wish them angelic lookouts
on vigil to transmit—brightening and moving—
the glory still forthcoming, still pending . . .
alert geniuses of anticipation . . .
in the pure moment prior to speech. . . .

Sadly, it's the dead themselves they resemble,
no longer fussing to be served better and more,
withdrawing their demands on our attention,
and are humble suddenly and patient, keep
to their places, and make themselves smaller
to give death greater room, and hunch down farther.
It hurts to see them so decent and poor.
And it does no good to scold them for it,
to shout at these newly impoverished relations
crowding timidly in the narrow hallway,
or recall to them the old extravagance,
or tempt them back with favorite morsels
and the glowing tales that made the hearth warmer.
Not once more will they rise from the table
or come laughing out of the vestibule,
kicking the springtime's mud from their shoes.
The little and the less consume them now.
What a fever it is, to make do with nothing.
And throw off every word they ever wore,
the metaphors that made them legendary
—as if anything not literal bone, not plain
matter, was illusion, delirium, conceit,
swollenness of spirit prancing on show,
this corruption ailing in their ligaments now.
They are dying to be the letter itself:
immaculate, and perfect in form, minute,
not ever again to be read into,
and beyond whiteness white, sole, invisible.

THEY WERE NOT ALIVE

They were not alive and were walking in the streets,
or they were in a bus, sitting still, and still

were white all over, were stone in the core . . .
This white plague expresses now the new boundary
of death, senseless, superimposed, suddenly there,
down, up, right here . . . unstable, treacherous, *jumping*.
And the plainly given, the unconjectured
dimension—faithful, basic, calm and ancient—
the horizontal no longer symbolizes
the dead in their lying down in the earth,
and the air without dimension opening
and opening and opening over them.
No one goes to tend the bulbs and roots and rain,
and be our farmers in the under-soil
—our other people in our other country,
where, living and dead together, we raised up time
time and time again in the fruitful order of seasons.
And no place is left for us to go.
                              Shall we, too,
ride around and around in buses all day,
and clog the streets in our aimless white parade,
over and over, each telling himself over
the bargains, the bargains he found and didn't buy?
They keep on crowding in, hang on, get in the way
—like the pensioned-off milestones of America
come in from the distances to be *mementi mori*.
We'll never let that happen to us!
                              No way,
we say, thanks, but no thanks.

                              And that's why all of us
who can afford it walk in a corporation
of interferers, a cloud of professionals
we hire to give Calamity the runaround:
phantom limbs we throw the circling shark,
live prostheses we dangle at the octopus,
foreplay forever for the heartless fucker
—*mucho* funny stuff to tie Fate up in court
or in hospital, let it hemorrhage in the head
and break a spine before it gets at us and ours
—let it never leave Intensive Care on two feet!
Our experts' hubbub and consultants' *cha-cha-cha*

are going to make it damned expensive
to jump us in the dark and without a warning.
Why, just to know we're giving Trouble trouble helps.
And what a comforting sight your doctor is,
healthy and pink in a nice starched coat,
or your lawyer with your life in that envelope
he's having fun balancing on a fingertip,
while one crossed leg swings idly up, swings down,
and someone's insurance agent waves a fat check.
Their luck could rub off here, you never know,
and their immortality-of-office, why not?
—Our doctor's gonna die, but not with us,
our lawyer drop, but never in our place,
our priest lie down in—thanks—his own grave.
Yeah, if that's where the action is, we'll grab a piece,
take some tumbles up ahead of the big parade
with the rest of the white face, white collar clowns.
Am I my lawyer's doctor's priest's accountant's lawyer?
You can bet your bookie's life we hotshots
are flashing in and out of each other's shadow,
luring death toward us for the other guy and for
his palpitating fee—while our thumb jerks back
and our whisper tips, "*Him,* he's the one you're after.
I only *work* here. *He* put me up to it—he *hired* me!"

Because, let's face it, folks,
we'll never be together again after this.

OR PERHAPS IT'S REALLY *THEATER*

Or perhaps it's really *theater* of deprivation,
and here we've wandered onto a movie set
mocked up from famous stills of fifty years ago,
and we're free to walk around and rub elbows with
these lucky white stand-ins for the tardy stars.
Why, of course, we could be extras here ourselves!
And look, there's the strange moment before the MIRROR,
the gruesome all-nighter around the KITCHEN TABLE,
the DOORWAY where she threw him that funny look
that stayed with him his first weeks off in the army.

At last we'll get to see the backsides of everything,
and find out maybe what really was going on
—no poverty so poor it has no secrets!
And so, having these scenes for our inspection, at
our disposition, is sexy, exciting;
here's fame and nostalgia and something else precious:
seeing the machinery and yet not losing
the illusion . . .

            But haven't we seen this flick before?
You know, the one where . . . right out of the 'thirties
. . . the bodies sagging among CHAIRS and WASHSTANDS
or plodding by COFFEE URNS and BUTCHER BLOCKS
through the grainy atmosphere, and gloom that suggests
perpetual confinement to amateurishness
. . . these coercive images of life after hope
. . . a century's terror by sentimentalism
freights the scene with yet blacker glooms of bad faith
—since candor alone is lighthearted—
somewhere a butcher's blunt finger is rending hearts,
while, faint, sweet, *crescendo* from the phantom soundtrack,
the still, sad music of humanism—so-called—
is symphonizing on the dark Stalinist fiddles . . .
Yes, the little people are appealing to *us*
to lead them into history . . . are dying to enlist
in the great cause of our generosity,
and, cap in hand, they come to us and say
with a shy dignity we simply can't resist,
"Here, good sirs, is all of our misery
—do with it, please, as you see fit."
. . . Careers open to idealism!

It all comes back, however faint, that redolence
of another era, but with the smugness cuddly,
the deception almost affectionate, affordable,
almost a joke—somber and improbable camp
that feels right at home in our living room.

Whatever can we be so famished for?

1

The bystander at the massacre of innocents
might have seen his own innocence among the dying
had not his distance from the spectacle of slaughter
(not all that far off, really) given him the space
to entertain a doubt—while it wrenched time backward
and made everything appear unalterable and past
even as everything kept on racing ahead.
He might not believe or come in time to what he saw.

Murderers and babies and frenzied howling mothers,
everyone crowded forward onto the picture plane
when he dropped to a knee to steady the camera
—yes, they could come this far but not a breath farther—
and now, for all their mutual horror and panic,
their cudgels and knives and the scream-saturated sky,
they are unable to smash their way out, although
repeatedly he stabs his finger into the photo
as if to verify something incredible there
or at least to render the illusion palpable.

For his is the spectator's essential doubtfulness,
this feeling that among the sum of appearances
something important doesn't appear, and may never.
At precisely his distance—standing by, looking on—
he can't get close enough ever to be certain
reality isn't some extraordinary matter
not yet glistening on those dull upturned faces,
that running about, or gray sky ceaselessly screaming.
Of course he *knows*—who *doesn't* know?—even *we* know
that terrible things are going on out there.

2

Is it curiosity? or a kind of revery?
or recollection of the city-dweller's pastime,
watching people busily, simply, living in their lives
—what can have stopped us here, like angel emissaries
to a doomed town, to view them while they muse or walk

about or work at their machines on a sunny day
torn from the archives of the ordinary?
Their entire absorption in whatever they're doing,
the feats of diligence and attending by which
they materialize, and gather in, being
—it seems recreation enough to observe them,
and almost a blessing that they take us for granted,
our gaze unchallenged, undeflected by any other,
as if, unseen, absorbed in our purest looking now,
we, too, could enter their sustained communion
and this moment should become the life we are living.
And so it's oddly flattering to feel welcomed
by being ignored, as if we belong here like stones
and trees, are features natural to the scene,
and haven't come this way disengaged, freewheeling
between one city burning and another's tinder,
and with that uproar—our names screaming—always
in our ears.

            Each in glowing concentration here:
the one of the DOORWAY, the one of the TABLE,
the one of the RESTAURANT WINDOW, the other one
and the other one and the other one, and each one
stitching, tapping, a little by a little
making it indubitable and good,
an artisan of the whole creation
as it was—streaming ether of their concern
for one another—before the slaughterers came.
Before the slaughterers come,
we can have no other way
but to make our way back
into the city, into the center
where what happened is happening now

—or our evasion expands to enormous
complicity, explodes in the spectator's rage
and demented scream for more bigger quicker death,
and we rush toward the time when, not lifting a finger
—and yet we may fairly claim it our creation—
we spectators are gathered into the act

and—for a second's intimate stupendous fraction—
everything is beyond any doubt real.

THE WHIRLWIND WE WOULDN'T ENTER

The whirlwind we wouldn't enter of our names
beseeching us from the sky . . . is far away now,
thunder over Disney Village to which we've come
. . . a green room somewhere in the wings of its heaven
where enchanted souls in whitewash await their cues
—the proto-Mickey, as it were, and ur-Donald—see,
there's Hughie Human, Percy Person, Cindy Citizen
in Santa's workshop before the color goes on for good
. . . to illuminate within the nihilist blindness
the sentimental vision . . . and look, we're kids again!
simple and pure in heart, healed, grateful that we're us
—because right now nothing ever really happened,
and life never asked more of us than innocence—
our new eyes behold not absence but color, our ears
hear Mickey's sweet squeak, Donald's stormy funny grumble!

Mickey and Donald want us to be happy,
they'll do anything to make us smile, laugh, clap our hands
—look how silly and harmless, not big and scary,
they make themselves for our sakes, we *have* to laugh
—because they love us as we are . . . happy, being good,
and want us never to be any other way.
Wide is our way and lined with clowns from here to forever,
from kindergarten to life and back again.
All we have to do is to enjoy the entertainment
and watch our mouths on the monitor screeching out loud.
It's hilarious and fun and interesting, too.
Donald is famous, but Mickey is famouser.
They can make *anyone* be charming to them.
Just because of who they are. It's magic.
How no one's boring, mopey, dopey, ugly, rude.
They'll even come to where we are and walk around
like living statues bigger than life and shake our hands.
"Hi, Mickey!" "Hi, Donald!" we practice on their names

over and over, even when they're not around.
And Mickey loves Donald and Donald Mickey just the same
because they're in the family of everyone famous,
who every day spend their time being nice to each other.
They go back and forth into their houses to visit,
and still whenever they meet in restaurants and places,
it's just like they haven't seen each other in years.
And all the time they're getting and giving out prizes.
You can see from their smiles they're completely sincere.
We love you, Mickey and Donald, with all our hearts.
And we'll never change. We promise.
For all you give us, it's the least we can do.

Sweet puppy self-love, the paradise of white lies is
the one paradise always in our power to achieve.

SURELY THEY'RE JUST SO LARGE

Surely they're just so large as their burdens allow,
and no smaller—yet—than the task at hand requires.
But when the light is right these figures of old earth
—the stooped pedestrian, the huddled subway rider—
are roused in their sad ghetto of anachronism
by today's untoward sun—and we see we've rolled down
the abyssal slope to a lost academy,
some dusty museum basement where plasters of
the classics have slept tumbled about cheek by jowl
in nameless peace all the minutes of these centuries:
heroes, athletes, titans in everyday clothing
who come racing in place from all the way back
to stand in no time at all—all of them, all of us
together here—at the abandoned finish line,
our fleet forerunners in prospective elegy,
champions, pioneers of the missing future:
this Laocoön braced against the supple void,
Atlas bearing up under a genocide or so,
and Sisyphus, his sleeves rolled, ready now to start
getting that apocalypse out of the cellar

            .   .   .

—the stooped pedestrian, the huddled subway rider,
such shadows flung at speed of light across the world
by enormity, just peeping around the corner.

NATIVE SOIL, WE SAY

Native soil, we say. But soil is debris,
blasted or broken loose, carried off, deposited,
its affiliations casual, crumbling
—a huddle of strangers from the old country,
arriving by wind or ferried over on
the water, carried away again . . . Of such
alluvium we are formed.

Our voluble streets
send the natural drift careening forward
at unnatural speed. You can glimpse the smashup
down any awful *cul-de-sac* you're driven past
—a litter of outmoded styles, old headlines,
fungible events, public gossip, rubbish news,
the *caca*-literature we generate, consume.
This is the slang and hot slurry of time, at once
traffic jam (trapped by one another, jeering)
and freeway shooting range of zooming moments
—the medium where you dare not set your foot once.
The rotting of the homeland's establishments
lays bare—underneath—our condition as clay;
nomads of words, our urban vanity is
our freedom of speech, the booming rumor of names
on which we make our getaway from earth
toward the high, airless, astral zones of fame.
A multitudinous gabble sweeps us along
—our ambition is to let nothing go unsaid—
while we go on talking as much as we can,
keeping up with what we accelerate.

Some obscure nostalgia for dumbness and earth,
for easeful insignificance, draws us back
to these dioramas of a vanished species

pasturing in half-dismantled habitats
—archaeological digs, you might say,
of the old neighborhood a generation back,
providing views of the crude artifacts,
the charming and un-selfconscious folkways,
a vision of life without the fuss of life.
How odd they didn't foresee their anachronism.
Now they seem revived a bit by the fracturing
that frames—and refreshes—each *mise-en-scène*.
And if these figures don't exactly welcome us
—but it wasn't precisely them we left behind,—
they seem, well, to have left a place for us.
How easily we take our stations beside them,
near the SUBWAY SEAT, at the COFFEE SHOP COUNTER.
It feels funny but right—we fit here,
we fit right in. Whatever our bewilderment,
our fear of having checked too much at the door,
our bodies, at least, have forgotten nothing,
except how deeply they mourned these other bodies.
So this is how it always was,
how it has always been meant to be,
the kingdom that should have been our heritage,
this pastoral standstill we've returned to flesh out,
reviving the *cultures mortes* as *tableaux vivants*.

Our soil is technological—our things, our ways
with things, our words about them—but rich and deep.
These are bits of pulverized place we pose among,
the solemn junk that was New Jersey and the Bronx,
and shall be what land our shatterings are lofted toward.

DUST, PALLOR, DRABNESS

Dust, pallor, drabness of the tomb.
                            The air in here
feels dated, stale, as if some special apparatus
—spiritual gills, say—were needed to get
into our lungs what little uncombusted time
is left, someone's been embezzling it so long.

These plasters, perhaps?
                    Impossible! Dis-animate,
they look like coprolites, a species of giant dung
left whitening on the ground with dignity and age
—of what unimaginable, departed gods
the sacred excrement, divine residuum?
No one else is around—just them and us.
Or not quite—there are the *things* they live among:
LADDER, SHOWER STALL, DENTAL CHAIR, BUS DOOR, EASEL . . .
Entirely literal beings of wood, glass, metal,
they lord it over the poor torpid people,
hardly persons at all, crude plaster copies
and nameless except for their jobs, locales, or gestures.
Surely, we feel, they were entombed to accompany
and attend these Things, their brilliant masters, in
the afterworld—as we, perhaps, do in this one.
A little lower than the Things, are these figures,
are we ourselves, just minor matter, *choses manquées?*
—lacking their hardness and impassivity,
their quietly unanxious single-mindedness,
their on the whole cheerful sense that things turn out,
sometimes someone boards a BUS, someone else climbs a LADDER.

It seemed rude of us and wrong—a profanation—
to come barging in on their cryptic privacy
with our contemporary bulk and breathlessness
to cast this public light over their dusty lives
and lesser idols from the Age of Industry.
But now a second thought suggests we are indeed
the afterworld they always intended to reach.
It's touching, really, heartening and heartbreaking
at once, that all this was arranged for our eyes.
Then we're not some grayed-out weed-choked local stop
the splendid silver *Rapido* of their Time Capsule
would always be roaring and barreling past
on its shining errand with important cargo,
but the very Terminus for which it set forth
aeons and aeons—a whole decade!—ago.
And how well we understand this—we, too, wish

only to be immortal in their modest way:
to be delivered in time to be tomorrow's news.
—See yourselves in us and weep, free us and be glad!

Wherever we are, whatever place this is, it, too,
is in transit, thing after thing flashing by, falling
into the past—for us immortality can't be
to last forever but to have a second chance,
another time over the littered quickening ground,
one more try at getting into the flow . . .

Skeptic time runs through and discards this and that,
goes through everything in time, as, in this case,
the glamor of sheer materiality.
These Things are less impressive than they should be,
or *were* when, reigning lords, they were launched toward us.
And if they thought to fall to earth like saviors
with final words on single Form and simple Being,
it seems to us now no great thing to be a Thing,
of rather less importance than the flux
and prompt delivery of information about it.
Painful, but the enchantment was lost in transit
—only some beat-up old secondhand furniture
has come bumping down.
                    And after all, we *have* gone on:
children of change, our birthright is skepticism
—total and unearned, but paid for afterward.
Like a man who ten minutes too late clutches at
his lifeless pocket—Oh my god, the wallet's gone!—
we gasp wildly as if to ask the fugitive air,
for lack of anything else to accuse,
What have you left us that we could wish to endure?

ALONE, ALIVE IN A TOMB

Alone, alive in a tomb, who doesn't dream
of despoliation?
                    —The sudden shockpower of
impunity: these leavings are helpless, they're *loot*
—let's grab it, let's go! And then the hot sweet

transfusing firewater of something-for-nothing
is like an extra life, like *more* life in the veins.
We're bigger, fiercer, twice as many as when
we came running in just ahead of wind and fire.
That was something—we really got our asses singed!
And look at us now: fine, fat, free, *untouchable.*
Whatever grocer god left this sweet stash, it's ours.
We'll put the useless stiffs to work: our land
factory livestock slaves—we'll milk them good.
Inside their suits our nakedness will be in business.
And it's all good stuff, man—it's *merchandise.*
Hey, they should be happy we save their heritage.
So let's go for it, let's cash in again quick!
And just for luck we'll dump a pile and leave it,
a love-note to this here immaculate horror,
a message from the good guys: *Goombye—and thanks!*
And we *gone.* See, wind die way down, fire black out.
It quiet, real quiet, outside . . . Shh . . . you hear that?
—*Who, regarding the dead, does not feel himself*
as purely needy, as simply honest as a flame?

But suppose that dream of our survival's a joke
and we've really been kidding ourselves along,
that we didn't just step in here to escape
a sudden shower or the street's whirling-burly,
but by some fluke—I know this sounds crazy—
it's *we* who are transfixed in a trance so deep
that everything around has stopped dead in its tracks.
Only Terror moves . . . its million eyes over us,
slithering toward the final advent of fire
—that twice before made a city its cenotaph
and scared us into this impersonation of stone.
If we should move, the world would end,
but the end of the world is us not moving.
The burning jelly everywhere is united
in a single burning, a single eye.
Inspector Fire looks us over.
The moment of the end is unending ash.
Illumination we dare not move to utter.

                    .   .   .

Nothing stands outside the dream—unless that is you.
Look at us, don't you see what we're trying to say?

LOVELY TIMES, HEROIC

Lovely times, heroic decades, happiness.
These we offer up to claws and kindling,
to the fierce gods who covet flame,
the prosperous with their sweet tooth.
Sacrifice is our panacea,
even for the illness of being well.
And this science comes so naturally,
measuring out ourselves for immolation.
The ash we keep: the bad nights, failure,
wasted years numbered in the catalogues
of discontent we poormouth at heaven.
And our deliberate evil, isn't this
our last *hopeful* offering to a god
who has despised our goods?
                                        Take them! Take these!
Take me! we cry to any possible spirit,
finding ourselves uncertain, fearful,
strangers in trespass on a god's ground.
Millennia later we are latecomers still,
squatters fit to be driven off by
trembling earth and thunder of the just disaster.
Something in us howls with the gods against us
even as they blow our bewildered cities down.

Hearing ourselves as we think the gods must
—our mimicries of divine displeasure,
our *amor fati* raging to become
fuel in the gut of the greatest power,
our cry to make us light without remainder—
no wonder we beg the elements, *Restore*
the chaos of your overwhelming concord!
No wonder we're merciless to each other.

Led off a little way from life,
and splashed with white all over,

symbolizing exsanguination,
prepared and yet to be offered,
or offered and not yet taken:
all of them halted halfway between
the world and the consummation.
And we feel we should do something about them,
bring them back to life, perhaps
—or step forward with them into the fire,
sensing ourselves also to be
sacrifices in search of a god.

—IT'S OBVIOUS OBVIOUS

—It's obvious obvious obvious!

—That one is so strange and sad,
I'd like to adopt it, give it a nice home.
—There you go again.

—Go ahead, call her up.
What have you got to lose?

—Is George Segal a famous sculptor?
—You bet he's famous.

—Mommy, I don't see any children statues.

—A beautiful day like today.
We could be in Bloomingdale's right this minute.

—Well, you took your time showing up.
—I'm skipping lunch just to be here now.

—We'll have to come back when it's not so crowded.
—This is the first time I haven't seen someone I know.

—I've had enough of you and your yapping.

—Did you hear what I heard?

. . .

—I like the way the line of this *arm goes*
with that *leg, and with the beige* TABLE. *See?*
—That's really fascinating.
Are you an artist yourself?

—My doctor said to stick with the treatments.
—Come on, you're kidding!

—Look, the sun's out.
Can I buy you a drink?

—Are you sure you're warm enough in that raincoat?

THE LIGHT THAT TOOK THE SNAPSHOT

The light that took the snapshot of the world
shows them—with a clarity not granted in
this life—poised in sober expectation at
the intersection of the ordinary and
of Something Very Important, which has stopped them
to ask the way, then turns back with a question,
What were you doing when the world ended?

The woman in the RESTAURANT WINDOW is saying,
I was lost in thought, and then
I was just about to lift the cup
when I saw the wavelets in the coffee
that were the world ending

And the driver of the TRUCK,
I noticed the signal was changing
and then saw up ahead the end of the world

The PRINTING PRESS operator says,
I was busy freeing up a lever
that ended the world

SIMPLE OUTLINES, HUMAN SHAPES

Simple outlines, human shapes, daily acts, plain poses
—exhibits for the Museum of Humanity,
the place to take the kids on Sunday outings and show them
how it must have been to be, once upon a time,
a common man in the Century of the Common Man.
"Eternal" and homely, final but merely roughed out,
gentle and not to be budged from their perplexity,
and blanching still in the calamitous afterglow,
they're like completed destinies that are at the same time
just poor people who couldn't get out of the way,
whose names have been exalted into allegory:
Exile, Homeless, Refugee, Unknown, Mourner, Corpse.

And if we surround and see them from every side,
all the while we can't help putting ourselves in their places,
suffer for them their vulnerability to our eyes.
Life, defenseless life—with nothing left to defend!
We understand: so everything must be looking at us
with the sight that seeing too much burned from our gaze.
And if we, too, now lack inner refuge and outer force,
are the very horror your generation strolls among,
we *will* arise from these tombs of hoarfrost and ash
—if only for the children's sakes who've led us here
by the hand, and over and over touch their small faces
and crusted staring eyes to our stone fingertips—
we swear it . . .

—Surely they are saying over and over again
inside their black white silence *something* like this.
But what they suffered, they also did,
and we can't find it in our hearts to pity, or forgive.

STRETCHED OUT AT LENGTH

Stretched out at length on the ground
—one might think them dreamers in a meadow—
how young they all appear now,
as yet unbent into characters,

but as if at any moment they
may climb, grown and whole, out
of the cracked open molds, and step
lightly into other worlds . . .
Who wouldn't follow them there!
But their dust is old,
earth is old and craves
a sense for its shambles,
why it should be this and only
this broken, low horizon of clods
the empty furrow cast up
in the course of defining itself.

And we, have we no sense to offer
to ease the torment of this earth?
—standing here, craning necks, squinting,
twisting ourselves half upside down over
the puzzle of these foreshortenings,
these fevered limbs, knobs, bulges like
the scrabbled ware of a potter's field.
But for all our triumphs of contortion,
we can't resolve the clutter into
figures intelligible like ourselves.
Or they refuse to make themselves clear.
A hidden life—turned low to endure—
persists in there, and contends with us,
with itself, with *everything*
for the meaning of the life.
And will not let us rest
though we pursue it down through
the last scattering
                    —ourselves suddenly
landlocked here, at our limit,
grappling for our own coherence
among clots of dirt, rock, soil . . .

Even as we rouse ourselves
from the spell of earth,
even as we straighten up and start

to disperse and move on to other things
—something, perhaps to gather
itself in prayer, perhaps
to touch its life
to the life of dust,
something sinks to its knees in us,
something falls all the way
and doesn't stop.

THIS COUPLE STROLLING HERE

This couple strolling here beside the BRICK WALL
look the way we might look if it were us
in raincoats walking slowly in the city dusk
—but how much better at it these figures are!
Their effortless mastery of the clichés
of everyday life—which we, who almost never
fit in anywhere, seem to go on missing—
serves them perfectly again and again,
when they sit down side by side on a PARK BENCH
or lie in BED and twine peacefully together.
They always manage to achieve the right pose,
without insistence or abashment or cleverness,
a gesture left over or one aspired toward.

We should envy them, no? Immortality
experienced from within must seem just such
imperturbable ordinariness as theirs,
repose deep in the simple heart of averageness,
which death, raiding along the frontier, must take
forever to reach.
                    The eternal verity of
their middle way nourishes with safety and seemliness.

Then *ils sont dans le vrai?* Well, it feels that way,
as if a truth too large for us to see at once
has brought our bodies to fall in alongside theirs
in easy, even, companionable pacing.
We go along. Turn and look again. And all go on

together. So, we think, it *is* possible
to be comfortable, large, happy, in the right.
And it grows on one!

       The mirror they hold up to us
is tempered with a gentle curve of revery.
And whether it's they or ourselves we see
doesn't much matter. Whoever's there—presence
and person and apparition and absence,
the once, the actual, the not yet, the never—
we don't want to be halted by identities,
we want to go on becoming in wonder.
About these figures we don't ask, "Who are they?"
We ask, "Who, who is it they remind us of?"

DID THEY LOVE ONE ANOTHER?

Did they love one another? Were they good?
So we ask about them, the old ones, the old people,
these questions that abandoned children send
toward the dark to follow their elusive families.
—Even the child whose way the stars made plain
may never be certain his coming was awaited
or that he is himself the child they intended.
But we're no longer children, have children of
our own and some title to this ground, these walls
—and yet find ourselves on a dark road downward
on an urgent errand to an uncanny past
after the fugitive powers through which
we are at all and may be reborn, renewed.
But it is so difficult to understand
the coherence of, say, fifty years ago,
to see that theirs was a world entire and not
a scattering of stray evidences, odd things
worn with use, habituated to their presence,
enriched with their sociability . . . this chair,
or this cup chipped, mended, left behind, this table . . .
If we could go back and see them as they were . . .

      . . .

Then recall them in the time of their strength,
the brothers and sisters then, their husbands and wives,
the landsmen, the large neighbors, the friends—as if
each one was a country and all of them the world!
Remember their enthusiasms, ceremonies, card
games, big voices, jobs, what headlines, politicians,
comics, rumors, music moved them, what laughter, and
how seriously they took each other and themselves
and us, and were wholly and profoundly at one with
the terrors and trivia of the century.
Heart-stopping to see it this clearly now:
bone, soul and song, they belonged to their time,
refuse to be transported into any other.
And dwindle as we look, move away farther, lost
at last among the multitudes of the era,
unknown in the crumbling society of clay,
the sands of the earth where we scratch, inquire . . .
How small our giants were and by how many had
been multiplied to become historical!

And then remember how we looked for them among
the horde on park benches as if in some sunlit
encampment of sorrows beside a black ocean
—their white heads like every other white head,
their clothes, coat for coat, dress for dress, the same,
their voices as low and unevocative.
A dog that day—had they a dog—their little dog
would, without a second's delay and joy
in each leaping step, have found them right away,
though barking through the sky of a whole galaxy!
But we, blind in the sameness and the sameness,
could not imagine by what power they
—so small, so indistinguishable themselves—
had singled us out from among the vague unborn,
and seen in each one the one original
each of us knows is named in his name alone.

But even there in the land of the dead,
lost not in time but out of it, in timelessness,

among the quiet, whited and nonchalant crowds,
where nothing moved but our shadows' vague passage,
a steady gaze of recognition from afar,
the happy affection glowing in those eyes
as we approached, announced who lit our way
and who it was there among so many:
it was they, themselves, and we were ourselves!
To have found cause, in such a place, for celebration!
Then *See, see who's here!* their eyes said in greeting.
And *Only you were missing, the last to arrive.*
Look, now there's not an empty chair at the table!
their eyes exclaimed what their voices could not
—while we looked into the bright heart of living coal
from our cold threshold in the bitter white dark.
And, heaping our eyes with their gift, each time
and time and time again they send us forth.

THEY SAY TO US

They say to us in quiet voices,
matter of fact, hushed with feeling
(to which we murmur our responses),
Here, this is the one.
Of course, you never met him.
And this is his wife.
This one is her brother.
He *passed on a year ago July.*
Here she's holding her eldest.
You can see she's pregnant.
That would have been
with little William . . .
To which we murmur,
Yes, yes, I see.
I see him. I see her.
Yes, takes after the father . . .
No, I never met him.
So, that's the brother!
Where is she now?
We are passing photos from hand to hand,
the living and the dead,

who mingle here
as nowhere else.
Almost we heft
the squares of shining paper
on our palms as if
to ponder better
their weight of being.
And yes, truly, they
appreciate under our gaze,
augment in our considering.
It is all very important.
This ritual is profound,
solemn, religious—we feel it,
become weighty ourselves,
judicious, like gods:
even and merciful in judgment,
simple, courteous and worthy.
Now we hand the photos back.
There they are—"little William,"
"her brother," "the neighbor's girl"—
all of them pressed close
in a single pack in dark
and radiant density.
All of us here
are deeply satisfied.

Our Father

In memory

This stranger whose flesh we never ate,
who, rather, sat at table with us, eating,
who for our sakes clothed himself in pelts like ours
and went away far all times to everywhere until,
clambering down starways into our street,
he stood in the door, the dusk-loaf under his arm,
and unpacked the lamplight of the parlor corner
where he called us to him and told us we were his,
and lost in thought led away our little army

of mimics to parade the deep lanes of silence.
Of our mother we ate always and plentifully,
her body was ours to possess and we did so,
thoughtlessly, yes, and also in adoration.
But how shall we understand this stranger?
And how are we ever to make amends to him?
—who had the power to eat us and didn't,
who consented to abide in one house with us,
and hailed the sun down to make the dinner hour,
and bid bread to rise daily out of white dust,
peopling it with mysterious vacancies,
and new night after old washed the odd smells
from himself with sleep and forgot his strangeness
and was, one moment at dawn, little again,
hungry like us, like us waiting to be fed.
How then can we renew his acquaintance, that boy
lost in the man, this man missing in the world,
walking among all that must be inexplicable?
And how are we to thank him properly?
who salted our cheerful, selfish tongues with farewell,
and gave us his name to ponder, to pass on, to keep.

River

Swift at its outset, ebullient.
And later on a wide majesty.
And always irresistible to itself.
And here, flow on its flow, the moments chose
to mirror themselves—or were helpless not
to be refashioned on its wayward glass.
High, up-ended clouds unloosed
their tumble of images, swallows were
at dusk and dawn, and wherever
someone looked
the moon went wavering,
the dark old towns swam slowly at its edges.
Day after day, seeing's brave flotilla
rode entranced on its motioning.

Whole civilizations found their trope
in its character and progress.

Under that,
and under that all,
it is feeling a way,
sightless, dark, small,
mere water
moving by touch, trickling
in fine deviations, in
precise intimations.
It gravitates
toward, it values, each
suddenness and resisting.
Stone, snag, hollow,
one by one
—it comes and savors them
as it can, disturbs minutely
to be saying, *Stranger? Or
friend? Do you prefer
to stay? Or come along?
Here, let me see if I
can help you on.*
                    Mentioned,
mulled in its divinations,
the old things startle into
life after life, entering
the water's disseminations.
The rusting auto and charred pleasure
craft, this silted loop of tire
—what we have abandoned,
or is abandoning us,
is the knowledge by which
the water goes along.
And had it words,
the water would say it is joy
to know the grain by grain
of its ground and, knowing it,
to be beginning
afresh.

An Atlantiad

Who is this great poet lapping near our feet?
—this shaggiest dog that ever swam ashore
and shook its coat dry onto the dull pebbles.
The Atlantic itself? at Rockaway Beach?
Mumble-master of toneless sublimities,
who won't stick to a point or even get to one,
always talk-talk-talking with its mouth full
—impossible to tell just what it feels
and, therefore, to understand why it goes
on and on about itself so, and in
some clunk's vocabulary restricted to
the slurps, thumps, bangings, rumbles and whooshes
of onomatopoeia.
Like a drunk trying to count his wad of dough,
this big lug is all thumbs and tongues,
helplessly unable to divide sound
from sense, or content from form, "organic"
with a vengeance, and woozily puttering
its fluent thumbprint over every shore.
Like the ungifted who invariably swear
(hand on heart before Art's customs agents),
"I only write for myself," it achieves
an exclusive sufficiency, which—whenever
we sit on the beach or wherever we dip
into it—goes on "relating to itself."
And why *does* it prefer its company to ours?
Surely it hasn't arranged this exhibition
—in broad, horizontal, full-color
centerfold nudity—just to be looked at!
Of course, one happily concedes its "greatness,"
and one did come prepared to admire—still
we might wish for less conceit, oh, a touch
of vanity, say, some little hankering
to hear applause, a wink of willingness
to, well, uh, meet us part way, and put aside
the indulgences of its "song of oneself."
—Obsessed old salt blubbering to our damp lapels
flecked with by-spray and bad breath from its brine maw.

Tell me, What damn duck did we ever do in
to be pummeled by all this humorlessness?
The bore is father to the solipsist:
feeling unperceived—since unresponded to—
one loses confidence in "reality."
Oh, we might call it "awful big poet," except,
unwilling to say anything large by way
of any little, it lacks, precisely, scale,
being a multitude of behaviors
that can't or won't get an act together.
And how can we know this poet from its poem?
—with its naturalism of mental contents,
its "whatever I happen to be thinking now,"
its queasy slipslop of selves, wobbling riffraff
of fish and turds and tarballs, of orange rind
and old hats, kelp and tires and glittery grit
—all this churning visionary trivia
and stuff, this "stream-of-unconsciousness,"
this lost topography that's left us "all at sea,"
this pounding platitudes into subtleties,
this diluting any old sludgy cliché
to the palest world-hue, this everlasting
running running running running away . . .
Oh, too grand to blush for its banalities,
and grandly disdaining fastidiousness
—this poem that cannibalizes all its texts—
look at it guzzle the palimpsest of foam!
Incapable of pretense, of stepping back,
as we do, and taking thought, of putting
itself into (for example) *our* leaky shoes,
it ignores us perhaps from fear that we
may interrupt its droning and give it pause,
impose the artifice of closure, and beginning . . .

The Judgment of Diana

Blesse us then with wishèd sight.

I

After the slamming door downstairs had rattled shut
and excluded her along with the oblate moon
and darkness and leaves scurrying in the street,
long afterward, her archangel's pallor, pure,
disembodied, chill, lingered in the half-lit room
—the young never quite know when to leave—
rougeless lips as if bled dry, her eye
bright blue and unitalicized, that timbre
—unplaceably estranged—her stilted voice,
the spooky, expressionless, would-be baritone.
In surplus army jacket and green fatigues
(did they camouflage a lurking roundness of thigh?),
those work shoes strictly for show; graceful almost,
spare, strapping, tall, she'd seemed a spear carrier
of Diana's out slumming on the night shift
to spread, *noblesse oblige,* her godawful pall
of radical solemnity—or was it,
after all, just the old gloom of forest and fen?
But suppose she *was* off somewhere laughing at us
now, back, say, on Artemis—or whatever
her pitiful planet was called—laughing . . .
if laughter ever transfigured that grim
utopia's ecstasy of being right . . .
her voice bassooning in a lost green glade,
or rocky enclave, its tale about how
those bad old dads had nearly got her
—while, self-exiled in their nunnery in the wild,
the martyr brides of ideology,
maddened by the crimes and misdeeds of men,
crouch nodding and snickering over some bones.
"The bastards! The shits!" they would be hissing—and
they would be right.
               But my companions that night . . .
did they, too, eavesdrop on that imagined scene?
And saw themselves with her implacable gaze
still eyeing us from the vacant chair?

And saw our ordinariness bemonstered by
the savage banalities of caricature?
—loose, clubby, bickering, comfortable, sort of,
with our insider's tolerance and gossip,
our vested disappointments and tenured failings,
middle-aged cogs lazily getting around
by rubbing elbows and scratching backs,
Charles, Andrew, Arthur, Melvin, Sidney, myself,
our gang of professor-poets who'd gathered,
as we did each year in leaf-troubling November,
to police a corner of the culture-feedlot,
swapping old nags or pushing a pet ape
—poets we hired to come say their verses—
by way of exchanging, with all due gravity,
our cards, scumbly and dog-eared, of identity
—Charles, Arthur, Andrew, Melvin, Sidney, and I.
Wherever pigeonholes are, pigeons must be,
and spats and bespatterings of the dovecote
—a roocooing featherweight hierarchy—
where, hoisted on the shoulders of the years
to our modest perches, we loafed alright
in a living room, each of us floating out
upon the perilous divan of his dossier,
or *vita*'s leaky, pneumatic pouf, out along
the whirling margin of a great unknown.

2

                                     God knows
what that lone student rep was doing there
—saving the world? or us from ourselves?
(and if so, to what end?) or doing right
for womankind? or for poetry?
                                     Certainly,
salvation obsessed the air around her
—as if everywhere the *bête blanche* she hunted
must be vanishing into any stirring leaf
—as if these millenarian centuries
had made each breath she held climactic:
The End of History would simply not abide
one more course of after-dinner sherries!

—or exempt an evening of cozy politics.
I suppose—no, *of course!*—her zeal discommoded,
and we resented the judgment it implied
—she meant to save *us*? to save the world *from* us?—
and were bemused how she confided in her powers,
envied the years she'd have to learn better,
envied her the passionate singleness
that draws the bow and sets the arrow straight
—however its conceit may stultify the aim.
Page-like, princely, in her androgyny,
image of our youth surviving to mock us,
surely she accused this too palpable gender,
in which we were decaying, *of* which we
were dying—rams, bucks, bulls, boars flabbed out
from domestication, all those hot dashes
to the fat trough and shoving a way in first,
getting and begetting. And she asked for nothing
—was our patronage not worth the charming?—
refused to play weak daughter or warm darling,
to have us old bullies set between her and harm
our moral authority, our mortal bodies.
Then she would be intruder and stranger both?
—with the menace of one, the other's nakedness?
Who or what was she really? Why had she come?
And now her liability inflamed us?
Whom bully doesn't guard, bully will batter?
So one saw her—mere girl, the creature itself
divested of allure or standing—and glimpsed
in her *our* nakedness and estrangement, *our*
jeopardy, works swept into nothing, words
forgotten . . .
              I am trying to understand
what happened, rather, what *didn't* happen next.
Our slap was inertia, discourtesy, silence.
Impassive and frivolous, we froze her out
with mineral indolence deeper than self-love
—that gladly would have seen the stars go snuff before
it chose to move one inch. The stars that night shone true.

                    .   .   .

—And glimmer high above her cohort of the hunt.
(So it is I imagined the harsh event.)
Black branches at midnight in the hostile grove,
stones some women grope along, and famished wind
tears flame from the meager fires and out-howls
their cries; they huddle and with warm bodies shield
the white-daubed effigy of the goddess their queen.
Poor and frightened, unprotected, prey themselves,
how it crazes them to have to keep alive
in their own weak words—like a seed of outrage,
a violent growth—the abandoned consciences
and lost concern of unprincipled and selfish men!
And now she comes in, gasping her story, she feels
she must, she must give birth to a chunk of metal,
this humiliation she bears and never,
not so long as she lives, forgets.

    3

                    She stood.
It was not what one had expected, that look
around the room that said she could as well
go hunt in a barn as do her hunting here,
potshots that we were, pitiful sport,
and really couldn't give a damn about
us dodos either way—redeemed in spades
or sent to bull among the shades—we were just
in the way of the chaste and fierce pursuit,
shutting her view to the clear way and great use,
and deflecting with our huge, torpid auras
the shining crowd of spiritual arrows
sweeping through the high trees.
                    Naked, bright, serene,
something moved there (I saw), someone swift—tempest
of moonlight—pattered over the leaves and lit
the lost traces to delight where they were touched.
Darkness came rushing after.
                 I rejoined our pack
—Sidney and Charles, Melvin, Arthur, Andrew—
to hound and lacerate with muttered slurs

the high arch and light heel of her tall,
unsullied shadow where she descended
the creaking stair—as if we wished to merit
in full measure the judgment against us,
and with negligent, grinning jeers dishonored hope
for that rebirth we could not cease to crave or fear.

4

Or was it only an evening
of moral melodrama we craved?
I'm not that certain what went on.
I got carried away—let's say—
but not so far that I don't wake up
mornings to Diana's mantle lost
in sun, and dailiness everywhere,
our comedy-as-usual,
the world just chugging off
down the laff-track of the days,
rollicking on regular—you know
the blend: optimism and bad faith,
or something too muddled to be quite that.
Sometimes I see her in the corridors,
taping a placard to the wall
or loping along, her old fatigues
resurrected as white overalls.
Let's see, it's a feminist event
the posters cheerily advertise.
Or announce her poets' workshop
for women only, Wednesday evenings
in some *not* suburban living room.
I think she likes the business
—her greetings (across a distance
neither infringes) now feature
a neat, cryptic nod. *Cosa nostra.*
She could add a smile, it wouldn't hurt.
Her new poems seem not all that bad,
though hardly less conventional for all
their energy. Why tell her that?
Her thesis—so Ginny says—progresses.

"Venus and Nietzsche in Paris."
Maybe I didn't understand a thing.
And Melvin, Sidney, Charles, Arthur
(Andrew now bulls among the shades
—in Berkeley, where else?),
when I ask them what they recall
of that evening and do they think
it was wild or what, every man jack
answers, "Huh?" while an innocent blank
endearingly dulls his everyday face.
Is one to infer that after all
other versions are being versed?
Almost anything seems to go
—if you don't lose faith in yourself.
You can screw your neighbor, okay,
but keep the old conscience clean.
I suppose you think that's sad.

Of course, I see the moon, too,
every now and then, still shining so
I have to lift up face and voice
and blare to her with open throat
the full song of my heart's adoring
—as any one of us might want to do.

Summer's Sublet

(hath all too short a date)

He felt he was carrying her whole place
uphill on his back, bearing it in mind
. . . the badly gored leather of the easy chair,
the scratches flocking along the tabletop,
or the fridge's all but terminal *râle*,
the slim venetian's elegant droopy slat
—these fragilities of a large "efficiency"
which he was shepherding for an old friend,

taking them to feed in the high summer pastures,
preserving them for one more season still
from time's furtive, undelicate claws,
or his own never ill-intentioned carelessness.

Still he was bumping into things.
As if blindness had redecorated the room,
nothing there seemed meant to put itself on view,
the watery, green mirror was so shy a thing
he kept on losing it in the cloud-white wall
because nowhere could he find himself—and yet
he stuck out painfully, that much he *felt*.
How one is *de trop* in another's life!
—not the blank mermaid of fairy tales, of course,
waiting to have her features drawn in fresh ink,
but a face already complete with erosions,
such vaguenesses, regrets, apologies . . .
Oh, on the contrary—he found himself
wanting to say, hand splayed over his heart—
on the contrary, it is I *who am too solid.*
Imagine, talking to furniture like that!

The furniture found a way to talk back.
The phone spent all one night calling him up,
and then pretended not to know his name.
Surely it was alive, he could hear it breathing.
The fridge, too, played dead, though its body was warm.
He wasn't fooled, not for a second—but
how a small thing can turn you upside down!

Another night someone hammered suddenly
on the door, shouted *Help,* ran down the hall
to the next door, pounded again . . .
In this metropolis the cry of distress
terrified more than the terror it fled . . .
One more midnight dropped blackly over him
like a hanged man's hood: the loneliness was
absolute—but soiled, used, full of last breaths.

. . .

Things were in that room he could hardly approach,
and places shuddering with life of their own.
He felt an infant Jonah battered by
the peristalsis of her spirit's labors,
by soundings cold and sharp against his ears . . .
Here she'd sat doing the sums of her life.
Or lay on the narrow cot under the stormy
air conditioner, praying for her daughter
that she might be happy, and less brusque with her.
At this small, white table, eating alone,
she reviewed the ranks of her obligations
and found them present and in proper order,
then forgave this injury, renewed that pardon.
Her magnanimity once more surprised her.
For one happy moment everything was clear
and able to look after itself—she was free,
truly free, as maybe not since she was a child.
Between coffee and a last scotch-and-water,
she canceled as entirely inconsequential
a long-standing debt of her own.
Halfway to the sink on the worn parquet,
a sudden thought rattled the cup she carried
and she sat quickly to catch her breath.
"A life, a life, a *whole life*," she gasped, "*my* life!"
Where did that happen? In that chair? Or in this?
He jumped up, walked, stood, couldn't sit still . . .
Like a pet turned suddenly savage, one favored,
old regret bit her deeply while she stared,
over the faucet's roar, into the corner of
an empty shelf . . .
                          And late one night
he saw the white invisible gardenia
on the inside of the refrigerator door,
the photo lost from the dresser drawer
she mourned like the child itself . . .

Every day now he found something else missing
—books gone from the year before, he was sure of it,
paintings bartered for emptiness . . . and what remained

had that remnant look: of being no one's,
or nothing, dispossessed of identity,
like orphans, at once touched by the gods—sacred—
and dispirited . . .
                        But why was she doing it?
Was it restless old age in her, impatient
to harry and rend clear through its withered root?
a kind of mad rushing around—so little held
one down—in a rage to tear loose completely
and be swept away. . . ?
Or her abandonment of the day on the day
she understood it could take place without her?
that her consciousness no longer was required
by the world for the world to be the world?
He pictured her off in her northern summer now,
unencumbered and concentrating all her thought
to lower the doorsill, to ease the step down.

How calm she seemed just then, and high—shining out
to him, like a pale flare drifting luminous
over the vacant sea long after . . .

"But *why*? Why *me*?" He looked around the room again.
"And whose little boy are *you*?" he asked the one
in the mirror, bereft, startled, one hand half-raised.
It was too much—more than he could take—to be
the recipient of her eternal good-bye
aimed vaguely toward the place where he happened to be,
too much to have to stand here and wave back slowly,
relinquished though he was with the rest, and all
his human powers reduced to helplessness
by life that didn't want to be saved . . .

He gave up his sublet suddenly, and fled.

The Call

On the phone from Florida, it's Louie,
nearly a cousin, almost long-lost.

There's something important he wants to know,
after all these years. I hear it in his voice.
It's like he's put a package down and looks up
and he sees sky, horizon, trees, something
empty, endless, peaceful, always the same.
"It hit me all of a sudden.
Listen, Charlie, don't worry about me.
I don't second guess myself anymore.
I'm sure I made the right decisions.
Really, people can envy me,
I've been as lucky as hell:
I got my health and all,
I'm like a bull I'm so strong,
I could live forever if I had to,
Charlie—honest I could."
But underneath, there's something else.
Shy, puzzled, urgent is how he sounds. I find
I'm bending over the phone to get closer.
"So how are things? What's going on?"
and then so low I've got to hold my breath
to hear, "Charlie, tell me," he whispers,
"how . . . how's the weather up there?"
I guess he's asking about the family
he left behind—do they miss him,
the wind and the rain and snow,
the immortals from long ago? and after all
what good would it be to survive alone?
And so I tell him what he wants to hear,
"Lousy, Lou, the weather's worse every year."

The Flight from the City

> *Each man on the street insists he is himself, but all
> have in common the same double: Disaster.*

*"Very good.
Now, once more.
Your name, please."*

. . .

"Kleinwort.
I mean, Hummingblood.
Yes, Hummingblood!—I *think*.
Because I, too, was asking,
'Who am I? Myself? Or my double?
Hummingblood in fact or "Hummingblood" in quotes?
The real one or the substitute?
—who shadows me at a distance sometimes,
or stalks me from inside my clothes,
jostling to take over my flannel trousers,
my blazer, my boxer shorts, my spats.
Well, I may be either one, or both, in fact,
a shadow in shoes and socks, so to speak.
This book will know . . . '—this very book you see.
Names have been in here since time began."

Since time began . . . had I seen anyone like this?
—Orange hairpiece like a haggard cockatoo's,
some dribbled calligraphies of greasy fard
that glossed his eyes' effect of fevered death,
the Doric sideburns daubed in sickening shoe wax
lifting heavenward his temples and his brow.
And this was the pitiful material
my "workshop" had to make do with
—some manikin on whom the heavens had fallen,
who was himself a splinter of crashing sky,
a giggle rippling the face of the void.
But I was patient. I went on.
"Splendid.
Very good.
Now, what happened next?"

"I was a wobbling rim around
a cinema's bright spokes and went
wheeling up the smoky night. Then down from
the zenith, weightless, blind, my body unreeled:
the screen over which empty spasms of light
and darkness staggered through unending war.
My way was that occluded, obscure—as if

I dreamed it all inside another's sleep . . .
till nightmare—mine or someone's—of consciousness
without remission woke me to a world without
dimension, or limit . . . out of nowhere
images came crashing into my eyes
under the clicking cold sidereal grid . . .
Traffic lights patrolled the heedless dark . . .

"On the street I saw these things, these things.
Live graffiti rotted on the walls, writhed,
throbbed in dark peristalses, then slithered,
convulsive arabesques that shivered in place,
went nowhere, waved their flagella, wove
their ornaments, invited one in to the heart
of their rouge insignia, the bold misspellings
—all lip, cilia, tentacles, tongue summoning you
to be the substance in their self-caresses . . .
Rats and jackals sat looking up,
slavering for them to drop . . .
I had awakened—not to shut my eyes again—
to disaster. And fire everywhere."

"And where was this? Where were you?"

"Marauding beacons overhead ravaged the dark sky
or smashed themselves on cloud into high headlines
about the famous strangers we would never meet,
their names the common prayer in our divided night.
And sudden—now incessant—criss-
crossing clamor: sirens claxons wailing bells.
The acoustic graffiti of a savage officialdom
were tearing clear across the shuddering rubble,
a vast sheol in which the City lay foundered.
Was it already blasted and trashed?
and surviving as the audience spellbound
before the footage of its legendary demise,
wailing and applauding as they died?
As for me that night, although I was there,
nothing there seemed my own experience

but just more news, things neither true nor false
but life at a long distance arriving as
the morning headline folded beside the coffee cup.

"And then the street assaulted me.
The mugger messages came for my soul,
pressing their hot slogans to my throat,
whispering, '*Give* it to us, *give* it to us!'
I turned my pockets out. 'Empty! Empty!'
my pockets cried, 'See, I have no soul.'
I disclaimed ever having known me.
Sundering myself, I surrendered him and sped on,
deaf to the scuffle and screams behind.
Who me, a victim? Never! I'm the *other* guy!
No, I proclaimed my predator's grin and whistle,
my hard logo of self-advèrtisement
—violent of color, virulent in stink.
I became inedible like an auto.
I posed as an identity posing as
a value—but what was I worth to anyone?"

And what was the meaning of his sudden smile?
Slugging assassins with pillows, was he?
Putting down murderers with mental weathers?
My associate and I exchanged a glance
—Have we gotten our hands on the wrong party?

"A thrill of silliness went lilting,
then sank itself to the hilt in me.
I was hysteria in slow motion,
transition in transit,
a shattered mirror shambling down the street,
setting one image before the other,
consuming and relinquishing sight after sight.
Constant voiding and betrayal of the past.
Panic of consumption, flight through things.
It was so hard to be serious,
to see how any life could matter.
If the world had decided to do itself in,
it wasn't up to me to tell it no.

I could go along with that.
I mean, Was I *supposed* to mind?
But if this really was the end of everything,
somebody out there ought to know it,
and surely it was worthy of transmission,
the roar and outcries and lamentation thrilling
outward on empty airwaves beyond the stars.
Maybe the media that catered reality
were beginning to cater the apocalypse.
Hadn't they pointed sparking wands and all at once
it occurred to thousands, yes, really, they
were feeling tired and would—as if it were
the most natural thing in the world—lie down
on the street in broad daylight and, well, nap a bit?
Such a good idea: to just drop dead right there!
And what harm if one should steal away too soon
one's little winks from all eternity?
It was montage anyway, lamination
of shadow and flame—the difference between life
and death was immaterial, just no big deal,
a budget item in someone's big bucks fantasy.
Then the street blurred, and ran like ink.

"There was no sensation of touching ground.
Adrift in a soup of lingos, sloshing
severed tongues sliding all together
or soddenly ironizing in my cheek.
Things I meant I didn't mean I meant.
The words I kept taking back were not my words.
Had I been expropriated? No self now?
no prohibited sanctum? merely a set
of always negotiable positions
of diminishing liability?
To be at last immortal and a nought?
And in my skull's bare ruined cinema,
now what low insistent hissing hushing?
whose sweet sinister hot licks?
        Sucks.
        Say what?
        That stuff sucks.

Huh?
Get with it, Chuck!
You ain't you
—you just your jive.
Same as I.
That's why we gots to deal it, daddy.
You hear me talk?
I mean, you hustle it, baby,
put its ass to work!
You dig me, Buck?
Hey, Humanbutt gots to die,
but *you* some other guy—dig?
'Cause, shhiiit, son,
when that mother don't cut it,
you dump him, pops, you split,
I mean, scrap your rap, pappy,
blow yourself a different riff,
get you some *new* sweet nut.
I said, Now move it!
You *dig?*
Get your shit together, Sid!
Get with it, Chuck!"

"Oh yes, Hummingblood was up for grabs."

"And you, it appears, had loosened your grip.
Or were you perhaps someone else
—if you were anyone at all?"

"Yes, of course, there might be two—or
there might be two thousand—of me,
but only one Hummingblood *by right,*
and all the others a nonce vernacular
dying on the air, poor wanderers
shaken nameless from the exploded town
who would be Hummingblood to be anyone.
And all are lost if one is lost,
and no one saved unless all are saved.
That night the elements were running for their lives
—while I thrashed, jerked, shook, fell inside my clothes,

struggling to bind again the missing pages of
our *Book of Every Name of All the People,*
where, leaf by leaf, life by life, we were
awaited and greeted, and our names and place
reserved and lavished to us before our births.

"But somewhere I, too, was being quoted,
somewhere they were saying, 'Hummingblood,'
somewhere commas were being inverted about me,
excerpting me from the context of my name
and rendering me a sign to be interpreted
to myself, whatever any noisy expert,
all the suave managers of meaning,
would say I was."

He twisted his neck as if
he meant to look around: half of one wide eye
rotated my way, half his mouth spat words at me.

"But your henchman here, this Hurtingbrute,
who wrenches arms from sockets, breaks heads apart,
this Hurtingbrute scrapes his horrid pate caustic white,
sculpting from a human brow the skull's abstraction
—being sergeant of its dismal ultimate cult,
into whose long ranks he crams his limp recruits.
He calls it sacrifice, calls it *self*-sacrifice
to boot: having renounced the right to exist,
Hurtingbrute acquires the right to be lethal.

"So this much I knew:
I had to recollect the book in which
we are and I am—and then, wherever
my eyes would take me, flee with it!"

He sagged abruptly—in lieu of toppling over—
but drew himself up before assistance reached him,
with courage not unequal to his suffering.
Nor could I withhold my admiration
—a feeling almost too fraternal.

. . .

"Then graffiti again.
Gorging on the verbal detritus.
Would nothing else survive?
All night long empty trains rushed
in narrow corridors underground.
Of course, the furious graffiti
had set them going, drove them on
—thunderous fugues of script,
a last vandal hand's grimy shriek
to the far termini of the City.
At eye level, in dawn's new pearl, I saw
across the towers' flickering imagery
a sludge and flotsam of names was stretched
—as if the tideline of a tarry surf
had left a heraldry in living carcasses,
a reef
of rabid telephones and raucous codpieces,
coral carapaces of logos,
and lurid solipsistic flora,
and raw genitalia dripping initials:
unanswered messages vexed to reiteration,
to self-elaboration, to self-quotation.
Jungle of identities without being.
(I stopped my ears and broadcast a din inwardly
—my head bloated with noise that might be me.
I'm no fool, I wore my coat of graffiti
and strode about like a public urinal.)

"A nobility of the poor had flourished there.
Warrior-poets clutched their juvenile scrota
and screamed their primping names at nothingness.
From the foot-square kingdom of a scrawl,
they bawled their barbarian's nostalgia for
the lost heroic eras of property.
(The poor are always with us, always out of date.)
Their baffled scribbles were demanding answers:
Who signs and authorizes reality here?
Isn't anybody *boss* in this City?
Why only *managers* everywhere?
Who *owns* this place?

What blind bitched-up fucked-over god built here?
—the unfeatured blocks where nothing loves the eye,
this big dead stone page, its desolated names
of reality, and smooth facades praying, Gouge,
give me life!
    —This was the unresisting blank
they desecrated: they staked their claim, they dared
the absentee god in his bland disguises.
Sly or shy, the god would not come out
or show any face but their own defacings."

He seemed more thoughtful now, better spoken,
less nervous, silly, inconsequent
—or, rather, less undemandingly obscure,
as if it might matter to him that his words
might matter to others, for all that his fingers
continued drifting through invisible pages.

"The gods had absconded from our city
and carried off with them the good words
enchanting the altars and effigies.
Animals through whom we joined the whole
of creation had run away from us to hide.
The elements all were lost in darkness.
And ourselves in our multitude, the crowd
of us pulsating and alive with our
individual visions of the crowd of us
—was now its negative crowd panicking in place,
among whom I turned aimlessly in the plaza.
What then might elevate our miserable cries?

"I, too, felt the city's acquiescence,
and rapture, in ruin. I, too, wished
the end to come quickly; our concern
and constancy—our being human—
had been too little to hold us together;
so many abandoned, so much forgotten.
Then let the city be one again in destruction!
I prayed for the unbinding of the elements,
the wind unable to overtake the wind,

the wave wandering lonely in the street.
And went out with the others to welcome disaster,
obliteration of our disheartened sentences,
the devastation of our indifference
—let this debris of feeling be offered to flame!
I stood with the jubilant ruined survivors
exhibiting our wounds—See, here fire
touched, here earth's heavy hand came down—
while we gasped, I have . . . lost . . . *everything.*
I, too, in the crowd escaping toward ruin . . .

"But who was this choir I howled among?"

"I hope, Hummingblood—or Kleinwort,—you don't mean
to embarrass our proceeding with confessions.
If so, you have misunderstood, I regret
to say, the purpose of your interrogation
—as you seem still to comprehend imperfectly
that your search to recover your originals
is itself quite sadly unoriginal,
a shadow of the initial fall and fissure.
—'Accept no substitutes'? That is the motto of
a world where there are only substitutes.
Now, think where you are, to whom you speak.
Reply accordingly. Consider that
it may not be your answers we require."

"A little word pecks among the blowing pages
of the scattered nomenclature . . .
Just Kleinwort, doubled over, trying
to put this and this and this together.
An insect circles on the facade of ruin.
It was somebody or other on his belly
in the slime and mother of origins
—it was me
where I lay and listened for the first story:
New Life Out of Old Death,
a spring in the dark stubble,
the birth bubbling up.

Stubble? Shadows were leaping
from the tall flame-towers, dust
sang in the mouths of the choruses,
burst, the matrix spilled brine out,
the clans and quarters were shattered.
A world was in ruins.
But nothing moved and grew in death.
Neither was death itself there.
—Ruin had become the system.
Irresistible to itself,
the manic short-circuit was wheeling
through perpetual motion pictures where
a world of fungibles whirled in a dead flame
—shadow and darkness, substitute, shade . . .
Terror was to know nothing outside.
In terror, I knew I was a manikin
on whom the heavens had fallen
and was myself a splinter of crashing sky,
a giggle rippling the face of the void.
In terror, then, I understood
I was the system thinking Hummingblood.
Terrified, I felt it spoil my lungs,
the final excrement of stone-filled air,
clotted omens I would be compelled to become . . .

"Was resistance my way out
—refuse the labyrinth,
be unthinkable, become
silence, cipher, grit, be
the word lost from every language?
Be namelessness?
Then no one would be Hummingblood.
I hid among my shadows.
I was scared.
I wished I would die right there.
There they found me.
I was hurled in spirals
winding in to a navel, a narrow pit.
Nose to wall, spread-eagle

against the clay, naked—here
they manacle me, pinion, mock, flay
with questions."

                    "Welcome—once more! We have
so few visitors. Few come this far."

                              "And who
are you to whom I owe my salvation?"

"And why not your salvation?
Aren't these rags I wear the rags you wore?
Aren't the pages of your book
this tremendous autumn on the floor?
Isn't mine the name you were looking for?
Don't you recognize me?
*Inspector Harmingbad—*à votre service—
formerly your baby brother, now
of the City's constabulary.
You are, as you understand, in *the City.*
You never left it.
The City dreamed you . . . child,
arrayed you in a dreamlike flame,
foretold your long way stumbling here, and told
you over and over. You *were its story,*
The Lost Redeeming Enemy: suppressed revised
corrupted purged rewritten forgotten revived
mutilated robbed botched burned scattered interred
forged falsified denied—and in every version
true, and each time more true, its only truth
and one hope. Therefore the hope it sacrifices.
Now the City salutes and embraces you
with its most ironic citation: Spikes Paired.
So, say you are pleased to see me!"

"Better pleased now than yesterday,
since sight has scratched away my eyes.
I have hid my silence in volubility.
Now I brandish it for all to hear."

                    .   .   .

"Indeed. I hear you perfectly.
Of course, I wished—I wish—to know nothing.
This inquiry has undertaken, rather,
to establish the integrity of your
resistance, which I require—I demand it—that I
may capture myself at the wall of your will
and know I haven't vanished in my system.
My 'paranoia'? Spare me the vulgar drivel.
I hunt down and persecute my enemies
in order to resurrect more murderous mobs
of howling martyrs beyond the system.
I press their execrations to my throat,
am justified by their just indignation
—these are sweet air and green ground to me, I
the living pinnacle on the heap of your dead.
Here, now, I rise in the dark margin
—this danger—and I shine between
the everlasting day of the system's
entire annihilating illumination and
the flicker of my enemy's moonstruck knife.

"Like you I am famished,
like you I rage, for reality.
Terror is to rage unopposed.
Poor whoever-you-are
(your double's double's double, after all)
who this last evening of earth
have learned in your little flesh
how—deep within the City, beneath
the system's ghostly totality—
driven by the voltage of domination,
the old technology ticks on:
one man is beating another.
What do you feel? What are you?
—when my demiurge strikes.
This fascinates as if it might hold at once
the secret of freedom, the secret of fate,
something unnegotiable and mortal in me.
To feel what you feel at the point
where flesh fails and mind faints

and my will is nothing but my will:
so I submit to my power
so I resist it.
When the gods vanish, pain becomes the god,
the indwelling alien,
the purest resistance
to the shortest circuit,
term to every terminology.

"And you imagined no substitute
would follow you this far, little one?
or follow and not go farther?
Yes, I am running on ahead now . . .

"Now give *it to me, your silence . . . brother!*
Say nothing more—whatever may occur.
Be my witness I neither flinch nor squeal.
Quickly: nod if you don't *understand.*
Good.
      Come, Hurtingbrute, your tongs . . ."

BUT HUMMINGBLOOD SCREAMED FOR THE SAKE OF
HARMINGBAD'S SOUL.

Art of the Haiku

His finger then, now yours
here, where master stopped, went back,
counted syllables.

From *The Life and Letters*

The Dream

Once, years after your death, I dreamt
you were alive and that I'd found you
living once more in the old apartment.
But I had taken a woman up there
to make love to in the empty rooms.
I was angry at you who'd borne and loved me
and because of whom I believe in heaven.
I regretted your return from the dead
and said to myself almost bitterly,
"For godsakes, what was the big rush,
couldn't she wait one more day?"

And just so daily somewhere Messiah
is shunned like a beggar at the door because
someone has something he wants to finish
or just something better to do, something
her prefers not to put off forever
—some little pleasure so deeply wished
that Heaven's coming has to seem bad luck
or worse, God's intruding selfishness!

But you always turned Messiah away
with a penny and a cake for his trouble
—because wash had to be done, because
who could let dinner boil over and burn,
because everything had to be festive for
your husband, your daughters, your son.

The Life and Letters

I

He got taken quick. Then he hung around.
And anyway, he never really wanted
to be anywhere he was—so why not?
Then from out there and for years the prodigal
wrote back to them—indolent letters, lying

about jobs, a wife he found, kids they had.
Things he used to hear people talking about.
He never even bothered to make it up.
Or tried to keep his stories straight.
His wife? A harem of hair colors.
Kids fizzed up like bugs, then fizzled out.
Well, that's the way his life was, in pieces.
Sometimes his head flashed on something fat
and beautiful. He watched it shoot by.
Then he listened for the crash.
Mostly, he was in the dark, drifting.
And, within limits, less of a chump.
He walked away from a lot of stuff.
There were some things he did. This and that.
Lucky, real dirty work never came looking.
Once he dumped a woman. Later she dumped him back.
That's how the game was played out there, where he was.
So that was that.
Well, just say he was down on his luck.
Or starting now to get it together.
Or he was taking things one day at a time.
Sure, one day at a time—for years on end.
One more also-ran playing out the string.
Or, staring straight ahead, out of the blue
he'd tell whoever was drinking alongside him,
Don't look back, champ, your crap could be gaining.
To which—years later—he took to adding,
And don't look up—you could be overtaking
the next guy's you-know-what . . . (Solo guffaws.)
So, what did they think of him, out there?
Joke. Embarrassment. Eyesore. Take your pick.
But how could it matter what anyone said
in that rasping, hissing, clanging tongue of theirs?
To tell the truth, since he'd first come to their country
he hadn't heard a thing that stuck to his bones.
Then every once in a while he sat down and wrote.

2

His words returned—in another's hand:
everyday things people put in their letters,

and howlers only a mother would believe,
and reassuring fluff about the weather,
as if sun were sun, and his rain, like theirs,
could fill the cistern and make green things grow.
And here they were, grinning back at him,
every pitiful, dumb phrase he wrote,
copied over like a holy scripture
in his mother's homespun penmanship
that made his snarled, uncontrollable scrawl
round and plain and easy to read.
Her ABCs were good enough to eat
—bits of dough she'd squeezed, patted, baked
slowly in the little oven of her hands
and strung into necklaces of script.
But if he read those letters at all,
his eyes scribbled some glare before he fed
the page, balled up, to the dark, muttering
demon of trash chained in the corner,
when, drunk or stoned, he plummeted straight down
—with the bulb he never extinguished burning
above his swollen, already aging face.

    3

And then. And then. And then.
And then no letter came back.
And soon no letter went forward.
Why listen now to people talking?
The demon settled into self-consumption.
And everything was still.
Dust silted over the phantom children
he'd never wanted anyhow;
at the end of its rainbow his wife's hair
came to rest on red—forever;
their house faded in the manuscripts.
Though old now, he was still a son
—though no one's son. A promise, then,
without witnesses anywhere to say
if the promise had been kept or not kept.
But didn't he, having no lands, no house,
no wife, no child, no works, didn't he know

what he had done with his heritage?
Then let their silence mute the judgment,
hush the accusation against him!
And now this little corner where he sat
need be no worse than any other
little corner of the universe.

4

And then one day a witness came forward
—from an old pair of pants, from the pocket.
An old piece of paper.
Wrinkled. Worn.
Smudged with the dregs of big numbers.
And under their blur, in palest blue
—blue of the veins of a vanished wrist—
his mother's hand at its homework
was being true to the words it found.
But there, between the words, in the smeared void
he saw his sentence spelled out.
Of his waste life: pain. Of falsity: pain.
It was a lash. A lifeline. *His* lifeline
—flung out to him, laid on his hands, *in* his hand.
With a pencil stub he traced the faint line
of her letters across the yellowed page.
As faithfully as she, as patiently
—as if he need never reach their end
and the words might now become his life—he wrote.
He wrote the date. He wrote, "Dear Son." He wrote, "We're glad
the children all are well again and getting A's."
He wrote, "We're also happy that you like your job . . ."
He, too, was happy. He, too, was glad. He wrote.

Immortality

The tropical, vast, velvet, star-struck dark.
The surf, black to white, against the seawall.
San Juan. Between Christmas and Epiphany.
The Casino's creamy, moonlit premises

—Spanish tile, marble, marquetry, high wooden beams.
And here the august Academy has convened.
On the swept parquet (where last night's happy hundred
debutantes salsa'd the sun up from the sea)
are forty folding chairs (metal, gray) on which
are old friends, the old wife, old lovers of
the old poet, the lone inductee, standing on
a little, low stage—Don Ernesto Pla, once
Romantic-Marxist-Nationalist-Christian,
now abstracted by age to a shrunken gesture:
this last of the octogenarian magi
blinking, smiling in perplexity
at all the kingdoms lost along the way.

Easier to bring a dead man back to life
than make an old one young? But if he's not
rejuvenated, he seems juvenile, at least,
with that tremulous certificate he clutches,
a large, important, parchment report card,
its message from muses to mamas
saying, "Your little boy's doing just fine!"
—whose text, in full, is being cabled to
the *Times* of Jupiter and Saturn's *Evening Post*
and other shining capitals of heaven,
because, as everyone knows, knows too well,
the ceremony is pre-posthumous,
garnishing the florid necrology
with one sweet ultimate puff, one bloom, one blurb
to bear in hand up to Helicon's gate.

Her smooth brown hand poised above the ivories,
María Vargas at the upright is ready.
Refugee three months from Castro's Cuba,
she's ardent, patriotic, eager
to pulverize the keys to divine confetti
in honor of her newfound home, her country.
Now from the sack of Uncle Santa's heart
she hurls down avalanches of Recessional,
pseudo snows of yesteryears that never were.
Thunderous tinkling riots there: it's "Jingle Bells"

rollicking so fast it's running out of sound
—as if ghostly herds of Bobtail rose from nightmares
of knackers, and ran ran ran in the traces!

Now here's a pretty kettle of kitsches
—all bubbling along with evident good humor,
while inducing moral motion sickness.
Everyone's getting a little queasy
from all this heartfelt inauthenticity.
It's so provincial, really—so colonial!
It's embarrassing, it's disheartening
to see the here-and-now is, here and now, *nowhere,*
not for real, doesn't count, unless, until
the Eagle's lime comes down and whites it out
in whirling blizzards of his being there and then.

Oh, but at this killing tempo, even
the piano's begging to have a heart attack.
Stop her, stop her! everyone wishes.
María's indefatigable, oblivious.
But look at Don Ernesto now—he's dancing!
Oh, it's not the tedious Eternity Mambo.
And it's not the sad Mortality Tango.
It's something else, something else entirely!
—something grotesque, perhaps, no, uncanny,
a halting hop, sort of, a hopping shrug,
or lurching shuffle, a kind of stumble *upward,*
as if, thigh-deep, sinking, he fought huge billows
of this jolly white plague of musical sewage
—up there, in New York, treated as "camp," surely,
and yet on him descending here in all
the fury of its raw banality!

No. Don Ernesto Pla does not break down.
Not in helpless weeping, or hopeless laughter.
He goes on being faithful to the farce,
in courtesy to María, to everyone,
granting as a grace what his moral weight
—his mortal history, his life lived out to be
this decay, this dying—rebels against.

Yes, he goes along with the music, he does more,
inventing the dodder-dance-and-stumble-walk
that keeps overcoming its own refusals
down the little staircase's six enormous steps

one by one by one by one, not swept away
but giving chase very slowly—until
then and there on the snowy parquet before
his white-haired cohort Don Ernesto catches up.
He reins in María's runaway piano.
He silences the tumultuous black box,
the hissing runners and muffled hooves
right at the black and crumbling brink
—silence the audience crushes between its palms,
then lets fly up toward the rafters, and up
and up to the heavens significant with stars.

Street Scene

Greenwich Village, Summer 1979

Like bulls trotting on their solemn rounds
over the cow flops, daisies, clover,
checking out the maidens of the meadow,
the barnyard's mud-bedappled beauties
—on Friday nights along Bethune
slow black Caddies with Jersey plates
(and lonesome *mafiosi* at the wheel)
cruise the action off the avenue:
mostly, three guys in ladies' rigs
marvelous with fringes, flounces, glitz.
One babe is black and six-foot-three
with fullback shoulders and halfback hips,
and the stricken lope of a wide receiver
whose skirt's tackled him around the knees.
The pigskin he fumbles is really a purse
—Pandora's, possibly, and full of tricks.
Up on those spikes he's six-seven, easy.
Pale and faint, crashing, malnourished, broke,

a dark decade of turf patina-ed over
his floral camisole, he looks just pulled
half dying, half dead from an orgy's heap.
(But who's that flitting through the tumbled gangs,
the terrible high pile-ups of all
the fall's leavetakings—is it Bully there
with somebody's life tucked under his arm,
unstoppable Death squirming toward the goal?
Why, that wise guy, that big son of a b.!
Hey, you bum, give the lady back her purse!
Knock him down! Jump on, boys! Bury him deeper!)

So, say it's a stretch: long like a hearse;
say wet bar, throw in TV, stereo,
figure phone, figure fridge, deluxe this,
plush that, power *everything*—the works!
Well, this randy Caddy wants to sniff.
Four door locks poke up together. Click.
Gleam of gold wig, then white stiletto of
a shoulder strap, a satin dagger of slip
stick the little mobster where he lives.
Car door cracks open. Slams quick. Click. *Vavoom!*
Thunder. Squeal. Odor of Vesuvian dung:
The Underworld burns some rubber—splits.

Beneath the clinging, rumpled number,
the baddest garter belt you ever saw
extends four lacy, fatal pseudopods
and grabs two stockings in small pink jaws.
And where strange nylon becomes plain leg,
a tiny hand on a hairy thigh rides
across bad borders of things forbidden,
over boundaries of race and class,
to Avernus—the hideout of Pluto
(il capo di tutti capi) . . . right here
at the foot of black-eyed tenements,
factories of night, boutiques of soot,
between tarred pavements and tarry roofs
. . . just around the corner on Washington.

.   .   .

Under plucked lamptrees, pools of pitchdark.
Lava spurtlets blup from Caddy's chrome pipe.
Then, motor killed, inside the limo
one fat bright roach floats back and forth,
before descending to the ashtray's dust.
Near some cans, some studious shadows browse
on garbage: urban serfs whose whole harvest
is the dump they harrow; city scarabs
doomed to grub for death with their guts.
                              And now
the *thud thud* of hearts bursting in the void:
Bully is sucking up all the air in town
for one climactic blood-curdling bellow
—his come-cry the bad news of an ambu-
lance's dreadful ululation's long approach
with its dark burden of appalling semen
that always always pulls up at your door—
when Bully rips off, rapes (again again)
the shocked bones of gofers, heifers, heroes . . .
hogging for Number One what life there is.

Don't tell me that it doesn't take lots
and lots of spunk—and maybe some speed—
to get yourself into a spot like that
poor, bedraggled person carried off
(by one of P.'s *junior* goons, to be sure,
some minor ruffian, some lesser punk)
to reenact Proserpina's story
—and never having heard it told, not once,
of knowing (yet) the happy ending!

Always a world of earth away
and digging from their male antipodes
with such unlikely implements—and yet
these two guys huddle together over
the strange equipage, the soft, sacred stuffs
—so delicate, and mortal.
Dumb fingers miss a catch, fumble
a button, persist clumsily, touch
thread, investigate the material,

delve the spun silk, velvet, lawn, looking
to release the miracle in the rags:
not this broad or that babe or bimbo, but
The Unspeakable (and still one nearly
stammers it out: *She, Herself, Woman*),
The Unseeable . . . and one wants to look . . .
But the revelation rewards the reverence.
Against all the odds:
sometime glints (perhaps)
somewhere gleams (maybe)
something glows (almost)
then shines out: She *shows*
—what Death (the boss of all the bosses
and bossies and bullies) had wanted hidden—
haunch and breast, hair, womb, shoulder, children.
The World is Woman's Self-Celebration!

Car door bursts open, out jumps—*wow*—
someone running—golden cornsilk . . . a wig!
in one hand, in the other . . . green . . . a wallet!
And runs "not as one who loses" but as
the only guy who'll score tonight.
Bang. There he goes! *Bang.* On the double
two bullets take off after the pullet
who lets the wig fall . . . lifts up the skirt,
whizzing zigging head down in a hurry,
streaking for dear life through the broken field.

The Runners

Here or there hundreds of them, phantom-like,
bobbing in place at street corners, then
lifting their knees suddenly and leaping
into the densest, loudest traffic
(of briefest trajectories, of shortest views),
in transit yet at ease, breathing, loping,
like bearers of distance and pure direction,
darting half naked out of nowhere and

where, where in the world are they running to?
swift and solitary, silent beings
who, should you now step into the path,
have dodged away, or, if you raise a hand
to stay them or speak, immediately
are gone: who are these runners who create
in their gliding such fine, singular spaces
among the street's vociferous jargons?
—as if each one were a still, wordless message
or question one would answer if one could grasp it,
this one, that one, sliding past, going away,
while you stand there, your hand raised to no purpose,
your hidden heart rejoicing that the quick heel
won't soon, won't ever, be overtaken,
although you, as you have longed to, suddenly
disburden yourself and follow follow.

Warm Enough

I

Down in the lobby's dim fluorescence
of dankly air-conditioned underworld,
Eddie the grizzled elevator man
never sees the light of day—except
whatever poor benighted puffs of it
are flung in by the revolving door.
Still, however sweet or crazed the weather
—monsoon, blizzard, inferno, May's loveliest—
Eddie, like the local monster lurking
neck-deep in darkness, pounces cheerfully at
anything that dares to hope to cross his turf:
the wayfarer getting there, the errand boy
bearing coffee and danish, the passenger
daydreaming his own particular business,
face forward in the cage, standing, waiting.
Once and once only the primal command
told Light to be, and it was, and *is*,
forever, in glowing self-sufficiency

—but every working day it's up to Eddie
at his humble post to put the primal question
and bring the high light down to earth.
"Warm enough for you today?" he asks, his tongue
thrilling to touch once more the sacred cliché,
his ear attuned to your personal frequency.
He smiles that yours may enter a world of smiles;
his lips already foretell your answer—and
in mankind's history has anyone ever
repeated himself half so brilliantly
as Eddie asking now, *"Warm enough for you
today?"*

        Then, any unruly and surly
and downright truculent brute, yes, Big Boss
Ego himself, hopelessly entangled
with Eddie's gossamer banality,
like Hercules fettered and baffled by taffy,
even he stands there helpless and grunts
something halfway civil to this Hermes
—to Eddie the soaring sinking psychopomp—
or forks back to Charon with interest
his dialogical lead penny.

And you, facing into the teeth of Eddie's grin,
you sense how his five small words subtilize
the sledgehammer sun and raw winter's ripsaw,
tilt the level mediocrity of most days
—having set you and your taste in temperature
nonsensically, with witty irrelevance,
at the very center of the universe.
"Warm enough for *me* today?" you ask yourself,
not ready yet to be the measure of so much.
And what *can* you answer? How *can* you name
your preference, your self—when you are,
yourself, as mercurial as the weather?
That hardly matters, for while you hem and haw
with interesting introspections, Eddie's grin
continues to insist, *The password . . . sir?*
And then you recall the weeks and months and years

of responses twice daily, and you blurt once more,
with mock profundity and sincere irony
and startled vehement noncommittal pleasure,
"Oh God, yes!"—or else, "Never, no way!"
Or "Eddie, you have got to be kidding!"

2

But just when you think you're getting warmer,
you catch the chill at the end of his question.
As if its ritual inanity,
its quick little idiot snip, has dropped
your trousers to your ankles, to your toes,
you sense out there in the dark beyond the tip
of your nose you've been had: hoodwinked, hobbled,
exposed—your answer lacks good faith, good humor.
Impatience, feigning, sarcasm, smugness—yes,
that's you all over: intemperate, unbalanced,
too hot too cold too light too heavy smartass blind.
As if the revolving door, enacting judgment,
has gulped you in and spat you out again,
your pounding heart knocks for admittance once more
into the fellowship of good standing.
Oh, but everything has been turned around.
You were the patron, are now the postulant;
the servitor has become the gatekeeper.
Think, then, think of another answer.
Warm enough for me today? Of course, it is,
Eddie—as you can see, I'm shivering,
I'm on fire. Eddie, it's me, a soul
in transit, someone who is dying.
Warm enough for me today? A minute ago
I was in the street—a free man, everything
was *perfectly* warm, I could have told you so—
and suddenly I'm here in this freezing lobby,
trying my best to board an elevator,
look, I've got one foot on already!
Somewhere between I lost track of myself.
Did I come in to escape the weather?
To go about my business? To chat with you?

I'm so ashamed to tell you, Eddie,
I don't know if it's warm enough for me
today.

Who is so naked as someone lost?
Better, then, to go adorned in sores and vices,
and flaunt your map of spiritual surgeries
whose scars have tracked your body all these years,
and better the bruises of the harshest judgment
—than to stand here gaping your blank confusion!
Oh, go on, make up a story for yourself!
But before you can, as you want to, cover
your embarrassment and offer to walk
the few flights to where you are bound,
Eddie slams shut the gate with a wink
(lofty? playful? keen? conniving? forgiving?),
and with one elegant white-gloved pinky
prepares to punch the button and send
the swift cage squealing on its way
Eddie's held your soul on his palm.
He has put down the number of your story.
You've watched him do this and heard him say,
his skepticism too delicate, of course,
to lift a brow—the merest pause, or less—
and yet great enough to hoist you all the way
or else, fastidiously, to let you go
plummeting head over heels after your pants,
"Mr. Feldman! . . . Warm enough for you today?"
A second chance? A new beginning?
Some might call it that—at least for now
you understand that wink and where you are
and what this dying is, and so at last
you answer him, "You tell me, Eddie.
Is it warm enough for me today?"

Only Then

She'd just reached that moment in her trip
where she would ask herself why in the world

she ever bothered—coming back to find
that ancient scrim of badly drab mountains
going on and on and on eternally
about themselves while keeping their distance,
and then the foreground's littered, frumpy jungle
huffing and puffing with *significance*
as if it had marvels up its dark sleeve,
a momentous something meant for her alone.
But all that ever came from the foliage
was a little clockwork tabby "pouncing,"
obligingly, for whatever passersby.
Did *she* then count for nothing? Really!
Still, there were photos in her camera
and bright, teasing little captions to say
—so it wouldn't have been total disaster.
After all, a story where nothing happened
to you was still a story—*if* you told it.
"Well, there I was, I was turning to go"
. . . so there she was, suiting gestures to her words,
when something odd brought her up short.
Something was there, stirring in the squalor.

Dull, small, chill, huddled, yowling—it seemed
a creature just reborn as its own ordure.
Too grotesque: a species of baby excrement
—at once furious and foul and feeble,
some awful thing that misery consumed,
consumed and voided continually.
But suffering this queer only left her blank
and burdened with unused sympathy.
Oh, she supposed it had a mother—lurking
nearby, no doubt—who loved it, as mothers will,
cooing and coddling until the little pest
believed itself minutely, vastly precious,
the best thing that ever happened to heaven.
Eat her heart out over the likes of that?
No, *there* was a woman she couldn't envy.
Imagine, sucking up to your own brat
—and then the thanks she was going to get!
As for herself, she'd give a poke with her toe,

see what it was made of, what it would do.
God, the stink was higher than heaven!
Useless for it to try its charms on her.
Mother *that*? *She*? Never! Not for anything!
Enough to know it could no longer harm
a soul on earth. And now, finally, firmly,
she turned to go.

                Who that was! Who that was!
struck with the clarity of a blow.
Exultation blazed up in her.
"Monster, I wished you here. I wished you so.
Now face me, look at me, if you dare,
and see what you've become in my eyes!"
The wretch knew better than to answer back.
Then let it rot here—since something so dank
could never catch fire—and *she* would be light
and show the world the darkness this thing was!
And then only, drawn up to her full height,
powerful, justified, radiant, whole
—a moment so pure would last forever—oh,
then horror, horror she couldn't let endure,
of that lovely face's hideousness!
And now once more, and not in pity of it,
but in pity of everything it had meant,
loveliness and largeness and wonderment
gone out of the world, oh, to bring them back
she, she herself would take its place in horror
... while *it* would grow up and go forth and go on
and go *everywhere*, grand, carefree, admired,
the great one—dining out on her story;
she could see it fill its mouth with her life,
"That madwoman witch fright pursuing me,"
and its glib eyes were filling up with tears,
"but oh I hurt her, oh she suffers so!"
And all the while it sat there swilling praises.
The sensitive ax weeps—and bites the tree,
then spits out, confesses, as devils do,
to seduce and filthy. But she saw through it:
void; heartless vanity ... And then, only then

knew she was the mother and the misery,
over and over devouring her own mess,
and was herself, and truly, in hell.

Story

One day she said, "Oh, babysit Michael for me,
will you, Joe?" Some things she had to do—you know.
Well, why not? Sure. Okay. So, fine, he stayed.
Besides, he felt it for the little guy
who had this look of being freaked—completely—
so uptight you'd swear his *ears* could scream,
an only kid, and no real dad around
to set him straight—which Joe related to.
Well, they hung at the house awhile, and then
he had this bright idea, took him to the zoo.
One thing and another, they got back late,
after dark, and she'd been home for hours
and getting really ticked, as he saw right off
—even though the kid was okay, in fact, great,
happy instead of hyper, for a change.
And here he'd even brought a Cracker Jacks
which he handed her with the sweetest smile,
like it was a special joke they had going,
and got her to open it and show the prize.
She wasn't having: not the stupid popcorn,
not the dumb prize, not Joseph playing cute.
"Where was you?" was all she said, and gave the kid
a good long onceover, checking him out.
So he went, "What, didn't you see my note?"
and took her by the arm and nicely walked her
over to the fridge. And there it was, of course,
under the purple fish magnet on the door.
She looked at it hard, like for minutes, thinking,
and then all she went was, "Oh." Like that. "Oh."

You would think that was that. It wasn't. It was,
you could say, the beginning of the end.

Oh sure, they had their good times after that,
when she'd seem to lighten up and go along,
but it was nothing like before, because
more and more she had this mean look on her
or he'd catch her looking at the wall when he talked.
"What's eating you?" he'd say. "What's biting your ass?"
Once she answered, "Nothing *you* could understand."
And he never did, not which or what or why
or how he got put in the wrong or what
he spent so much time trying to make up for.
All he knew is that he could honestly say
—and every so often swore it to himself—
he never once meant anything but good.
And look what it got him. Tell him it paid!

Oh yeah, maybe she *would* tell him *what,* as he
so couthly put it, *was biting her ass*
—except she was too smart to say anything,
was sorry she'd let on as much as she had,
because that time he brought Michael home late,
that was a message he was sending her.
There she was, not thinking anything special,
tidying, putting away some things she bought.
She asked herself what kept them, where were they.
She went to the door three or four or five times
and looked out into the empty driveway.
She sat down again and tried to eat.
Back then when she was still a prize fool.
Suddenly something started clicking away,
like the night was typing itself into her head.
And then she was reading the words.
Then she saw black. It was Joe telling her:
I can get at you anytime—through your kid.
So it didn't matter how good he might be,
and he was alright as far as people went,
or didn't realize what his actions told,
or that she could be mean, distrustful, sneaky
—she had to be, because he had it easy,
but she was fighting just to survive,
she was fighting for her life!

Right then she decided: when she was sure
he couldn't get back at her, he would *go*.

The Affair

"It *was* love at first sight—at first seeing!
That instant in the street our eyes met
we knew, and *saw* we knew, and foresaw what we
shall never understand—the dark oneness
whose shape whose grandeur only our months,
our years and years together would reveal.
Our passion, pining, our pain, our ecstasy,
the wonder of our feelings, of *feeling*,
the wonder we told each other: everything
two people possibly could live *we* lived.
Our final parting was like death. We died.
And neither was himself, herself, or whole, again."

So she said, so he said, to herself, to himself,
in the street while their relinquished gaze
was severing itself into two glances
they followed past each other, two strangers,
though moved alike, satisfied alike, renewed
alike, each having for one instant lived
as wholly as he could, as she could.

Variations on a Theme by May Swenson

In memory of May

"Feel me to do right," your father whispered
to you out of the blue of two silences:
his shyness, his dying. How beautifully
the words bespoke their reticence, implying
they said all there was to say . . . only doing
remained—to do—and feeling, to be felt.
And surely he felt he'd said enough and was done,

and turned his thought elsewhere, for now he read
once more from the pure page of his closed lids,
translating as he went into Absolute.
His clear gift became your clouded legacy
—for there the riddle of his remains lay open
and shut to your anxious conjecturing,
and here were all of you trying to reach him
by following instructions, asking and asking,
"What do you mean? What is it we're to do?
And is that your order? Or supplication?
Or both together?—as if you are at once
above and below us, nowhere, everywhere . . . Dad?"

Alone among the stragglers and bystanders at
his bedside—the late beginners, you his children
moving by timid inches into middle age—
he had, though lying here, accomplished already
his first great stride toward rebirth: he was dying.
And now he was running to get there, each step
swifter, less encumbered—he'd thrown off every tie,
was breaking free, while your infinite regress
of half measures pursued itself vainly and
your sorrow clung uselessly to his soaring, to
his skidding—endless, sickening;—a last point
of life in him, unloosed, swelled into terrible
momentum, massive, too fast, dragged him gasping.
Would he never crash and come to a stop?
He flailed for foothold, handhold, anything . . . he prayed
for mercy, to be as light as nothing is
everywhere, a lucid serene transparency.
He was plunging, falling into an enormous
dark loop and a narrow corner where he caught,
lying there, frightened, failing, an old man
who couldn't get through, to whom nothing was clear.
But he grasped what grasped him—this knot, riddle:
his life, whole life, this moment, here. Pulled it tight
—"Feel me to do right," he cried out in the blue,

his voice so low it might have been a last breath,
his words adrift among you in a dream sentence's

phantom clarity you were wrestling toward sense
—but though it clung everywhere in the room,
again and again it ran away from your hands . . .
"Dad? Dad?" you called to him to waken yourselves.
Empty, estranged, powerless now to invoke,
the word passed over his still lips, his closed lids.
He seemed, so intent was his serenity,
so austere, to be listening for something else.
And you, struggling under the pure gravity
of his indifference, unable to bear him here,
you understood at last that understanding
him meant you had to do as he was doing.
All of you were falling in place like the dead.
And now it came and gathered and clarified in you:
so in a mother's heart a name swells and grows,
a droplet of its infinite preciousness
her murmur instills in her sleeping child
to be its own soul—so you and you and you,
his children, were whispering into his silence
now, " 'Feel me to do right'—is that it, Dad?"

Before the dead we are all in the wrong,
although we know and swear we've done nothing wrong.
We shift from foot to foot, fidget, stare off,
unable to grasp what doesn't hold us,
our sheer life too impatient, too clumsy and loud
to feel anything not itself, to enter
with them into a world without dimension.
We hurry away, abandoning in our turn
the scene of our abandonment, saying that
every one of us shall be put right again when
our separate ways gather at the end of the road.
And until then?
                          —you kept returning for him,
but he was not to be found among his words,
or waiting for you, a meaning at the end
of the broken, dim path of their expiration
—and yet like a name these words could summon him
into your mouths on your tongues from your lips:
droplet and knot, clear droplet and dark knot,

too clear to see, too enduring to untie
—your talisman with you under your breaths,
carried everywhere to be whispered when you
are in the wrong, alone, bereft, dying
to give yourselves up for undone, mud, no one.

Revolving the parts among yourselves,
you will go on saying to one another
time after time, "Remember what Dad said!"
"What Dad said? I *don't* remember—honest!"
"Dad? What Dad *said*? Hmn. Did Dad say something?"
"Yes, I . . . feel . . . it's right . . . here on the tip . . . of . . . no!"
"Oh, we give up. Tell us! What *did* Dad say?"
—you will (smiling in darkness) say as if to stop
the earth from turning, playing to delay the sun,
the sun's rising, and protract night and death
in unendurable unendingness until
the moment all of you shall join your voices
and Dad sings out of your mouths, 'Feel me to do right.' "

The Little Children of Hamelin

Pewter, then silver, the palest gold, an almost
silence we almost could hear, dawn led us out.
So light a sound had lifted us from our pillows.
And to hear it clearer, there at the end
of our hearing where it licked at our ears,
we crept softly away from the sleeping town.
What was it singing, ringing, piping, saying?
One more, one step more, and all that we always
were overhearing at last would speak to us
—where the world, whispering whispering, was.

✦

Like a reed, hollow green tender heaven-high,
he played, and the world sang out of his mouth
in flowers; crocus and columbine and daisy

and rose the iris the lilac the lily blew
and scattered and flew, arrows we chased after
in the light in the wind into the world
until we had no names left to call them only
our shouts and cries that burst from his mouth and bloomed.
The stones in the road clattered and clay laughed.

◆

We are little children. Our parents say.
And everything happens. Sun brightens the sky.
We play. They call us in to supper. We sleep.
We wake to promises they made to us.
Today we'll visit Auntie. Tomorrow we pick
flowers in the field. One day, we shall go to school.
And always through the porridges and pennies,
the playthings and pettings, a question scurries
out of sight down small black holes in our dreams.
What do they need us for? What use are children?
—so easy to overlook and leave behind,
too weak to draw a dogcart up a hill,
who own nothing, to whom nothing is owed.
Let them say they wanted us, we don't believe
in grown-ups' love, but in the mercy of their whims.

◆

We knew the sweetness of power, it knew us.
The road coursed along, coursed through us, like song,
smoothing our way. All the words in the world, every
thing, all that our parents held aloof, became
the tune's single word. Because we had nothing,
we who had nothing else, now had the word.
We were his children, and he was our champion.
And so we followed him, column and tongue
of sunshine and sound, of revelation,
to know how high how deep how far life could lead.
And nothing nothing resisted our song.

◆

A mile or two gone by and we understood
the one we followed in the golden tatters and
the green patches of a roaming tree, he knew,
though it was strange and jolly, a single tune
he piped to himself alone over and over
—lonely as we should be had we never been born.
How sad for him—his only playmate was a song!
And so we trooped along and kept him company,
and knew then that not everything is made clear:
secret within each secret a darkness keeps mum.

✦

On the last hill we looked back a last time,
and saw a town shining beside its silver stream.
So that was our village, where we'd always been!
See, we exclaimed to ourselves, to each other,
there in the tiny streets, those little people
so much smaller than we are, those must be
our parents—just see them circle and stamp
their heavy feet as if battering down the dirt
of a grave into place. And spring aloft again!
Look, their heavy pockets are leaping up, too!
Are they dancing their dismay, having seen us
go marching away? Or skipping about in joy
since we are all the little coin they had to pay?
Look now! like living things the gold swollen
inside their pockets grows bigger as they leap!

✦

Within a wall of wind a well of water rose
enclosing a void where one unbearable noise
was a crowd of voices roaring all at once.
The dark tongue drew us up into its song.
And there we floated while the sweetest voice sang,
"Only you can save them—*say* you will save them!
Even now they think of you and say, 'We were deaf,
heard nothing, not the piping, or the patter and
chatter of our babies leaving, going away,

and kept our coins because we were afraid to die.
They knew better than we the right way to live.
We'll follow our children and be like children, too'
—for what you left behind you gave away,
and what you shall refuse to claim is more and more
abundance you bestow. A world so abounding
is a world of innocence and a world
without death." Oh yes, we will, we shouted,
but tell us, How much must we give away?
"Everything," the voice sang, "everything. And yourselves.
And at the last you yourselves will be given,"
sang the voice fading, letting us down, "away."

✦

Mouth a darkness, pipe a cracked bone wheezing
bloody spittle to the ground his back was that bent
down, mound of rotting rags like a walking grave
—an old man led us, piping himself into
the earth, and we his raggletaggle funeral.
Helpless, compelled, we clung to his suffering,
knowing a thing so horrible must be holy.
Sometimes, wanted to comfort, and dared not touch;
sometimes, tootled on our toy pipes to please him;
or ran ahead, howling, taunting, Old man! Old man!
Catch us if you can!—adding our children's mite to
whatever power it was had marked him for its own
and danced a mad jig now on his miserable flesh.
Life could lead as far as deep as he had crept
—then left him good as dead, and still he lived:
Complete. Real. Past help, hurting. Alone. Accursed.
Powerful with what rejoiced, destroying him.
From this final milepost every step must start.
We vowed to carry him with us everywhere
we went, and felt on our heads blessing descend.

✦

Suddenly the pipe was still, piper was gone.
In the place of his mouth a river squirmed, squealed

—one endless rat of one million rats drowning
and drowned: Rat River, cobbled with sleek rat backs
and wet rat bellies, where little rat feet slipped,
and caught in the thatch of rat whiskers and tails.
Black bubbles boiled up gleaming and looked at us.
White foam raged and gnawed at the night for breath.
Abandoned by music, and frightened to death
by death, then and there we'd have turned and run home,
but the wind at our backs brought us happy sounds
of children who scraped our bowls and rolled our hoops
and called our pets—laughing, golden children grown
from gold coins our parents hoarded when we left.

◆

"You can, you can, come over here, come over here,
if you are light enough, slight enough, faint enough . . ."
little voices were calling out, and calling out
from over the squealing river, "I'm lonely here!"
—runaway children, abandoned and lost children,
stolen children, and strays, and foundlings, and poor waifs
sold to be someone's slaves were calling out to us;
and the ghost children we children would never have
from the distant shore were singing, "Please play with me!"
But when we crossed to them, we found no place at all,
no children there, but voices saying, voices singing,
You can, you can, be music too, be music too,
forever, and forevermore. And so, and so, we were.

◆

If on a summer's night, unable to sleep,
you throw open a window to the starry sky,
and the softest air from far off enters your head,
and life is wide with possibility again,
before returning to the sweetness of your bed
and the charmed oblivion of your dreaming,
remember us lost on night's farthest shore,
and linger on a little while at your window
to hum, though faint and broken, this story you hear.

Buy yourself back, father, mother, you can,
you can, for the price of a song, you can,
from death—and take us in, feel us, feel
us, give us a home here in your breath!

Malke Toyb

When she was still a tiny girl,
well, not so tiny, a *little* girl,
one day her mother's lips were speaking
and saying nothing, birds were mute,
she saw her father clap hands at her
and shout no louder than the sun
cries out crossing the heavens. That night
the lightning stroke buried itself
in the sand as silent as a snake.

She grew. She grew. And heard no better.
Grew. And heard no more. And understood
she must be so always, forever.
Now she knew: God the righteous one
punished her for something she had said,
said or heard—did it matter which or what?—
something bad, for sure, for God is just.
Nothing less could justify the God
of this affliction that took from her
her mother's dear voice and the voices
she had never known—nor ever would—
of her daughters. And yet she heard
well enough her own voice saying
always within her, "Punished. Punished."

An old old woman died, and brought
her faith into the presence of
the face of God, which was kindly
and spoke to her so, "Malke, dearest,
you've suffered grievously enough.
Shall I restore at last your hearing?"

But Malke was humming, humming.
"Malke, beloved child," God's voice grew
more tender, gentler, more urgent still,
"let me restore to you your hearing."
But Malke went on with her humming.
"Malke, please," The Divine One whispered,
"just a taste of the honey of hearing
—surely, one little taste can't hurt you."
And Malke was humming, humming,
"You forget, dear Lord of hosts, I'm deaf.
I can't hear a word you're saying."

And so for all Eternity
The Divine Lips plead and Malke answers.

The Knot

After the Fate has snipped the measured length,
the seamstress, my mother, licks her fingers,
and around and around twirls the severed tip
between her fingertips until it's smooth,
and then creates a darkness: hiding the thread
within itself, she ties a tiny knot
that I may catch in the cloth and hold.
An inch of tail dangles—she bites it off,
she takes it between her teeth, she rolls it on
her tongue, she hums to herself while she sews.

In the Manger

Sacredness is present
also in this:
the hushed regard imposed
by animal seriousness.
Dumb among the kine and fowl,
once again we approach

the wonder of their purposes,
and kneel here to see
how the lamb stands up beneath the ewe
and eats.

Good Morning America

"Snuff a senator for a wart?
Well, why not?
For weak mouth
for puffiness
for talking too much.
You talk too much!
Vulnerability sweats and smiles there.
He knows it, too.
He knows he can't return my look.
Okay, I pull the plug on the sucker,
zero in my laser eye:
I see through him—entirely.
There's nothing there!
You blew it, buddy.
You're down the tube. You're *gone.*
Senator *who?* Senator *what?*
My remote flushes him, and welcomes (please)
a president, a comic, a killer, a kid
with (Laughter) and (Applause)
—such phantoms shadows images
in some unplaceable space without
consequences, hiddenness, the once only
of dying . . . but I keep trying . . .
Gotcha, fella!

"And that was entertainment, and this, too
—to sit back now and savor the repertories:
the sniff, the pause, the leer, the shudder
drawling itself out to an epic one-liner,
the pop-eyed gulp, the bespittled guffaw,
the gleeful bouncing up and down, the quick buss

on the cheek, the lingua franca of clapping.
Some do it better than others,
or better than they did it before.
But not one of them sees me here,
sees me get up, walk across the room, come back,
crouch in my chair—lord of the effigies,
so absolute in my living room my applause
alone can keep my solitude company . . .
(Bring palms together. Nod. Like so. Like so.)

"Or I pluck poor victims out of the air:
a numbed relative is poking through wreckage;
a sudden tear-spoiled face occludes a burning house;
next, some people are running around crazy
—no hidden ventriloquist is throwing *those* groans
into what looks like empty ditches . . . that's for sure!
Something terrible happened somewhere.
And I let it all come into my eyes,
receive the blessing of the authenticity.
And yet—is it *my* fault?—last week
a *worse* orphan was on the news . . . looming
out of the universal darkness of horror
to blend into the medium's universal
pallor . . . and last season's starveling was somehow
more poignant, dearer, than this morning's sad cub.
Sympathy, of course, will have its caprices,
and suffering its connoisseurship . . . as though
it were leisurely, minor, something genuine
perhaps—why doubt it?—but really sort of trite
—like shouting, *Help! Help me!* while going under.
One might like to freshen up that phrasing a bit,
and then—*maybe*—toss the drowning man a towel . . .
Morass this wide this deep is Chaos again—see,
the crouching connoisseur gasping in his high ditch
can't discriminate air from earth from water.
Nor do I, tilting, turning my cup over him
in the common ceremony of the era:
Outrage is anointed by levity.

.   .   .

"But did my viewing it so long give it sight?
That wide, white eye has come to low, dull life.
I'm haunted by a constant, blank regard, in which
I'm not the god it sees but a fool it shows
going through my motions, who gets up, walks
across a room, comes back, crouches in a chair
in miniature—Is *that* me? Is this *me*?—and where
my words, *these* words, are a show of talk merely
—confessions broadcast to an eavesdropping void,
a planet of strangers on unplaceable chairs
somewhere, saying, "Hope the next one's better!"
But *I'm* not getting better, I sicker, more
shadowy . . . am losing my place and matter . . .

"Well, and let's say that Jesus assembled here
the thousand thousand bright dots of himself,
and Buddha came from his green room as Buddha
—then if they thought . . . if they thought me *worthy*,
they would give me something to do but watch.
As *flesh* they would walk into the room!
Their gaze should temper, should contain my glare.
. . . I lean forward, raise the wattage of my eye.
They, they burn up in my vision . . . they revive
in my Christ-impression, my Buddha-bit.
Having emptied myself of experience, I
know better than they the works and the boredom
of life without content, life as pure performing.
(Open your mouth. I open my mouth. Sing. I sing.)

"I lack patience. My teeth hurt terribly.
The cold volts of our loose-wire age zap through me
whenever I touch the ground . . .
Is it any wonder I'm mad?
Who gave me motionless omnipotence?
power without resistance?
the governance of inanity?
If I could have him right here in my sights!
Yes, I'll lean forward, I'll look some more . . ."

        .   .   .

When Arthur goes out, his stare prowls before him
—lion on a leash, too powerful and rude
not to reduce to shadow the oncoming crowds,
not to challenge the faces in the street:
What do *you* care about?
Prove to me you're *not* a performer!
Can you *bleed*?
You, you did this to me!
And then it turns around and scans Arthur from
the eyes of each of these impertinent
and utter and somehow familiar strangers.

Outrage Is Anointed by Levity, or *Two Laureates A-lunching*

> *"How can one write poetry after Auschwitz?"*
> *inquired Adorno . . . "And how can one eat lunch?"*
> *the American poet Mark Strand once retorted.*
> *In any case, the generation to which I belong*
> *has proven capable of writing that poetry.*
> —JOSEPH BRODSKY in "Uncommon
> Visage," his 1987 Nobel lecture

In any case, (or, as our comedians say,
"But seriously, folks"), has Adorno's question
been disposed of, interred beneath the poems
written since Auschwitz?—rather than raised again
and again like a ghost by each of them?

In any case, one would like very much to know
how one *can* eat one's lunch after Auschwitz.
Can you tell me that, please?

NOT, let it be said, *fearfully*
Certainly NOT *despairingly*
Therefore NOT *painfully*
NOT forgodsakes *starvingly*
NOT *weepingly*

NOT *resignedly*
NOT, please, *horribly, hideously, moribundly!*

HOWEVER, should one, *bizarrely,* encounter
difficulty in eating lunch after Auschwitz,
one can do it in the following manner:

First of all, HEARTILY and CHUCKINGLY, as an example of
good health, infectious optimism, faith in humanity.
Then LOVINGLY, SAVORINGLY, to show one is lovable, always
a delight to observe.
And CHARMINGLY, assuring one's food of one's civil intentions.
Then it will *wish* to be consumed by one.
And CONVIVIALLY, since company always adds zest, even to a
menu of sawdust.
But also LANGUIDLY and as if POORMOUTHINGLY, not to
attract the attentions of the envious or the merely hungry.
Yet INNOCENTLY, because like, man, I didn't do it—I mean, I
wasn't even there!
Which is to say, FEELINGFULLY, because one *has* feelings—
doesn't *everyone?*
And so, RETORTINGLY, even QUIPPINGLY, and (seriously
folks) RIGHTEOUSLY, since poets *must* keep up their
strength if they are to prove capable of of writing poems "after
Auschwitz," being mindful of the mindlessness everywhere
about them, for it is their singular task to promulgate the
deepest human agendas.
And therefore, GENEROUSLY, since one is eating (whether *they*
know it or not) for others, for civilization itself. One is (to put it
in a nutshell) *lunching for Auschwitz.*

◆

"And how can one eat lunch" after Auschwitz?
High, high is the noble dais where godlings sup
and from hog heaven splat down their pearls on us.
So outrage is anointed by levity.
So levity is solemnized for the world.

. . .

And all we shall know of apocalypse
is not the shattering that follows but
brittleness before, the high mindlessness, the quips.

◆

This
poem
doesn't silence
silence
one or the other—this poem
or silence—interrogates
one or the other
how can one
how could you
silence
every all
the voices
—this page
I write and
the silent
who couldn't cannot
whom silence
and I
cannot what nevertheless
I nevertheless
how can I
write
this poem silence
doesn't interdict
only has made
impossible
this poem
asks
how could you
how can you
silence asks
this poem
unable to answer
silence

unable
and yet writes
the silence
out

No Big Deal

1

Well, Anthony starts to hit on this chick.
How about let's knock off a piece or three?
The old story: *First, I'll see him perspire.*
And then we'll see. No sweat. Clee suddenly
is hornier than she cares to admit.
'Cause the stud went, "Hey, babe, it's no big deal."

2

Washington Attila Mozart Elvis God
old Albert with that funny wild hair of his
cute little Pablo the *duende* of Elmer Fudd
—all the biggies, right? the whole pot pourri,
unforgettable names, franchisable faces—
you know, Madonna Shakespeare Andy *whoever:*

Playing the Palladium, or playing the Mount,
or sitting with her dead kid across her knees,
or modeling tux for the Swedes' Academy,
or safe between walls of shuddering water,
or standing one sweet frantic week over
the brand-new ball of wax, the world—*wherever:*

No way they said: Sail on, guys Eureka
Like hell it don't move My cup runs over
Mine eyes have Give me liberty. *Whatever!*
Because even God is a nihilist.
Underneath the hype, their hearts don't beat twice,
and all they ever go is, "Hey, it's no big deal."

3

And when Joe Blow forgot to check the gauge
(or turned some effing valve—who the hell knows),
so it just so happened this reactor blew
the sky right out of the sky, I mean, it blew
the atmosphere to shit. Then Joe said it real
real slow to calm those sobbing maniacs
who're grabbing up each other's legs for crutches
and making noises like you wouldn't believe.
Joe goes, "Hey, don't go getting your balls
into such an uproar—it's NO BIG DEAL!"

In Theme Park America,

the mugger raises up his hand
for no reason

in theme park america
every tree is a museum
every leaf a monument
each flower a flower idea
this slum a garden of garbages
the world a world still swelling with

its first inhalation of eternity

everything is larger farther apart
the squalor spacious clearer
composing a picture of squalor
misery is misery with the pure glow
of something like forever

by whose mild light we see a gleam
sharpen in the killer's fist

look the other one twists away
for our information
those wide startled eyes

are for our information
for our information
he is screaming
can you hear what he's saying
he isn't saying anything
he's just screaming
so that's how it's done how it happens

it's interesting

he's not screaming now
he's doubled over

and we don't have to worry
what it means
nothing is supposed to mean
that will come later
when there's more information
about the information

and so we walk around
in families and couples in shorts
and jeans and t-shirts and sneakers
solemn and docile
eating our ice cream

because everything depends
on going through these motions
the whole fragile revelation

once
we worried sweated I worried
once a black revolving thunderhead
opaque enormous glob of clenched fists
of motives and intentions
wanting wanting wanting wanting
each hidden behind every other
battering to get out
demanding to be imagined

            .   .   .

it hurt unbelievably
it was horrible
that everything wasn't what it seemed
promises broken things blocking the light

we didn't deserve that not us
we were still good
in spite of everything

all that's history
a long eyeblink ago
then america became
theme park america

every tree is a museum
every leaf a monument
each flower a flower idea

who would have dreamt
a miracle could be so
easy

everything is so simple
so transparent
one intention smiles from every face
to be pleasant and to please
to please for example *us*

who simplify ourselves
to receive simply gratefully
what brilliant good people who have
the franchise on reality
thought up and made for us
this wonderful truly wonderful
and give us our role to play too
we please by being pleased

and showing it
            .   .   .

addict
batterer
suicide
insomniac
senator
mugger
drunk
the baby with the cigarette burns

wherever in this great park

look at that one
look there
look over there
how amazingly like themselves

nothing has changed
and everything is different

and let's face it
no one *needs* poverty anymore
it's not *doing* anything
we don't need these poor people
so it's very nice
if they're kept on as the poor

things our eyes say
when we pass in the street

I mean we're poor too
we're visitors ourselves
look at all we gave up to be here
we have nothing but our wonderful faith
in all this wonderful
truly wonderful
we're doing the best we can

and because behind the scenes
another hand

is moving the mugger's hand
it doesn't hang baffled in the bright air
it's doing it

right now
right here
across the street

and later maybe we'll know *why*
our wounds our woundedness so deep
they keep crying out for some eternity
right now

we never
not us
oh no

every tree
every leaf
each flower
a flower

look look he's gasping
look he's looking over here
don't look
look on the ground collapsed
he looks awful
like a messed up balloon
look at the mugger he's crouching
he's feeling around in his pockets
I think he's smiling at us he's showing
it's terrible it's interesting it's nice
it's not dangerous
in theme park america
we're grinning we're
grinning back

look at that blue sky
it's a perfect day
it's perfect here alright

. . .

if only the whole world
of everyone everywhere
could see us
see how good we are
truly good
they would be happy
they would want to be good

please god let's not blow it
again
let it stay like this
forever

oh did we see this one before
it looks familiar
I don't remember
I bet you he gets up and walks away

please move over I can't see

the knife the knife again
plunging
for no reason
but it will not rend no
it will miss entirely

the innocence of everything

The Celebrities

Not themselves, but like photographs of themselves;
and their faces, whether puffy, sleek, or wrinkled,
are faces we cannot imagine anyone
gazed at with love ever—because they are angels
burned to fierce neutrality by the billion stares
that make them immortal: great, impoverished beings
sprung whole from the eyes of strangers.

Interrupted Prayers

The sun goes, So long, so long, see you around.
And zone by zone by zone across America
the all-night coast-to-coast ghost café lights up.
Millions of dots of darkness—the loners,
the losers, the half-alive—twitch awake
under the cold electronic coverlet,
and tune in their radios' cracked insomnia.
A static craziness scratches and buzzes
inside the glowing tombstones of talk
—some crossed wires' hodgepodge dialogue,
or Morse and remorse of garbled maydays
of prayers shot down by Heaven's deaf ear.
Heaven itself is crashing tonight.
The signal breaks up, it fades. Silence.
Then static, then chatter. Then silence. And still
—poor peeves and griefs, poor spirits—from all
the alien area codes we phone in
our cries . . .
            "Hello, Larry?"
                        "Go ahead, Cleveland,
you're on the air!"
                        "Larry, this is Don in Cleveland.
Longtime listener, first-time caller,"
                                    booms a voice
that could float you home in a hurricane
—that big and rich, that cheery; its billion bucks
i.v. directly into the bankrupt heart.
It's one A.M. and, God knows, I need it bad,
just one little hit of hopefulness.
I dial Don down to whisper, curl closer,
plug myself into the keyhole of sound.
Feed me! Be me!
            "Great show, Larry, great interview!
Loved it, Larry! My hat definitely is off
to you."
            And mine to you, Don, I whisper, for
the lovely pure bullion of your accolade
—this gift you bring to Being's bright mountain!

And, rising in radio space, there Being *is*.
My heart's successful twin—I look up to it:
the whole rock, passion amassed as majesty.
Don out there in Cleveland (and Bruce in Duluth,
Duke in Dubuque, Harry in Gary), you show me
that Being is praise and praise is Being,
and how amazingly possible life could be.
So, I'm piggybacking on you, voice of Don.
Carry me home! Take me where I want to be!
In my heart of hearts I'm praising Larry, too.
Yes, I'll phone him up and say, Larry, you are
the greatest! This is me, Irving—you know,
in Buffalo!

        Flat and harsh—Larry's voice
interrupts.
      "No names, please!"
                  "What, Larry? What?"
"No names, please. And please turn down your radio."
"What, Larry?"
           "I said, 'Lower it, sir—your radio!' "
So Pluto puts down the upstart corpse.
Silence. Don off-mike fumbling in his room.
And silence. And silence . . . until silence one
dead second too long rips it open again:
the jagged gash black in the heart of Being
—the secret fissure where the whips are kept.
Suddenly, he's back—though not all of Don
has made it through the communication gap;
something's missing: the fizz, the zip, the good gism,
which night by night he's hoarded drop by drop.
"Sorry, Larry. I am absolutely sorry."
Silence. This silence swallows mountains whole . . .
—Don in limbo awaiting acknowledgment,
put there by Larry on eternal hold.
But then, "Great show, Larry, great interview!"
Don booms, re-running his spiel from the start.
I almost see it shrivel, the hand he's held out
to Larry taken in hand by the night instead.
But what a fool he must feel, hearing his words

grimace at themselves in the mirror of silence
—like starting over your interrupted prayer,
As I was saying, God . . . or, shouting now
to your beloved's bad ear, I said, Darling,
I love you!

        "I have a comment and a question,"
Don plunges on, "and then I'll hang up, Larry,
and listen to your answer."

                What is your question?"
"My comment, Larry, is just this: Larry,
if anyone's out there, I mean, anyone at all,
who's contemplating suicide—don't do it, please!
I tried it once. It's not worth it—believe me.
So please, I beg you, please get help, get help fast!
See a counselor, a minister, a *therapist*!"
The marvelous T-word sizzles on his tongue.
"I can't emphasize this enough. But Larry,"
he segues smooth as a pro, right on beat,
"I'm really phoning in to ask you this.
Historically, twenty-two major leaguers
have played in four different decades in the Bigs.
Larry, can you tell me how many of them
are active now? And can you tell me their names,
Larry—please?"

        They're playing our song again
on the suicide trivia hotline.
Once there were worlds, and now there's entertainment.
So let's just relax and enjoy the void-noises
of the whirling debris of shattered places
drifting apart in the wide ocean of air,
calling out, trying to get connected.
And Larry? Lord of soul dumps, Larry trolls
the airwaves for trash fish, for flounderers.
He tingles when the stricken vibes imply
a flat one's on the line. With his gleaming hook,
he'll play him good, he'll pluck him out, he'll toss him
flopping onto the heap beneath his hams
of the used up, the washed up, the obsolete.
Larry is jocose, superior—a winner.

His tone announces, Hey, everybody, do I
or don't I know a jerk when I feel one?
"Bat around, fella!" he says.
And *"Hit for the cycle, man!*
Touch all the bases, baby!
Go, go, go! Go for it, guy!"
                              "Larry,
Larry, am I getting through to you?"
He's getting through to *me,* alright.
Ex-drowned man, Don's into survival.
He's got longevity on his brain.
Oh, he's making his comeback alright;
and this time he's going all the way
—if only he can die completely.
He's opening his veins to America,
his heart he opens to the blowtorch,
the supple, the darting, greedy eel of flame:
Once you were cold like us, but now you're hot.
Larry, do unto me as you did for Larry.
With these bedraggled facts I saved my life,
see, these last damp straws to which I cling.
Autograph them with your raging acetylene,
with your outrageous adrenaline—and bless them,
please, burn them, please, scald them, with reality!
Larry, show me how to be like you!
(I'll show you, fella. Here's lesson number one:)
"I haven't got all night, sir.
I have other callers on the line."
Larry's voice holds Don off at lash's length
—not to be contaminated by loser taint.
And certainly success owes this to itself,
to go on being successful,
and always be wanting more—not like ghosts,
who have to hunger for Larry's hunger,
who call and call in, hoping to please him,
because losers can't please themselves.
From admiration, we break our bones,
we hold the shattered stemware up to him,
we say, For you, this toast. I am nothing.
But drink my marrow—and be everything!

                                                  Oh well,
Larry is hungry—but Larry is picky.
For who will divide hunger from anger in him?
—because Larry is never satisfied.
(Is Pluto *satisfied* to rule a bunch of stiffs?)
And that's why Larry's a winner, not a loser.
Is success work? Is success luck? What a laugh!
Success is fury, frenzy beyond measure
—the lifewire dancing with its own power,
crackling, too hot to handle; admire it, buddy,
if you want, but get the hell out of the way,
because try to grab it, and you are zapped, you die!
Therefore, Larry scorns praise not fulsome with defeat
—anything less would be effrontery—
the meat of the broken only is broken enough,
and flesh that failure has predigested.
                                        "Larry,
'Consistency!'—that's the word. To go out there
year in and year out—like yourself, Larry—
and no questions asked just get the job done."
Don doesn't get it, he doesn't have a clue.
"You guys are the real heroes, true professionals.
You should be named our national treasures, Larry,
really—don't you agree?"
                        Dear tender wish,
sad furtive ploy: Don sneaking his shy fingers
to touch the handle while the tip flicks lightly
and leaves a little welt of praise on the air
—he wants so much to get a few strokes in,
to have his hand on it when the lash plays nice.
"What are you, some kind of wacko, sir?"
                                        "Believe me,
Larry, I'm doing the best I can.
You can't ask for any more than that.
So, look, enjoy your success, Larry,
you've paid your dues, you really have,
and good health to you, and lots more years.
I mean, as long as you've got your health . . .
Hey, Larry, am I right? or am I right?"
"When you're right, you're right, baby . . ."

                                        Some solar storm
or perturbation in the ionosphere
sweeps the air clear and blows those voices
God alone knows where, pelting down
their blight of white nights, their acid blizzard
on innocent cornfields and quiet orchards.

"Hello, Larry?"
                It's 4 A.M., and, risen from
static and silence, good old Don is back,
cold Lazarus recycled word for word
by courtesy of tape—still trying
to reach the Thaumaturge, still getting through
to Pluto instead . . .
                        "Go ahead, Cleveland,
you're on the air!"

West Street

            Exotic birds of passage, errant bits
            of bright nights dropped from heaven to hop
            here—in party hairdos at all hours,
            in hotpants and minis, and black or white
            vinyl half-waders even the wily trout
            and wary bass shall find alluring, sexy . . .

            might be models shooting on location
            in some slummy industrial setting,
            sucking in their cheeks and mugging funky
            goofy moody naughty haughty pampered
            —one of them now holding half a jelly bun
            and slowly eating, then throwing it down . . .

            but these early birds of six and seven,
            out to catch the early worms,
            are half a dozen hookers working from
            a West Street warehouse loading dock

—runaways with razors in the purse,
the missing girls next door come down

from miserable highs and home to roost.

The Girlfriend

It all began when poor messed-up Lara called.
Oh, the same, the same: boyfriend down the tubes;
mother throwing fits; job post-terminal;
biological clock in doomsday mode;
her men shrinks were bullies, the women were,
if possible, worse: critical, envious.
What didn't shrink was her laundry list
—the slights and frights, sobs, rages, gripes
wouldn't come clean for all her self-expressing.
And always always *she* responded, clucked,
cooed, hissed, howled, grunted, yea'd-and-nay'd, played
—like Old MacDonald's wife—the whole barnful
of backup sounds. Actually, she could have cried
—though Lara made it hard to *feel* your sympathy.
At last, she got the poor thing calmed down, sort of
—until tomorrow's "Lara life-attack."

And then she walked into the dining room.
There was Bernie, still behind his paper.
He must have heard it all, or caught her tone
of burbling harmony with someone in hell,
because he said, hardly looking up at her,
"Lara, huh?" It was one of those moments:
quite ordinary, and then everything
turns around. Her answer was to smile.
Whenever Lara's name came up she smiled.
And Bernie as usual returned her smile.
And she held hers an instant longer, until
it hurt, as if frozen in a second smile.
Smiling, she walked into the bathroom,
and sat down on the edge of the tub.

She wanted to touch her face, poke it, pull.
The plate, she saw, was still in her hand.
It was shaking. She'd *had* to sit, because
his smile might have spoken words—it was that clear:
he'd taken her smile to be telling him,
"How marvelous you are! How lucky I am
to have you and not be like poor lonely Lara!"
But no, she hadn't meant that, not ever
—her smile, it was only now she saw this,
in fact was saying, "How lucky *you* are,
you might have married some helpless bitch like Lara
('helpless,' that was a good one) who'd really
have clipped your wings and kept you hopping!"
So *that* was it!—and this had staggered her:
to realize her whole life with Bernie was
this constant, numbing, shaming apology
—for robbing the man of his precious freedom.
And to top it off—the irony of it—
he hadn't the least idea what freedom was!

Bernie was in the living room now.
He looked up from the paper and smiled at her.
The plate, she saw, was still in her hand.

Even in Eden

Adam was happy—in, of course,
that agreeably vague way of his.
After all, nothing could be less good than he,
and he was fine, quite good, well, wonderful,
in fact, and well intentioned—obviously!
At one with himself, solvent, splendid, whole,
he might well stand as the world's guarantor:
while he was, nothing should decline or fall.
And surely no less could be expected from
the president of the Club of Being.
Therefore, his bearing, his plain demeanor.
And let it be said that all in all

he never met a fellow in his domain
of starblossom and star, angel and angelfish,
who refused him the exchange of courtesies.
By query, by challenge, temptation, complaint,
by innocence, guile, by nuance, by gifts,
Eve, meanwhile, in every imaginable way,
to learn what worm of loss the future hid,
vexed the present into hissing signs.

She Knows

Abandoned, deserted, betrayed, cursing
and wishing him damned, damned, burning in hell,
ladies' man, womanizer, who lied in the crib
to his mother!—yet she knows, while she rages,
that somewhere at the end of the line of lovers
down which he takes his inconstant, destined course
as though passed on from one to the other
until his mystery is all rubbed away
and all he is meets any eye, oh she knows
that a woman, a mere woman, like her,
will, though numbered a thousand and four,
one day touch her fingertips to his lids,
will wash and perfume his blank body all over,
and dress him, as she might dress her baby,
her own dear baby, for his long night on the town.

Widow

The woman tends the fire
gathers sticks for it
shields it from the wind
she piles it higher
pokes it into shape
lets it warm her
explains its virtues points out

its brightness to others
oh how she dotes on it
and vows never to let it go out
but is forbidden to carry
or even to touch
the sacred implements by which
it is struck
into being.

Now these are inert
and blackened forever
and it is she who bears them
proudly everywhere.

After Empires

The boots, the pompadour, the enigma smile,
the eyes following wherever you go,
motherly and kind, hard, demanding,
that bedrock jaw, that towering brow's
forethought stretching out to forever
where finally no enemies are,
the stature magically dwarf and giant,
like seen from faraway and from underfoot,
the nod that dominoes down the hierarchy
until all hell breaks loose or gets quiet quick,
the famous greatcoat for whose least little thread
how gladly we would die!
—this the emperor, resplendent icon
and cynosure of every blind eye.
But when a child renamed him Naked,
our laughter tore illusion from imposture.
We came to, staring at the shriveled image
of our miserable lives: some shivering imp
—who'd actuated the boots, the greatcoat,
the whole vast shadow play of good and bad
from which real blood ran.

. . .

That was in our long dawn
of seeing things as they are
and saying over and over what we saw
until we rejoiced to know at last
what we hadn't known we were seeing.
We pointed, stammered out our disbelief:
There, that's the little, vicious ear that sucked
the whispers snitching from our innocent mouths,
and then that knowing wink included us in
his debaucheries and blunders and scams and worse
—while it said yes to our fingers cunningly
to grab the crumb that came their way in the dark—
and that club foot good for kicking ass,
that secret claw which bloodied, caressed, bloodied,
and always got its own back, no matter what,
so cleverly you couldn't help but admire . . .
And all the while we were believing
everything they wanted us to believe!

Shame confused our faces, and we looked down
and hid from ourselves and each other.

But the nakedness of the emperor
is also the empire naked.
That little boy who dissented
from our credulous commonplaces
and our enormities of faith
and was beaten, mocked, medicated,
while decades long we looked the other way,
is an old man fading slowly into
the nothingness at which he points.
A hundred million of us who died
in famine in prison in fire in war,
have died absurdly, incredibly, as if
bulldozed nameless into the pit and left
unshrouded to the raw sky to devour.

Something's gone wrong with reality.
We know what we know now, but no longer
how to believe what we know.

Our lives are going to be better,
but somehow without our lifetimes,
without the meaning we lived through,
as if our history had never happened:
all of it a lie—and all the truth we had.
Suffered for nothing, sacrificed for nothing,
no sins purged, no future prepared.
What was our empire, then?
Desert. And wandering. An interim.

The enemies are back. Out of nowhere.
Whichever way we look, we see them
floating up and down in our retinas,
darkening our view, threatening our sight
—as in the good old bad old days.
Our laughter only laughed our world away,
and our rage cuts every way at once
and still can't make reality come out right.
It's got to be them: the enemies are
the difference that's screwing up the whole works!
We suspect they conspired, they conspire.
In that. In this. In everything.
In fact, nothing is more certain.
It's in their nature to get together,
send signals, understand each other.
They are patient, have faith, never tire,
their simple yet infinitely supple plan
is worldwide, stretches for millennia.
Without them, no empire.
How many enemies does it take
to build an imp? to fill a greatcoat?
There are theories.
And we are counting.

In the Mental Ward,

                    a little light
        from out-of-doors: a visiting child

intrudes in the darkened hallway;
he takes sweet mint toothpicks
from his pocket; smiling and beckoning
toward the patients, he holds them out with small
encouraging gestures: Are here. Not bad thing.
No hurt. Good thing. You do.
                              Comfortable
now, their terror drowsing after
evening "meds," bulked out
in pajamas and robes, curious,
companionable as kine, they come and flock
to him, the sad lean years, they take
toothpicks, they tear the paper off,
they clip them between their jaws
and stand with sage expectancy,
they turn and gaze at one another,
slowly, gravely, with perfect ease,
their astounded tongues divining
the secret, freedom! rousing the wild wood.

Poem of the Old Avant-Garde

Coming home, cut to pieces, but victorious
and looking forward—you write that, write it good—
after our rough times off on the frontier,
we met them going out the road we traveled back.
Oh, they were a cheerful bunch—and young, my god, young!
"Hey," they said, "your old king died or something years ago,
hardly anyone's left you would have known—and us,
we're on our way to do some fancy soldiering for
his son or his son's son, maybe, someone like that.
Boy, you old-timers are going to have it good!
It's all *history* what you done—we learned it in school.
You're okay, you saved the country. They'll do right by you
—same as they will by us when *we* turn around."

So back we went and got paraded up and down.
Strangers shook our hands, strangers kissed our cheeks.

Strangers shouted, "Marvelous! Congratulations!"
Strangers whispered to their children on the street,
"See the fine old heroes! See them marching by!"
That was us: marching, marching, always "marching by"
—the Immortals of the month, the grizzled darlings
of the snotnoses who crank the awe-machine.
And we, it shames me to admit it but
we gobbled it up, like we were good for nothing
except to blubber in public about "it's wonderful
to be back home" and "we're so grateful you're grateful."
And strangers took us out to see the monument we were,
and watched the teary, shining expressions cross
our scarred old faces when we saw what we'd become.
How happy they looked making us the gift of ourselves
—sponsors of our last shape, our final future!
Then strangers walked us into the pensioned twilight
where we no longer knew ourselves . . . and nothing nothing
nothing came back . . . only this feeling of strangeness
that kept you company . . . with everything spellbound
and going away because you'd come to a stop
. . . and then while you sat there becoming a stone,
you felt it—time was flowing over your hand . . .

You can take it from me, my friend: getting mad
is what will keep the sad songs out of your dick
—and your dick out of your hand . . .
Maybe our Old Guy was one mean s.o.b.
—who ever said that *we* were any bargain?—
and had nothing to give but his holding back.
But what good was everything we'd done for him if
we couldn't throw it in his teeth and hear him squawk,
"What in the hell ever made you think I'd pay up?
You did it—it's yours. Now live with it. Or don't."
So, what's it all come to anyway?
We saved his ass. He died in bed.
Or he got out of bed a thousand times more
and then one morning didn't. Just didn't.
And now no hand is left that's fit to lay
the "living laurel on their faithful brows."

. . . .

Me? I'm re-upping in the second campaign,
marching away to those kids in the old outback,
where we're dangerous still . . .
                              You tell them, tell
all those fine civilians our day will come,
the clarion's voice rinsing out the whole wide sky,
the wind stepping into the banners, and all the rest . . .
Till then they don't have to worry.
And if that's never, then fuck it, it's never.

Adventures in the Postmodern Era

Speedy said to Spanky as Spanky to Speedy said,
"Let's go out and beat up some old clichés!"

The chronicle of their war with the clichés
had for theme: Omnipotence in the realm of words.

No fact or feeling, circumstance or being
ever affronted their far reconnoiterings.

How unsurprisingly a world without experience
confirmed that "In the beginning is the Parody."

How admirably a world without transcendence
satisfied their master motto: Just us new clichés.

How perfectly a world without resistance
suited their single rule: Be arbitrary.

Their drafts on the universe were always honored.
Their women took whatever shape desire said.

Why counterfeit when your credit is unlimited?
Why tarry when all the girls cry, Yes, yes, yes?

Speed is a great enemy of feeling. "Faster, fool!"
"Harder, schmuck!" For shock is a fine anesthetic.

. . .

The spiel of clichés in their sideshow voices (Slash and Burns)
was hyping One Big Void to the crowd of little voids.

The French kiss of void and cliché is the mutual
accolade of tongues in an absence of sensation.

Those lowlife clichés could well afford to be pushovers:
they were infinite, all they ever did was reproduce

—by dissolving contexts that might make them more than woids.
(But Hack and Tack bore frameworks to death with solipsism.)

Therefore the armory of Slap and Dash had: *The Endless Work,
The Fictivity Fiat* ("It's all a lot of crap, guys"),

and the massive cliché-ingesting *Meta-cliché*
—metabolizable in turn by quotation marks,

themselves transcended by sly tongue-in-cheeks
(to coin a phrase (to coin a phrase ("to coin a phrase"))) . . .

Fast and Fist came to where the brightly various texts
all empty into one glum sump of Meta-text.

And here Hare'm and Scare'm sat down on the bare margin.
They covered it with crushed butt words, empty can words.

WWI (Writing While Under the Influence)

"When I hit New York it was all getting started.
Right away Ted became an influence.
Then I was out on the Coast and Robert was there.
He was one of my major influences.
Then Allen came and started influencing me.
And Jack was in and out a lot, and Gary
—and everybody was being influenced.
You could just feel it wherever you went.

Then Bill came back and the wattage zoomed.
Three four five influences all working at once!
That was a really incredible scene.
For three months everything was right there:
the whole future of American poetry.
Suddenly, Buffalo was the center.
And Charles was the center of Buffalo.
I was there maybe a year after Charles,
but anywhere you were it was like people
were saying, 'Charles.' So he was an influence
on me, indirect, you could say, but strong.
That was when I got heavy into ampersands.
God, I still love those little suckers!
I could talk to you for hours about them."

He set the empty tankard down. He sighed.
"I haven't been influenced since.
I mean, not seriously anyway.
Maybe *you* can tell me, kid.
Are the influences what they used to be?
And just who are the influences today?"

Terminal Laughs

Thirty years ago the young Corso in his cups
—*my* cups, in fact, my booze, too, on which, a gulp
away from getting smashed, he was loading up.
First, tagging along, he'd crashed the party,
then was everywhere making his presence felt,
depositing impartially—on rug, on couch,
on the proffered hand and the affable lap—
steaming little signatures of self.
Introduced to me, his next-to-unknown
and near-anonymous host, Gregory exclaimed,
" 'Irving Feldman?' 'Irving *Feldman*?' '*Oiving* Feldman?'
—what kind of name is that for a poet?"
He probably intended well: you know
—Touring Star Instructs Benighted Yokel in

the finer perks of fame, its *droit de seigneur:*
since one never knows who'll get the last laugh,
Maestro will make sure he grabs the first sneer.
Caught red-handed being *myself,* naked in quotes,
I contemplated the awfulness of my name
—undistinguished, uneuphonious, a joke.
What vocal apparatus would not collapse in
a fatal fibrillation of runaway yuks,
intoning those syllables with suitable awe?
Well, then, spare the world apocalypse by laughter
—just shut up, Irving, shut down, back off!
Oh, but now " 'Gregorio Nunzio Corso!' "
he tarantara-ed, nose loftily rising to
this high occasion, as if summoned upward by
the fanfaronade of its fantastic fanfare,
"now *that,* Oiving, is a name for a poet!"
Second paeon, dactyl, dactyl catalectic
—his name itself, alone, had heft and breath
enough to launch and swell a mighty fine line.
No way to know *this* poet from his poem!
—who, an hour later, crossed one line too many.
Ralph (red-faced, Anglophile), taking his measure,
tapped out deeDUM, the old iambic one-TWO,
and did a number on Gregory's nose.

It took a day or so, but finally,
gestating the guy's manners, mien, mug
while licking at my wounds, my "staircase wit,"
laggard though it was and lost in transit usually,
gagged up a fur ball part blood, mostly spit:
"As the poet said, Gregory, What is *in*
a name? By any other you'd be as Coarso."
The party, fortunately, had long been over,
and, bolstered by two tender-hearted ladies
covering his flanks as he retreated, while
his nose autographed in red a borrowed hanky,
the poet, faring forward, had stumbled downstairs
—to pipe his old tune in pastures not greener,
perhaps, but, for sure, far far grassier.

. . .

Skip thirty years. An eye's blink. The interim?
Some books. Some other books. Fade swiftly to:
Another party now (my son's). Another coast.
Same hubbub. Each newcomer turns the volume up.
Whom the gods would mock they first make famous.
Enter Thad. Young actor here in Hollywood,
dying for parts, money, acclaim, the glamor and
groveling and intoxication due to fame,
to be something more, but not necessarily
much more, than "just another pretty face."
He spots me there, singled out from the crowd
by the sudden celebrity that follows me
around, or maybe is leading me on:
this year's MacLaurels penciled in on my brow.
"Hey, Irving Feldman," he shouts across the tumult
of everyone madly talking all at once,
"you are a goddamn star of poetry!"
Has he ever read a word I wrote?
Still, I glow for a moment in his glee.
But somewhere behind my back I sort of hear
how Gregory, our Chatterton, our wingèd boy,
sloshed out of his cups now and into his saucer,
stubble-bearded, his underwear stained with pee,
his nose no straighter for being out of joints
though longer perhaps by a thousand lines,
half-toothless, and slowed to a sub-pubcrawl
—just the type, immortality's mortal bouncer,
to i.d. the gaggle at Parnassus Gate—
I seem to hear how, guarding the lowest stair,
he mutters in his despondency (*his*, truly,
having kept his lost promise all these years),
" 'Irving Feldman,' huh? Just another pretty name."

Kiss and Tell

"Dear Alfred Tell, Come back. We love you." Signed, *"The World."*
A little ink. Some paper. A postage stamp.
What would it cost them? They could all *chip in.*

But all that comes of my wooing, waiting are
solicitations aimed blithely *Tell*-ward.
Corporations seem to think that *I'm* "The World."
Wherefore I've come to frame my law, Tell's law,
to wit: Junk mail doesn't drive the good mail out
—junk mail *eats* it. Which explains why same arrives
engorged, glossy, upbeat, with dentition gleaming,
more comfortably at home *chez vous* than you are,
and feelers already caressing your wallet,
and bulging with metaphysical confidence
a world is out there equal to its diet,
while first class matter, thin, pale, self-effacing,
gets through—if at all—looking badly chewed.
True, that envelope jumbo-ed up on my desk
wasn't junk, exactly—had the stamps to prove it.
Still, it got lots of respect: the full *bill* treatment
—quarantine, and burial in the real stuff.
Forty days, forty nights later, I fished it up.
Hefted. Squeezed. Soft. It sighed. Gas? I sniffed. Mildew?
Ambergris? Shook. Listened. Rustling. Heavy-light. *Aiee!*
Moby-Dick? Or *Moby-Dick?* the drowning reader joked.
Oh, *this* could only mean pages, pages, pages
of stained, discolored, shriveled onion skin, on which,
battered through an old typewriter ribbon's ragged
palimpsest, a ghostly scurf of words had spread
—*rescu'd from death by force, though pale and faint:*
yes, more hopeless poems of Kenneth Irving Kiss!
(Before being seen by a critic, shouldn't they
have been looked at by a dermatologist?)
My X-ray vision foresaw what no eye should see:
impassable scrub of scumbled symbols, syllables
—before which, dreading alike what pokes at his eye
and what dimly he conjectures, the bravest reader
abandons hope of glimpsing starlight again.
So back to my labors at anachronism,
my one-man sweatshop of selves and memory,
picking through phantom rags, pecking away, shirtless
(nude author/naked truth), at *Memoirs II*
through one more week of dripping New Orleans summer
—until, jinxed, snakebit, bugabooed, I hit the wall,

I blocked. The thing was getting into my mind—and *at*
my manuscript. *Then* I grabbed the damn envelope.

Our correspondence had begun six months before
—a note from Kiss: he was reading *Memoirs I,*
how come he never saw my poems in print,
anyway he was pleased to see I had gone on,
he had, too (while remaining there in Gotham,
something in administration—grunt or gripe—
somewhere in the bowels of City government),
was pretty sure he remembered me, and did I
remember him, from forty years ago, you know,
that great Village scene right after the War?
(Miffed, was he, or pleased he'd been omitted from
my "scandalous me-mires"—one smart reviewer wrote—
or, as I thought I detected, both together?)
Well, yes, I recalled a kid, five years my junior,
around the streets, at parties, in bars, and a face
like other faces (freckled, unformed), and a name,
though one he seemingly had, or had had, bobbed
—something like "Kissoffsky," wasn't it?—and, hey,
though you didn't get around to saying so,
I'm really tickled to death you loved my book!
Kiss's answer was a poem, a modest trickle,
a lonely drip; politely, faintly, falsely,
foolishly, I praised it—and brought down on my head
a slew, a slough, a slurry, a deluge of verse
—oh, these pent-up, aching poets!—
and cuttings of reviews, mainly disdainful,
of his single, long out-of-print collection;
and stark xeroxes of letters to editors
with his outraged, unanswerable Last Word,
which had gone, of course, unanswered, unprinted:
wildflowers sacrificed between the leaves of
his heart's throbbing album, to which, commemorating
their bloody soil, they had, dot by doleful dot,
transferred the smudged stigmata of their type.
One *knew* he had it all by heart—but had his heart
shrunk to a postage stamp to harbor nothing else?
Then one saw the clippings in particular

were clearly not copies but originals
—the very ones that Kiss first read, and bled upon.
And what the *Times* hadn't punished, Time had,
flaying delicately the ink and paper
into a martyrdom of transiency:
"i"s decapitated, "t"s nakedly uncrossed,
the newsprint frayed and softened to a baby fuzz.
It was too much almost to handle them
—one felt that, yes, here, not in Kiss's feeble *oeuvre*,
one touched, too literally, his very quick.
But such precious, painful things as these . . . and I, I
was, after all, a stranger, really . . . No,
so much intimacy I hadn't bargained for . . .
I thought now I understood the onion skins:
not the poems blurred thereon but they themselves
were Kiss—Kiss's own epidermal sloughings.
I had been receiving through my front door slot
matter descended directly from Job.
Small wonder I'd felt their touch sacred, disgusting.
Were these, then, in the nature of his confession?
And, sadly, like most confessions impertinent?
But was he, perhaps, aware of all this?
And if so, did he mean to rub my nose in it?
Hadn't that kind of thing—the flaunted self-hatred,
the fond gloating over one's own misery,—
hadn't that all gone out of style in the 'fifties?
Now this mass of unrequited vanity, this soul,
this self-absorbed Kiss, was catching me up on him,
dumping decades of Kiss into my lap—I feared
each post would bring a c.v. updated to
last midnight's movie, this morning's raisins and oats.
(In our era of professionals and managers
art may be long but the *vita* is longer.)
Amazingly, Kiss had spared me (in fact as well
as in facsimile) current photos of self
—which I could imagine too painfully well,
or grimace back at in my bathroom mirror:
the hair gone white or gone altogether,
the baby fat rendered to a rigor of gristle,
and peeping out of the casual carnage,

341

the eyes—betrayed, startled, lost—of a boy.
I was grateful.

        Suddenly, I tore it open.
Out tumbled pages on which a faint subtext
of coffee spills, wine stains, paper-clip rust, ash
—the fading sediment of human presence—
had left the deepest, most enduring impression:
of all the reddened eyes that ever peered at them
darkly through a threadbare scrim of sleeplessness,
the wired hands that set them trembling, and blessings
sprinkled down of smokers' hacking aerosols;
and last the hopeless journey homeward in disgrace
in lovingly stamped and self-addressed envelopes.
And now I understood my turn had come.
Wasn't I being thoughtfully provided with
material for, shall we say, a *Memoirs III,*
a chapter, perhaps, on "Kenneth Irving Kiss:
The Poems, The Man, The Correspondence With?"
Exasperated, guilty, feeling doomed myself,
I was like the surgeon who opens and gazes
into the morbid heart of humorlessness;
he notes the lack of tone, the arrhythmia,
the total absence of proprioception;
everywhere he probes there are the tell-tale,
grim metasteses of mediocrity,
of obsession; praying, cursing, he capitulates
—to the inoperable, to mortality.
I gentled it all back into its envelope,
and resubmitted it to the raw dark maw
I'd plucked it from: my desk's final landfill of
verbivorous, logophagous literature.

Small Talk for a Sage

        "I seem not to have any small talk."—PAUL GOODMAN

Whatever stoa he strolls around
with other sages in blessèd dialogue,

may he find fit words though few
though minuscule to reply in kind
to amiable Aristotle's
"Well, where have *you* been keeping yourself?"
and to solicitous Lao-Tsu's
profoundly, touchingly cordial
"Hey, Paul, warm enough for you?"

How Wonderful

How wonderful to be understood,
to just sit here while some kind person
relieves you of the awful burden
of having to explain yourself, of having
to find other words to say what you meant,
or what you think you thought you meant,
and of the worse burden of finding no words,
of being struck dumb . . . because some bright person
has found just the right words for you—and you
have only to sit here and be grateful
for words so quiet so discerning they seem
not words but literate light, in which
your merely lucid blossoming grows lustrous.
How wonderful that is!

And how altogether wonderful it is
not to be understood, not at all, to, well,
just sit here while someone not unkindly
is saying those impossibly wrong things,
or quite possibly they're the right things
if you are, which you're not, that someone
—a difference, finally, so indifferent
it would be conceit not to let it pass,
unkindness, really, to spoil someone's fun.
And so you don't mind, you welcome the umbrage
of those high murmurings over your head,
having found, after all, you are grateful
—and you understand this, how wonderful!—

that you've been led to be quietly yourself,
like a root growing wise in darkness
under the light litter, the falling words.

Fragment

for John Hollander

The language isn't saved by style
but by a tale worth telling.
Not, then, to purify the old words
but to bring new speech into
the lexicon of the tribe,
to tell, for example, how they
received their names—the gods—
who die in every generation
—the world ends—
and are revived under new vocables
as yet unknown to us
and in other, still unguessable shapes
—that must be the world renewed, the new world.
Or even to tell—if we can tell
no more than this—how they came to die
and lost their names and their allure, were husks
hardly able to hold our whispers,
even this allows us a kind
of communion, a beginning of sorts,
a way to keep feeling alive.

From *Beautiful False Things*

The Recognitions

Not the god, though it might have been,
savoring some notion of me
and exciting the cloud where he was hidden
with impetuous thunderstrokes of summoning
—it was merely you who recognized me,
speaking my name in such a tone
I knew you had been thinking it
a long, long time, and now revealed yourself
in this way. Because of this, suddenly
who I was was precious to me.

Voluptas

Strange to be remembering how
—was it twenty-odd years ago?—
you drew back from one of our kisses,
your head turning half away so that
I saw in our bedroom's half-light
your lovely profile and eye staring
out toward and into a passing thought.
Then all of half your smile was for me,
and you put your mouth to mine again
with overwhelmed gentleness.
We both were overwhelmed and pulled under.

Strange suddenly to remember this
after so many, many kisses,
after such years of rupturing.
Caught in our archaic caresses
(you know, that same old, old thing):
a space of five seconds of fresh time,
when nothing was happening
and nothing was happening yet.
And I now its voluptuary.

"Sono un poeta . . . Scrivo"

At eighteen, nineteen, twenty years old,
my *Bohème* was a walk-up on Willett Street.
And I bolted up—two, three steps at a time
to my garret under the stars . . . where Mimì
came at me in the dark hallway, eyes burning.
I thought she'd strike me with her cold little hand.
Or darted back with angry mutters, and stood
in her apartment door, pronouncing my death
in hoarse, undecipherable arias.
She had lost the key—to everything.
Dark, small, white-haired, darting, a Fury
derided by minuter, madder furies.
Or was Catastrophe, the idiot Fate,
gibbering a million strands together.
Then swipe of the shears cuts a city short.
And all night just beyond my bedroom wall
something, newspapers, rustled into my sleep.
What is she doing? my sleep asked me.
Go to sleep, she's burning the building down,
looking by firelight for the key in the fire,
lost homeless wind groping among our embers.

✦

Garret? Star-infested? On the Lower East Side?
Near the middle of the twentieth century?
Charming had it been, oh, say, something like
a set for the real thing, the opera, I mean
—with underwear filling in for window glass,
and nesting icicles in the potbellied stove,
and tarpaper shreds festooned overhead,
letting starlight fall through with the snow.
And yet, whatever scenery was shifted on
or off, the thrill was in the being there
and singing out, "Who am I? I am a poet!"
The air we sang was city soil, tenement musk:
cooking grease, coal dust, mildew, piss, sweat, rot.
Ages of human habitation, failure, loss

—birth-cries crowding on death-coughs in the walls—
authenticated our art and love and talk.
Come January, hallway johns froze over.
And under my kitchen sink, lath bared its bones
—one tough rat had knocked a chunk of plaster out,
and perched in the hole for a good, long look around;
then, slumming god before my trite offerings,
turned up its nose, and faded into the wall,
as if to say, Keep it, kid—you need it all.
(Worse critics than the rat have condescended since.)
Picturesque? Of course—life imitates bad art.
Poor? Of course *not*—I was, we all were, *young.*

✦

Kid poets, painters, actors, our collected works
you could have flushed down the hole of a pin,
but youth poured out of the holes in our clothes,
youth poured down from the openings in the heavens
—and poured on everything its shining *possible.*
We knew we were the whole show and theater:
authors, players, and the audience that counted.
And if we preened and played to one another,
we were the world's own preening to the universe,
admired in the bright, galactic galleries
—Because, we sang, we have the key, the key is
ourselves belovèd by and beyond everything.
And all the while, Mimì, like the *faux-phénix*
—cloud of ash and dust dying as it rises—
Mimì, raving, scattered down on our heads
the starless, futureless snows of tomorrow.

✦

Josie hemorrhaging her bank account
—she wants to give it away, set it free,
transfuse the whole world's neediness.
"Yesterday I went back there.
I brought these presents for my friends.
I have to rescue them—they have beautiful souls.

Bad things go on there. They hit people.
They wouldn't let an ex-patient in.
He was smiling at me as if I'm crazy.
I'm writing an exposé."
Mania only makes her insanely
tenderhearted, madly idealistic.
Are girls still that way these days, burning
in the furnace of the marketplace?
Thirty years after the year of our love,
ringing me out of nowhere,
from a thousand miles away, from Miami,
at two A.M., at three, at three-fifteen.
"They're out getting pizza.
I'm upstairs.
My sons have me locked in here
—the boys say they'll commit me again.
My baby's charged with child-molesting.
Because he put his hand on that little girl's tushie.
He isn't epileptic anymore.
He's such a beautiful young man.
My older one's a doctor.
I'm sneaking this call to you—I'm sorry.
I'm sorry. They're coming!
The soul is beautiful. You know that.
If anyone does, *you* do. You showed me that.
Can you help me, Irving?
Good-bye, Irving, good-bye."
The year of our love in New York—the year
you were so confused, so tormented, poor,
the year I could have been an ant fiddling,
so strange to you the semaphorings
of my inflamed adoration that left you
out in the cold, in the dark, asking
yourself—I still see it in your heavenly eyes—
"What does this boy want from me?"

I want to fall to my knees in the street
under your window where you stand half
in shadow, or half of you is shadow,
looking out, your lips moving.

I want to consummate my stupid conceit,
be blind in the white light of midday Miami.
I have no right, no right to see your ruin.
I understand nothing anymore.
It's all a mystery. I never understood.
Is this what crazy old Mimì
was raging over back there?
What she remembered? What she foresaw?
I have to save a blessing from the curse.
Somewhere, it has to be here somewhere.
Throw the key, Josie. Throw it down.
The soul is beautiful, the soul is beautiful,
you cried out from the heart of brutality.

Beautiful False Things

Broadcast as if from beyond the grave, a voice
is stumbling through a new vernacular
—some barbarous mouthplace of stumps and swamps
and ruts and roots and gulfs of rubble.
And, lurching toward you, urgent, unearthly,
this voice—imagine it!—is Dante's voice:
Dante declaiming Pinsky's *Inferno*!
Melodious and placeless bliss,
Paradiso, hasn't prepared him for this
his other afterlife—of fame,
this straining to illumine from within
a text he is always outside of.
And where he struggles isn't dark woods
but a bright, hellish glade of clear-cutting
and splintered slash where once the sweet words sang.

So Krip, the much-belaureled Yusuf Krip,
imagined one night in the groin of night
—when Mother Sleep, embittering her nipple,
banished him to wastes of consciousness.
Starving, parched for consolation—to float
at ease, a soul in a sea of sound,

and sip the medium of his being—
now, the friendly lamp beside him unlit,
deep in his study, seated, fingers gloved
in night, old Krip bestirred the radio.
Fiddled at a dial; poked a knob.
It glowed up ruby-red, blared into flame.
A spirit spoke: somewhere close, Dante—so near
he might have plucked at Krip's pajama sleeve—
was speaking English, no, talking American!

An agèd voice, frayed, failing.
Couldn't praising Heaven save the poet's throat?
Or lift his speech from its local self
to pure and universal eloquence?
But, torturer, devil, dunce, Dante's accent
loaded words with chains, shoved cadences down
to where the frenzied Unintelligibles
—like tongues torn out by the root midsentence—
go on expostulating in their Circle,
furious to transcend the interruption
and once and for all time get it said,
clamoring (if only one could know it!)
for the mercy of making sense.
                      And Krip
felt lost and bound in circles of his own,
straining to comprehend the delirious scene
—Dante clutching at this newfound Virgil who
was dragging him by the throat toward exile in
a world undreamt beneath his circling stars . . .

       ✦

He came to, chilled, laughing at himself.
A testimonial to the translation
from the author of the original?
What could he have been imagining?
Oh well, at 3 A.M. anything goes.
But Dante risen—on the radio?
Too much! Revived, more likely,
for purposes of pasta promotion.

Something was being sold. And whether pasta
or poetry, *Dante* guaranteed it!
—Oh, not the *Commedia*'s prophecy,
but "Dante having the Dante-experience!"

Amused, Krip pursued the fantasy:
the great poet, he who once was Dante,
trotted out from deep retirement in death
to perform the poet he no longer is,
authenticate words he never wrote
—on the road somewhere this very minute
starring in "My Life in Irony"
or, ironically, "The Death of the Author."
Better, then, to peddle secondhand poems
in postmodern America than reign
supreme in irrelevance on Parnassus?

Krip knew it, too, knew in his bones
how far the way from the grave,
and hard the translation to new life
—all this vehement clawing into
the glib slope of meaningless words.
But past a certain point Krip couldn't go,
embarrassed for Dante by the raw desire
of his voice, its urgency, its striving,
like the salesman selling himself to himself,
to rise from self-impersonation in
a single-throated rapture of conviction—not
to make sense (to whom here could Dante *wish*
to make sense?) but only to be believed.

The fantasy that shimmered before Krip
turned and stood in his path, roaring.
Painful to face Dante destitute,
Dante stripping himself to ease the way:
lifeworks reduced to vehicles,
and his history, his gravity,
the concern that made him who he was
—all this realm now streamlined to
a repertory of portable emotion,

a shorthand, a rhetoric, a kitsch,
soliciting the common adrenaline;
that, and the will, faithless, inconsolable,
to survive.
          And then, sitting there, to sense,
behind the fever and banality,
Dante's mind was elsewhere, distracted, thinking,
Surely I wrote something once—but why?
Have I, too, abandoned everything to hope,
Krip asked, in order not to abandon hope?

"Hard the journey up and down other men's stairs?
Bitter to chew on, bitterer to swallow
other men's bread? But in this your new exile
you will be learning bitterest of all is
to savor your words with another's tongue.
Then welcome to our world, old wanderer,
where I, its resident exile, shall guide you,"
Krip rumbled back at the radio's rumble.
Not that Krip could savor much, not with
—rudely prosthetic on the stump of his own—
this stranger organ writhing in his mouth.
And he helpless, though he tried, to spit it out!
Sitting there, Krip spat dry-mouthed into the dark.

       ✦

Gently, he depressed a button, and put out
the radio. He wanted it to go away.
Embarrassed for Dante? Now he could lay down
that burden, and go creep under it from shame.
Guide Dante? That was a laugh. And no kind one.
Krip growled suddenly, not to laugh that laugh,
or maybe to scare off the thing he'd understood
when he heard his voice and Dante's fall in step,
then coincide, like two shadows that blend
and darken together into a single shade
—who was himself, alone. That voice was *his*.
That accent's blundering teratogen
was his Albanian, not Dante's Florentine.

And that performance of author ecstasy,
that "heartfelt inauthenticity" were his.

No, not Pinsky's Dante, it was Pinsky's Krip.
A poem he'd written years and years ago.
Or was it someone else from that translator crew,
perhaps that Feldman kid—his latest Englisher?
To his Albanian ear, they were all
one indistinguishable "Feldminsky,"
and their "Feldminskish" some hypothesized speech,
the nontongue of a nowhere—where, precisely,
personality is whited out, and into
the so-called and much beloved "works of Yusuf Krip."
Je est un autre? Oh, but in translations
je is beyond the incommensurate
—not sublime, just *personne*.

                        One leg, the left,
lay sunken and annulled in other otherness.
He willed it back. A shower of savage darts
got him out of his chair. Got him going
—three unsteady paces, then a lunging fourth
to the window, where he let the shade fly up.
One more infinite step beyond all this,
the "babies bright" of his infancy, the stars,
were afloat in their far-flung encampment.
All of it was sea. All of it was shore.
Where wanderlost is also homecoming.
Too early for dawn. Too late for sleep
—but lush and still, this hour of beginnings,
when (it was Krip's recurrent revery)

his sailors would be bearing Odysseus
out toward the circle of siren voices.
That crew a stepmother-tongue's wild brood
he'd scraped together from seaboard hellholes
in Egypt, in Lycia, and westward to Gaul
—day and night their dinning, brutish pidgin
drowned the water song, and tore the throat
from the wind and left the sky stifled,

world stunned with what they couldn't express.
Then midnight, once, plugging their ears,
Odysseus stopped their tongues.

Displaced and moving, and bound in place
unable to move, a pure desiring,
Odysseus, as blind, as large, as night,
listened—and music came, imbuing the dark
with his native speech, his mother tongue.
Everything he heard he understood
—chatter and tattle of water at its chores,
laving rock and laundering the stones,
in the warp of reeds, wind raveling
its gossip of laughter, shushing, whispers,
and spats and hisses and kisses and tears,
and wavelets' intimate tidbits of tidings,
water yielding to water enfolding water,
exchanging playful, sweet dependencies
—You need me I need you You'll feed me I feed you,
and song welling out from gratitude
the song was understood before it was song.
Odysseus here in oneness with
the world's eliciting intelligence,
the listening silence that moves our speech
—in the lush, still hour when, ravished, he drank,
and the speech that is the world came to his lips.

◆

Too late for sleep. But sleepiness was, Krip knew,
the greater imperative. He would go to sleep.
And sleep—and tomorrow would write about
this last of his adventures, spewed up
out here beyond the Pillars of Hercules
by Time, the monster at the edge of the world.
He could smell the Albanian speech he loved:
of charcoal burners' huts below the pine-tree'd passes,
with smugglers and pack ponies adrift in haze,
and the agile stream telling the stones, darting
out of high solitudes to the salt-sharp beach.

The old excitement came, and fresh courage.
Could *taste* the tongue of Chako and Fishta—and Krip!
What to call the poem? "My Life in Irony"?
No. "My Life in Translation." No. Something else.
So, yes, he'll do this, though this poem, too,
in time will be recorded—by himself—
and flung broadcast through the great American night.
And Feldminsky would have all the last words.

◆

And drifting, in the embrace, on the bosom,
of Mother Sleep, Krip, drowsy, murmuring
in the world's ear, You'll never know, but, people,
believe me, it's better . . . the original.

Solange Mistral

Ange, tu m'as connu!

I knew that silhouette elegant in black,
that arm upraised, hailing, and stepping toward
a cab in the furious street . . . who, reaching
to pull the door shut, turned in my direction
—but not, after forty years, the haggard rock,
the supernatural contour of her face, and eyes
as if they'd looked on the purely evil and
utterly boring so long that evil bored
and boredom was itself their only evil.
Then the charred gaze fell blankly on me
—from the blackened stones of a wayside shrine,
an empty place where someone once died
and a last gasp of smoke now clutches at
the luckless, halted passerby, demanding,
Did you think you amused me, fool?
Yes, I, too, had scraped my match, burned and moved on.
After trial by fire is trial by ash.
I bow to the verdict of the embers.

Testing the Waters

Daylong and then in dreams this testing
the waters—how swift, sweet, thick the course
of things, how cool, consistent, various,
and what the current bears, or bypasses—
so that we can go on and on in the swim
and still be staunch and other than this flowing:
not carried away, not left behind.

These Memoirs

Stumbling midnight tipsy in Jackson's studio,
who knocked black paint over into tomorrow
and throbbing rainbows of our morning after?
Well, thanks to these *Memoirs*, now we know.

When howling sounded over Rockland State,
whose Parker jotted the holy phonemes down?
'Fess up, Allen, and give the man back his pen!
—because these *Memoirs* tell us, and now we know.

In that smoky predawn dive *who* taught Balanchine
to do the twist, quoted since on scores of stages?
No thanks to Mr. B. we know about this
—down to the bubbles in the Veuve Cliquot.

There could have been dull Nothing, you never know
—bland canvas, numb poem, torsos untorsed.
Who, then, was the quirk at the lip of Oblivion,
the droplet that set the trembling source aflow?

But by what inversion of Fate the Ironist
have his loveliest strokes become his erasure?
Surest to remember is soonest forgot.
That's the awful truth, as these *Memoirs* show

. . .

—fitfully, from darkening pages, where one reads
how, years ago, overlooked, *his* drained goblet lay
tipped over, losing light, filling with silence,
far below the lid of Cage's black piano.

"And lies there still, flowing, lost, overflowing,"
our nameless author wrote. His last words are:
"Absurd though all this will seem, yet in these pages
Oblivion toasts Memory now—as we know

"this moment, overflowing, flowing, lost."

Laura Among the Shades

Honor, and excellence, and transcendent best,
I was the laurels I denominated:
diadem and queen and diadem's bearer.
Disdaining tribute from inferior hands,
I crowned myself *The Greatest Poet Alive*.

And died to pursue opponents far worthier.
I bore my distinction against the famous dead,
and grimly—not their rival, their enemy.
My evergreen shall overgrow their names
grimed on the black page of Oblivion.

My conceit was always larger than myself.
Not vainglory, it was ambition, and meant
to show my complete contempt for poetry.
Accursed the leaves I plucked and poison to me,
my laurels mingled with berries of the nightshade.

Lives of the Poets

Poor Paul—when he might have been kind
to a kid, he made a pass instead.

Well, literally zillions of passes
are launched all the time: by day and by night
hot dragon pantings, pawings, pinches, winks,
insinuating, sucking smooches like silks
ripping deliciously from throat to crotch,
lewd, obvious leers and gross eyeballings,
and quiet invitations to dinner, drinks
—all throng the atmosphere around the planet
till Eros gasps for air, blanches, blushes.
This very second dozens hundreds thousands
of passes are dying to get themselves laid
to rest in the worst ways imaginable.
And while most fall flat and pass away,
some, believe it or not, make out, connect.
And who's to say the world should be different?
Then was Paul's especially brutal? Hardly.
Undeniably importunate? Puh-lease!
Or something like a minor herbivore
trespassing on its munching way? Perhaps,
perhaps—if one could ask the grasses.
Really, as passes go, it was prosaic
—a small *éclat* of soul's wind, like the ghost
of affection absent, chill, and odorless
but for its fetor of self-absorption.
(If Eros heard it, did he hold his nose,
and utter some rudeness in return?
Or let it pass, as manners ask one to?)
Puff, it was present; *piff,* it was past.
But piffling though it was, and pitiful
—imagine, if you will, a pass on day-leave
from an orphanage or hospital—and brief
and too impeccably impersonal
to be malicious, still it wasn't kind.

◆

Sunny afternoon (May? June?) in 'forty-six.
Fifth-floor cold-water walk-up on Orchard Street.
I'm a student slash poet slash bohemian.

The world is all before me. I laugh a lot.
My spirits too high for whatever turns up,
and "greatness" the afflatus fluttering my tongue,
I'm at that age: unable to distinguish
ardent idealism from ambition
from rebelliousness from my sense of fun.
I add my dash of satiric slash fervid fizz
to the Lower East Side's postwar bubbling scene
—where my signature is swirled off into
the *Zeitspritz* of the many-minded foam.

Paul, at twice my seventeen, is slash nothing.
He's fully hyphenated, poet-novelist-
playwright-critic-teacher, but unstuffy, boyish,
and like a boy responsible to truth only
and to his pleasure. He's one of us, our best:
self-styled Socrates and wonderful *Überkind*
(whom success alone will save from ending as
resentful *Untermensch*): our David, our champion,
doing in the dinosaurs of Authority
—with uncredentialed, freelance brainpower,
the look-Ma-no-hands of the genial amateur.
His surefire dialectical judo pretzels
the bully in bully's own dumbbell hammerlock.
Once he shows those dads they're extinct, they'll just *go*.
He's got the word on everything—including,
quite possibly, me? I admire so much
I copycat this man I scarcely know.
And now he's dropped by, dying, as he says,
to hear me read aloud from my *oeuvre*.
Will I do that for him?
                              Why, certainly, sir.
Pages gripped in one hand, about to begin
—when suddenly he lunges for the other
like someone really dying, clawing for help,
drowning, going under, heart infarcted,
hand hemorrhaging mortality at every pore.
And I'm to lift him out? To stanch the bleeding?
But *no*, my hand's apparently a telephone
connecting heart to heart, and he's calling up.

Look! as if to filter visual static
from aural ecstasies to come, his lids have shut.
Charade of a soul in transport, wholly tuned in
—to whom I sit reciting every blessèd one
of my twenty, precious, tender, teen-y poems.
And all the while something odd is going on.
What he appropriates, promptly I disown.
My person redefines itself at the wrist.
If he wants whatever it is, here, take it!
My arm's offended by this stupid mitt.
Pluck it off! Anyway, I could care less
—I'll grow another, new, strong, articulate.
And the rest of me will get away clean!
(But if, nerve-damaged, numb, the stump should stay
humorless, unmusical . . .)

My reading done, I get to see Paul do
his Act II: reluctant opening of eyes
—tearing himself from the pure Ineffable.
Affably, perhaps myopically, too, a bit,
he talks down his nose toward where I'm waiting:
sly nods, knowing winks at my Unconscious,
things to make me doubt I am who I think,
have me think I'm a stranger to myself.
However distant his acquaintance with either,
he's willing to present us to each other.
That seems to be the offer. Think it over.

What I think is my hero doesn't play fair.
And doesn't understand me, not for a second.
I don't aspire to be an object of
his interest, or even noticed especially.
What I want is to hang around and admire,
and learn all his sharp intellectual moves,
those quick grips and nifty throws I can use
to flip the world over onto its back,
and hold it down until it cries out, Uncle!
What I think? Master protects disciple.
The slugger doesn't hit on the batboy.
And here he's put *me* in danger—from himself—

prevaricating interest in my poetry.
Oh, I'll go on admiring the guy, but never will
forgive him his treachery.

                    Is what I thought.

                    ✦

That, roughly, was fifty years ago,
and half these years Paul's been gone—and half
his mourners have by now outrun mourners
of their own, and taken cover in the ground.
And so here one is between two corteges,
Paul's past and the present writer's assembling
(slowly, gentlemen!) somewhere up ahead.
Well, Paul had his decade or so in the sun,
his nearly fifteen years of fame
—which at this distance seem foreshortened
to Andy's famous "fifteen min."
The times took his hand and walked with him
a while, a mile. And then walked on.
His coronary when it came along
was wholehearted, unrefusable.

Wisdom (Not for Beginners)

When I was ten and seven
I heard a wise man say,
" 'We err just to live on a little.' "

That would have been Paul, our Socrates, who
at thirty-five was swiftly approaching wisdom,
and would soon reveal to us—with shy aplomb,
as if requiring himself to tell a truth
too obvious to mention—his Sagehood was
rumored no longer, but full-fledged, in full flight,
and about to land not simply with good advice,
but also making itself available

to the world as an example day and night.
And, really, when you got right down to it, who
possibly would rather be wrong than be Paul?
(*Some* errors, then, were perhaps *extravagant*?)
It wasn't just the Goethe he kept quoting;
his *tone,* wistfully sighing, artlessly prim,
befitted wisdom suffered for, wisdom won.
And I, tenderfoot among the symposiasts,
I sighed louder than all the rest, and hushed
—to hear the feathered, strange *whoosh,* the susurrus:
Wisdom's wing was buzzing our coffee-klatsch.
Yes, yes, awestruck, we agreed, life is tough!
It never occurred to me to laugh and sing
seeing a stuffed owl cosily lecturing
—that self-pity warmed over by self-approval.
Because "we?" That would have been Goethe and he.
However thoughtlessly you and I screw up
our lives, and trash the people around us,
Paul, poor guy, had to force himself to err
—with difficulty outwitting his wisdom,
though wisely, of course, for the best of reasons.
And "err," that had to be the harmless stuff
that leaves you ready to go and goof some more,
the way a hobby might, or small addiction.
Persistent fools and great sinners needn't apply
—assuming they think they require licensing.
Then "live on a little" would mean: *less and less?*
A dreary kind of wisdom—though who knows
what might inspire the aspirant narcissist
to grand, to noble, to daring self-regard?

And me? I've lived on a little.
And now I am five-and-sixty
—with no idea where I've gotten to,
but know some things I should apologize for.

Honors! Prizes! Awards! Etc.!

Eternal outsider always wanting in
rattles the latch, enters the cell, rummages
for, reaches after, some unimaginable
innermost . . . lets the body drop . . . reaches into
your body, into mine . . . trying to know
what it cannot understand: ungraspable life!
Or we build a body here of many bodies,
a club, a corporation, a membership
of Immortals in a Muses' Institute,
closing ranks against, precisely, *that one,*
who (though widely acknowledged *mighty* and *dreadful,*
and present as the night—self-nominated—
between the lines of every short list
for all the prizes and honors under the sun)
is turned away repeatedly at the door
as inadmissible, as having this bad rep
for hopping into the sack with anyone
—muddy old parvenu dragging people down to
his level, into his unspeakable hovel . . .
And we make a party—a gala's galaxy
rubs the elbows it bends to toast itself,
and crowds together to a massive muchness:
no chink, no aperture, no slightest silence
where to enter, where to hunker in and hide
—only our animated, general hubbub,
and over us a more-than-mortal outcry from
the laurel branches of our green academy.
But who can hope to be more famous than death?

Oedipus Host

Blindman, cripple quarrel in a single body
over which one leads, which will stumble after.
Each step's disaster—somebody's trampled under,
half trips the other forward, half drags him back.
Back on top now, he kicks out, tumbles over.

Blind pride precedes the fall, lame pride plucks up
the fallen feller, and pushes him on ahead.
How long has this? How long has *he*? How much *longer*?
you ask—and love the man for all this way he's come.
And pity those bare and bruised and swollen feet.
How *far*? Twelve steps? Twelve *monster* steps, for sure
—farther than from Glorious Greece of yore to us.

The *Hindenberg* bursting into radio flames.
Welles's *War of Worlds*. Murrow covering the Blitz.
Welch lambasting McCarthy. Kennedy's cortege.
Now add the day that *he* first guested on a "talk."
Moments truly Great in Broadcast History.
And I was there. Tuned in. Glued to my set. Taping.
That video's in my personal collection.
And now he hosts his own I never miss a show.
Curtain rises: for one agonizing minute
a spot wanders lost, then falls on him, and brightens.
You could have heard the light creeping on the floor,
it was so quiet there. Now everything busts loose.
Even the cams get hot, can't pan fast enough, *bam
bam*, zap from face to awe-gone face, then shoot
the audience going off its collective nut.
He's in his trademark toga—sun-blighted, rain-splotched.
He totters, shuffles, wobbles, he staggers, lurches
—his old drapery coughs up centuries of dust,
like a winding sheet wind-uplifted from the earth.
As if drum-majoring a weird parade of one,
he waves, thumps his pilgrim staff. *Cudgel*'s more like it,
good for beating back the mean-assed roadside curs.
You can just bet that stick has busted up a few.

Whoever did his makeover's some kind of brain.
That mask he wore is gone; this face is mask enough.
How could paint improve the hollows of those cheeks,
the dark sumps pooled inside the sockets' crusty holes,
those hoary locks the gore has plastered into place?
They say his wardrobe stocks a dozen changes
—it takes that long to launder out, and *in,* the dust.
On screen some ancient rock, a gnarled old tree,

sun-baked villages, moonscape vistas frozen white,
where, montaged, his ghostly slo-mo figure stalks, stalks
—stuff so *un*contemporary you can't believe
one stringy hand is clutching on a microphone.
He's like oblivious, like he couldn't care less,
his stagger's that unwavering, his trance so deep.
One gentle daughter brings the guests onstage.
The other's in another show . . . she turns the wheel . . .

✦

I think those girls must love their dad a lot
to lead him all this way. I had daughters once . . .
Two were rotten bad; the good one went and died.
And once I owned a country, a little one
—the car, the house, garage, the job, the family.
Hell with that! Now look at me, bedridden
in Brooklyn, shut in, on disability.
Fate fucked me over. It got me good.
Feet don't work. Eyes going out of business.
Someday soon I'll be down to audio.
Twice a week Mrs. Pomerantz looks in
—my cranky lifeline; could be better herself.
Not that I let on she has me worried.

So when *The Oedipus Hour* rolls around
it's all right, it's okay. Job and Lear drop by,
dressed in the clothes they actually wore.
Or it's Don Q.—the piercing eyes, the broken lance.
Think you've seen a lot? They've seen it *all*.
Or Julius Caesar calmly matching up for us
the holes in his toga to his awful stabs.
So let 'em, those critics, jump all over the show
—for "bad taste," for "frankly, implausible."
Lots of losers from history come on
—also everyday survivors, sinners, ex-cons,
and handicapped, and freaks, and fatties so shy
they go transparent not to weigh on people's eyes.
And some real trash who piss on your sympathy.
He welcomes them—in, like, his living room.

Each guest's escorted to a chair. They sit down.
Hang out. Talk back and forth. Tell their stories.
Pain this one saw, that one suffered, other gave.
You see them let go, feel at home, forget their acts.
Forget to be impatient. Really listen.
Don't make faces, interrupt, drown the other out,
talk behind their hands. Show nothing but respect.
Like they're telling us, World is plenty harsh
—critical will only make it harsher.
Restless Oedipus goes silent among them,
a tall needle stitch-stitch-stitching it together.

And sometimes people's stories meet—then wonder
widens their eyes, the worry leaves their brows.
You were there? . . . So that was *you*! . . . Of *course*, I was . . .
That happened to *me*! . . . And me . . . Can you *believe* it? . . .
Now it happens to *you*. You're here, and you're there, too.
Because anyone's story could be everyone's story.
Something tremendous is going on tonight.
Everybody's coming out to everybody.
Even coming out to us, to *me*, out here.
Can anyone not feel what I feel in my heart
so strong the wave of it rolls back to *them*?
Because no longer are we putting people down
for creep, dog, dickhead, weirdo, whatever.
That's over. Done with. Ashamed I did.
The shut-ins, everything shut in, are coming out.
The fatties step in front of their flesh and shout,
Look your fill—I'm so big no closet can hold me!
Lying here, I stomp and hoot and high-five them on.
And feel America's big heart in my heart pumping.

A new thought thrills right through me—my precious power
I squeezed out and saved up from any scrap of luck
I ever got my hands on, got control of:
my secret privileges; leeways I give myself;
meannesses just for the hell of it;
rewards I'll take and nibble from my fingertips
—yes, my edge in life that puts me one up
on anyone who thinks that I'm this nothing

and can't do my chunk of damage, if I have to:
yes, goodbye my self-intensive-care unit,
I'm getting off you, my bitter, my sweet life support!
I, *we,* are saying,
                              Dear down-and-outers,
never again will you have to envy us.
Not you. Not you. Not you. Not you. Not you.
Do you understand? You . . . no . . . envy . . . me!
I spell it out like talking to a child.
Speaking the same words, but it's a new language!

    ✦

Sunday night. Ten minutes to ten. On the dot.
Spokespersons about to get into their pitches.
Noises scuffle behind. Bumps and bulges—like
the curtain's alive inside. Head pokes it open.
Then Oedipus pushes through. His travel cloak
looks mussed and crooked. He's erect, tilted forward,
fighting the wind and the dark way uphill.
Pounds his staff three times. Pounds it three times more.
Those bitter slits get right up in the camera's face,
look it dead in the eye. Just when we feel our hearts
surrendering, thunder—caught, struggling—flashes free!
All over America on millions of sets
Oedipus again now makes the same speech.

"God-marked, who looks at me
                              sees the god-power.
Apollo adopted,
                    marked me in the cradle,
breaking my feet;
                         marked me with my hands,
taking my eyes;
                       taking my eyes, my hands snuffed
the sun, the far-seeing;
                               not to see myself seen,
I covered my shame in shadow;
                                    shadow is
my greater shame

            —darkness I made lord of light.
On broken feet, in darkness,
                        feeling for the way
I came here seeking,
                now shall creep away seeking
never this suffering again,
                  but bright death
where (where?) your light-arrows
                      open my eyes,
Apollo."

         ✦

Gone now. They came for him, his mom and dad.
Out of nowhere. Out of the flies, it looked.
The pair of them were standing in this bucket.
People still talk UFO. Me, I think it was
a cherry-picker thing. I'm guessing, rented.
Down smooth as butter they ride to him onstage.
Whatever anyone wrote, no way they're dead.
Bloody-red, the bucket door swings open.
Blind, he hasn't a clue what's going on.
Broke my heart to see him standing stump-still,
except his old head, yawing like a horse's.
Like smelling at the sights he couldn't see.
Then out they step. Dad's beard is white, and trim
—around the purple zigzag of a cicatrice.
The mom is old enough to be his mom.
Gasp, the studio goes. I'm gasping, too.
Somehow, without our knowing it, we *knew,*
Something *major's* going down. And him?
All that pride is bent in one big question mark.
Like he's asking Fate, *NOW what you got in store?*
The old battler, he pulls himself together.
He straightens up, his whole body expressing,
I took your best shot once—can take it once more.
Suddenly, this big smile. It's like teeth can see.
Then sweet-tongued Ismene's laughing, oh god,
can't hold back her laughter—so bubbling-happy
with something she knows that I'm laughing, too.

"Surprise, Papa! Guess who's here to see you!"
Black pit of his mouth opens. He's speaking.
"Apollo, golden Phoebus, great lord of sun
and death, is that you in your bright chariot?"

Desiring Power Where Surrender Failed

RIDDLE

How can sharing bread not be true companionship?
When a shit-eater has you dine from his dish.

CEREMONY

More awful than the banquet of excrements
was his toastmasterly regurgitation
praising your compelled "collegiality";
then the brown buss of his lips on your cheek;
then 'round your neck and hung at heart level to hide
the shame and vomit: the cold weight of his medal.

HONOR

His one principle is this: he will accept
no wage or fee until he's begged for it.
So you see him shove forward, cup in claw,
and genuflect to the dribbling cloaca
—always the proud first in line for seconds.

"HE KNOWS THE SYSTEM AND HOW IT WORKS"

First, subsumption upward of the small fry
defying gravity in the next greater's gut;
then—presidential, chairmanly, veepish,
at every stage more pure, more unnourishing—
the voiding downward and processing of shit.
This is how it works, he knows, snacking below,
repossessing himself as this fungible stuff,
while his gloat says, "Who dines on me dines on dreck."

Shit Happens! the bumper sticker fleeing the scene
hurls back, thumbing its rear at the victim.
Where his mouth used to be, tire tread grimaces
the collusive smirk of his admit-it-Jack-
you-like-it-too, and a taste for collision.
Resurrected as the vehicle, brutal,
but weak, he's driven to revisit that instant:
its slow approach, then sudden wreckage,
when Power ran his innocence down
and had some buttered roadkill for lunch.
So he thinks to pass you through him
and serve you to yourself from his dish
—and observe you observing your principles
become secondary, lax, late, corrupt;
then self-surrender turns self-loathing,
and self-loathing a greed for more spoiled self;
then you fleeing your corpse in the road, grinning.

HAPPENS *NOT*!

No, you decline the company of Power: stooge,
suck-up, cynic, panegyrist, footstool, wrecker
—who, caught in some eternal happening of shit
in hell, struggle, and can't engorge, can't expel
the truth that punishes their enfeebled craws.
You give yourself, give more—do your uttermost.

ENVOI

Go, little poem, go far away from here!
—before he comes to covet your rebuke,
and butts you down and rolls around in you
and smears you over himself and gulps you in.
Run, little poem, run, run away from here!

The Switch

Each of us has it—the live/die switch:
oiled daily, recalibrated, kept ready,
hair-trigger, or unbudgeable—maybe—
until in one instant kindness, care, compassion,
love, self-sacrifice swing sickeningly
toward . . . *past* indifference, past hostility . . .
toward *nothingness*. It trips. And *"You,"* we think,
"you've been here too long, too noisily.
You're in the way. You interfere. Dying?
Well, don't just hang around here screaming
and pulling those sad faces of yours—do it!
And, yes, we'll tidy up for you a bit."

Even this child at play, he knows it's there
somewhere near or *in* his own dear mother's heart.
And if he can be a little bad, a little,
a little badder, he will *help* her find it
—in the dark, among tears, at the threshold where
an empty, thrilling *puff* replaces him.

Tantrum

From the doorway he saw the next room
was empty, so empty that if he *were*
to step inside, it would remain empty
—unless by means of this chaos he should
almost almost inhabit it, though never
in any form be able to leave.

Of This and That, and the Other, and the Fall of Man

This and that.
Here and there.
And me.

We're okay
where we are.
I want this and that—badly.
This is red and round.
That is round and red.
I've got this.
And I can get that
if I poke it with this.
No, I'll just have to throw this
to dislodge that.
Good shot!
Here comes that.
There goes this.
Come here, you luscious round red thing!
Poor this, it's gone now.
Absent. Offed. *Pfft.*
Actually, I was rather fond of this.
If only this had been that
—or that this!
Now I hate this.
You deserved your fate, this.
So don't blame me.
It could have been you, you know.
It didn't *have* to be that.
You could have made me want you more.
But no, you wanted to deprive me
of your red roundness.
Bad this, shame on you!
wherever you are, out there,
thinking you're just fine,
a perfect little this.
And now that is all gone.
No more that.
I want this, I want that—badly.
But this this won't be that this.
That that wasn't this that.
I didn't know.
I know.
Oh, I'm being lifted up.

Yow!
I'm being thrown!

Cartoons

Somewhere cars are parking any which way.
Somewhere else some cars are doing any damn thing,
getting all over the place and getting into stuff.
Some quarter- or half-acre of open space, some *lot*
—cars are going in and getting right on top of it.
And they're bringing bumpers and fenders *this* close.
Cars are coming and going *just as they please.*
Some cars are doing it day and night and *overnight*!
Doesn't anybody *care* what's going on there and *there* and *there*?
It's time someone put up some signs—*don't you think?*

✦

A whizz-by of words down a leafy street;
big red letters peering over the green slats
of the brand-new, bright, shiny pickup truck
—just loafing along and hanging out, at ease
in the still momentum inside the commotion,
just going with the flow of trees and trellises
and whatever else is streetwise in spring:
seven signs in search of seven sites,
where they shall proclaim NO PARKING to the world,
and—with two words and by the power to seize
chattels, assets, persons—make a sacred space.
But, for now, the prohibitions are as happy
as grown-ups who are being as happy as kids.
On holiday from making sense, and taken out
of every context, they kick back and hang loose,
take it all off, right down to their coats of paint.
Out of character now—as mere characters—
they're so mellow you could drive a twenty-six-wheeler
loaded up with universe between "N" and "O."

◆

PARKING RESTRICTED OFFENDERS WILL BE TOWED
UNDER PENALTY OF LAW ALL OTHERS KEEP OUT
Block letters on the sign's brow mean, I mean business.
Mean, None of your cursive crawling charm crap for me.
No Pretty-please-I'll-be-your-best-friend-I-promise.
No Tickle-my-belly-while-I-lick-your-hand.
This is monomania's forbidding scowl
—its pliers for getting a good grip on its head.
And it *must* be awful being ripped away
from the great ingathering of everything
and raised up high to tell the All to toe the line.
Meanwhile, cars flaunt their flouting, screeching out fast,
skidding on curves, squealing, when not crashing, to stops,
and honking their heads off every chance they get
—all to shout, Hey, make yourself at home with us,
and let your scarlet letters brighten our lot!
And air is airier, space more spacious now.
One corner of the sign sports a lost left mitten.
At its foot a hubcap *clank-clink-clunks* itself down.

Words Out of Place

Somewhere, say, a slip-slopping mash or mush
or bubbling bog of abandoned name tags
on a ballroom floor frugging the wee hours through.
Pop. Sigh. Balloons release their airy souls.
Prepare themselves for damper, graver spirits.
A streamer untwists its silvery slight being.
The silent flotilla sways to the gurgles
of the gala's ankle-deep, salt, cold champagne,
sloshes knee-high now in the great gashed vessel
—doing a last dance with A with B with C. . . .
Nearby, nameless swimmers in darkness kick out,
thrashing in the seawind-tormented wash . . . when

. . .

the stenciled life raft of a NO SWIMMING sign,
sky-high atilt atop the last wave in the world,
comes drop-drop-dropping into range, in reach.
Some avid readers—keen-eyed, and literate,
and literal-minded, and obedient—
get it brilliantly and for dear life hang on.

✦

And somewhere for a while a wind forsakes
a leaflet blown against some desert rocks.
Wind, wind has gone away—gone back for more.
One leaflet face up under the sunny azure.
Surrender! Surrender! Surrender Your City!
Or Suffer! Suffer! Suffer Consequences!
the page cries out to the populace of sand.
Gingerly, three jackals hearken, and sniff.
Lift up heads and ask the sun.
Ask wind, Wind, whereof do you speak?
Delicate, astute, tongue touches *S.*
Snake bit? Worm stung? Home.Quick.Tongue.Come.
—Smoke! And, yes, squiggle, of . . . mm, mm . . . *sangre.*

Alpha (first), then Beta, then Gamma initial
selfsame with showers of fine flourishes,
attesting Alpha, et al.—the real guys
and brothers, true owners, heirs and sole assigns
in perpetuity of turf hereabouts
and out as far as eye sees from boulder yon
to yonder scree—have read and duly noted *Stuff.*

✦

The fierce maenads of existence keep tearing
The Dictionary into deep, inscrutable
blizzards of Orphic confetti, swirling up,
and down on the stream parading its passage.
And, loveliest foam, the syllables, riding, sing
this moving beauty of the moment's novel body.

Nor will the river be as it was
before words were set to water.

The Lowdown

Remember when Jack changed girls year by year?
And how we talked it up—and talked it down?
Our tongues deliberated every sigh and vow.
Let no fact go unlubricated to its grave,
no innuendo stay unmaterialized:
real dirt was the grist our guts required.
Gossip grain by grain was how we earthworms prayed
—communion with clay that churned up ground of being
into sweaty partoosies of particulars:
Who was carrying the torch? Who was tinder?
Who had the ball? the balls? the gism? the juice?
Who had it? the speck? the spark? the dough? the power?
we wanted to know—since we *knew* it was *somewhere*.
And where was it going? Who'd have it tomorrow?
Remember that? And don't you remember when
dear Jill's affairs were *everyone's* affair?

Then history moved on, went off to live
in other loins and pairings of pantings.
Hear that furor of rumors rumbling underground?
Not elegies, for sure, but music of
the *new* historians' delirious mucosa.
Our chatter's like this here crumbling incoherence.
Our cohort's down and done for. So who gives a damn
about these temporary contemporaries
—not you, not I—now that Jack's nurse changes Jack,
and Jill, still carrying on, changes doctors!

Joker

"Call!" "Call!" "Call!" "Call!" "Call!" "Call!"
Thought I was bluffing. Wanted to see me.

I'm loaded, guys, I am fuller than full.
So, see 'em, read 'em, feed 'em, eat 'em—and weep!
Then, our heart-and-soul-satisfying smart sharp
snap-and-slap-the-cards-on-the-table shtick:
up on two feet, I cracked the buggy whip my wrist;
and the five-of-a-kind of the hand I held high,
one by one, Take that, *whump!* and Take that, *whamp!*
and Take this, *whomp!* I smacked down—notice served
to all the stiffs and to the Big Stiffer
by the woodcutter and master of the deck,
owner of the ax, last man alive and standing!
So I chastised Bad Luck's obstreperous butt
—the table back bearing up the scarred baize.
Ground of our gaming, I stung him good,
taught him who boss is and damn you hold still
while we game on, hand after hand forever,
our give-and-take sifting the lucre pure.

And leaned across, raking the heap home to Papa,
my forearm's enormous promontory engulfing
the golden louis, the silver simoleons;
and looked around, to share this big win
in my eyes, and saw what everyone was seeing:
my aces aging, fading, suddenly blank,
like the Killer Joker sprawled faceless there,

and on the loose now, and running wild
from the shattered room in the house of ashes.

Heavenly Muse

> *Et le regard qu'elle me jeta*
> *me fit baisser les yeux de honte*

Late, as usual.
And staging her entrance
—the flung-off mac flying into
a little storm of its own making;
wellies kicked to a corner,

as if reproached for the rain;
the flowered brolly dropped, upended,
weeping on the welcome mat.
"I'm drenched—*literally*
soaked right to the bone!"
Not that she couldn't do
without drama, but so intent
her sense of self
theater happened around her.
Things snapped to attention,
aware all at once they, too, were there,
and eager to answer her vehemence.
And I no less, no less so.

Subdivided, firelit, a crowd
of raindrops was the fine glitter
in the dark auburn of her hair.
"You're a little late, you know,"
I called out toward where she'd gone off,
sweeping the vividness after her.

"Sarcasm is beneath me—it's rude.
Make certain it's beneath you, too.
I'm *very* late, thank you
—as I very well know."
My john door at its most rumblingly prim.
And here she was in the room again,
refurbished, radiant, and ticked.
"Please to repeat what you said."

"I *said,* 'You've kept me waiting
—miserably, if you must know.' "

"Poor man! I pity you—or would,
if you left me the tiniest spot
beside your tragic cenotaph.
Forgotten, have you, I knew you *when*?
If not for me you'd still be bumbling away,
or back to being mutely unglorious
down on the farm I plucked you from."

"You need me, too. . . ."

"Oh, there are others . . . as you know
—who'd bite their tongues off to serve my needs.
Therefore, do not, I repeat it, *don't,*
lecture me about my obligations
—especially when *you* are unable
even to *begin* to imagine *what*
it's like to be a muse in a man's world!"

"A deal, then. *I'll* stop lecturing,
if *you* agree to end your complaining."

"Stop complaining? Our complaints are ceaseless
because we swim in oceans of maleness
—every instant refreshes our pain
with some new blunt, blundering obtuseness!"

"Uh-oh, here we go again.
Funny how always you work things
around to where you can't be wrong
—down here in good old gender quicksand:
you waving from shore and me drowning in
original gender sin."

"Oh, pooh, your jealousy's deeper than gender.
Never mind that my cabbie got lost;
never mind you live in the middle of nowhere;
never mind that every bell and mailbox
in this foul tenement says ANON.
You're angry that I've just stepped off
the Metroliner from Washington.
You want to be the only poet I inspire."

"Let's not argue, please, not tonight.
I'm blocked, I'm blocked bad.
My mind's a bitter blank.
My gift is lodged with me useless.
You've got to help me—and, besides,
you know that, feminist muse or not,

I find you—the quicksilver logic of
your moods—fascinating, inspiring."

"You think I'm 'cute,' don't you,
when I throw myself around like this?
And, really, I'm in agony,
and dramatizing my exasperation
to make a little space for myself
inside the too muchness of everything,
and that includes *your* (collective) exigence.
And always so impatient
—as if Time were your enemy."

"I'm sorry. I didn't realize."

" 'Realizing' isn't your thing, is it?
Honestly, do you ever think of me
from one little yen of yours to the next?
And then it's Woos, Spews, and Thank-you-Muse!
Do you even know my first name?"

"My?"

　　"That's terribly funny.
And it isn't Irving, either.
You male poets are all alike.
Because women have no place in your minds,
you've no idea how much space a man
—any silly little man—takes up in ours."

"No need to get personal."

"Or need for you to pout.
You've done nothing else since I arrived
—at great expense and peril to myself,
and on a dark and stormy night.
Look, I've even brought you this:
a bottle of the bubbly Hippocream!"

" 'Blushful' . . . '*blushful* . . . Hippo*crene*. . . .' "

. . .

"Whatever. And not that you noticed.
Poets are such a self-absorbed breed
—and so unconscionably immodest,
or would be, if you weren't such liars."

"I beg your pardon. I write the Truth!"

"Of course you do, poor dear.
And very solemnly, too.
If you managed a smile now and then,
you'd be a lot less scary
—or would that burden too much
your precious air and aura?
'So much depends upon . . .'
your high opinion of yourselves.
God, if plumbers carried on the way
that poets do, cold water would run
from all the taps of Hot.
Toilets would be gargling in our sinks."

"That's not fair . . . you're in this too, you know."

"Oh, lighten up; try charm for a change.
Or I may just go ahead and leave you here
'to wade the wide streets of the broken wave.' "

"That's '*white* streets'—you're misquoting me!"

"No, I'm misquoting *me*.
Or are you forgetting that, too?"

"If only you knew . . ."

"Knew what? Is there something I don't know?"
She was looking around now for a mirror.

". . . that maybe you make sense to yourself,
but what I hear's a garbled hash of sound,
some static of the spheres it takes me years
and years of labor to get into tune."

. . .

"That? That's wax in your ears, child.
You could be what's-his-name; instead,
choose to be his very common crewman
complaining that the Siren squeaks.
The problem's not me but your instrument.
Which is why I always tell my poets,
'Fingernails and ears, if nothing else.' "

"You're getting personal again."

"Am I repeating myself?
Very well, I repeat myself."

"I guess I might as well go *be* a plumber."

"Oh, come here, you poor man.
Sometimes I do feel sorry
for all I put you through.
I'll make it up to you this minute.
You may be a man, but you're not
completely useless. And tonight,
tonight you inspire me strangely.
Tonight I have immortal longings . . .
Quick now, sit down, write just as I tell you.
'Of man's first disobedience, and the fruit
Of that forbidden tree, whose mortal taste
Brought death into the world, and all our woe . . .' "

"Whoa! You gave *that* one to Johnny Milton
three hundred fifty years ago!"

"Picky, critical—that's you all over.
You might be a *little* encouraging.
I suppose we're too much alike.
Women and warriors and poets
all have a dainty nature,
living or dying by our morale.
I ought to go and find myself
a nice, steady fiction writer

—as, blessèd be her memory,
poor Mother always told me to.
But I, I had to follow my heart.
And now look at me, stuck with you
who want the roll, the rise, the carol,
the dictation—without your submission.
This is eavesdropping, this is stealing,
unless, until, you give yourself to me. . . ."

"Oh, all right. 'Sing, Heavenly Muse!' "

Les grandes passions manquées

Had she survived her immolation
and lived on in quiet disfigurement,
Dido would have hated the lost fire
and partial combustion and what in her
was earthen and too insipid to burn.

Bad Brunch

What got them started hardly mattered, did it?
Enough it was Sunday, endless, awful Sunday.
Or maybe it was that porky, dorky friend of hers
she hadn't seen in years and barely recognized,
photographed looking just too hopefully happy
among the weekend's supplement of brides.
And how long from now would be among the mothers?
(Unawares, her teeth began to interrogate
a ridge of skin inside her lower lip:
So, what have *I* got? And is it what I *want*?)
That gown might be set off by legible ruffs
of printer's ink offset from the facing page,
that gaze be disconcertingly bespectacled
(did the bridesmaids tackily do glasses, too?),
that thumbnail bio better padded than the dress

—and yet she felt that by some magician's trick
she'd been flung, had caught, here in her breakfast nook
that pudgy fist's brash bouquet of nettles, felt
so complexly wronged, so obscurely punished
that she could soothe one sting only with another,
and only then if she kept completely still.
He should have known that, irksomely did not
—rustling paper, clearing his throat, breathing loud.
Botched, embittered, ruined, hideous, lost,
the perfect day she ludicrously had planned,
had permitted herself to savor in advance!
Imagine, terrorized by brides and babies!
Everything undefined—she hated that, while he
seemed actually to prefer it this way,
deferring, shilly-shallying, noncommittal.
But she knew it in her bones: absence of structure,
chaos, is sign and origin of corruption.
She looked at him sprawl snug in his self-complacence,
letting things slide thoughtlessly, but then, perhaps,
such his opportunism, *deliberately*.
She startled herself by asking, Is *he* corrupt?
And if he is, mustn't *I* be tainted, too?
After all, Bluebeard's wife also had to be
at least a *little* aqua around the gills.
No, shallow people were wicked in a way
—simply didn't know the effects of what they did,
or whom they did it to. Did *he* know *her*?
And could she any longer say she knew herself?
Something here had gone badly, badly wrong.
That moustache was one fine line she should not
have crossed.

        Alarms sent his alpha waves scrambling.
His adrenaline got right up on its toes.
Backpedal? Plunge ahead? Take off? Lie low?
"Oh god, what is it now?" he almost blurted.
Her mood had caught him smack in full revery.
Ball scores stopped their calibration of glory.
He was too distracted to consider duly
the profound mystery embodied in stats.

Angels with shining tape measures in their beaks,
who hover over home runs, had all been blown away.
The crossword lay a shambles of cross words.
Not the Sunday for which he'd penciled in SEX
—horizontal, vertical, before lunch, after.
One more chance for fun-before-death gone down in smoke!

The whites of his eyes came fluttering up
from the fat, white trash of the Sunday paper.
He must have felt *something* of what she was feeling,
because he smiled so reassuringly it was
reassuring almost, and might have been but for
that eager—beseeching—grin it ended in,
his coy mummery of "I'm just a simple guy."
Apologize and not put it in words? How could he!
—as if she weren't worth the cost and effort
to exhale a few intelligent sounds.
He underestimated her, she knew that
—and she'd prove it to him if it was the last thing
she ever did!
            Little man, she thought, you won't,
although you try to, undercut till the end of time
my every effort to take you seriously.

Episode

Their quarrel sent them reeling from the house.
Anything, just get on the road and get away.
Driven out, they drove . . . miles into countryside,
confined and bickering, then cold, polite;
she read a book, or looked out at hillside pastures;
once, faraway life came close, and they stopped
in mist for muddy, slow cows at a crossing,
then, tilted, shuddering, a tractor came across;
coldly silent other hours of trees after trees
interspersed with straggling villages—then hot;
her voice pulsing, tempestuous, against the dash,
buffeted, blew up; she slammed her hand down, hard.

"You *let* it happen—you *know* you did.
And you make *me* the bad one—all the time!
I won't stand for it another second." And then,
irrationally, "Look at me, I'm talking to you!"
What half faced her was mulish, scolded sullenness
—who gripped the wheel and to scare her drove faster,
scaring himself; he felt out of control, dangerous.
Downhill, the road darkened, dropped out of sight.
At the bottom, racing toward them, three lights,
and trees. . . . Remember this, remember this,
she thought, the last thing I will ever see.
Diner, tavern, café, whatever it was.
The car spun suddenly into a parking lot.
She grabbed at the key, threw it out. Shaken, they sat
—while their momentum went on raging down the road.
They knew they might have been killed—by each other,
had someone been up to just one more dare.

Bust–up

Their thrashing in one another's clutches
sends out all kinds of vibes, makes more mess
the longer it goes on. Tooth-to-bone squeals
and mutters like quick crushings of something
—this thrill of animal alarm gives them all,
after initial shock, a sense of life quickened,
transcendent vigor: the friends, odd confidants,
new lovers, "ex"es, summoned professionals
—the extended family of disaster—
busy now about the place of damaging,
comforting, clearing debris, cleaning up.

After it's over, the half-dead agonists
and their seconds and helpers can't much stand
each other. Their revulsion's impersonal,
as if the rupture can't not go on tearing.
They flee the accursèd spot, woe-sown, barren
—though others will marry and, to warn evil off,
make the wedding party loud with clanging pots.

City of Good Neighbors Blues

"Impossible," Lionel chummily remarks,
"adultery in Buffalo." He's cheerful, though,
and grins—at his boomerang in mid-career?
Or at this married interlocutor (myself)
whose nodding head has deftly intercepted it?
Am I supposed to commiserate? Be wary?
Or just sophisticatedly flabbergasted?
He runs his A-list of obstacles by us:
Single homes. Deep front lawns. Barking mutts in back.
And bored, provincial, porch-potato busybodies
who hope a *soap* will come to sordid life next door.
And furthermore (pausing for effect) there are:
no cafés, no hotels, no apartment houses
—where one wide door opens to a hundred doors. . . .
Nostalgia, flirting, challenge jostle in the gaze
he flings at the rest of us around the table.
Well, who ever said transgressors can't do "cute"?

Before him a moundlet of crumbs his butter knife
bulldozes and bosses into swirls of eddies.
All napkins are stained, wine goblets lip-printed.
Down to its debris, the dinner party flares up,
its husbands put on notice to consider *now*
their positions on passion, order, family,
their wishes, their memories, such as they might be,
and the sheer logistics of getting to it.
And are wives being defamed? Or wooed? When in doubt,
choose the latter. It's the latter they choose: the wives
at table are the most at ease, the most amused
—bemused, perhaps, too, as if they're wondering,
All *that* impossible? Really? One would hope not.
And which sort of lovers do good neighbors make?
And what good fence could keep neighbor Lionel good?

New Yorker who owns no car and doesn't drive
(but has one or more positions on everything),
Lionel brings all his skewed experience to bear.
"Even the taxis here are monogamous!"

True, our cabs don't cruise, and look very yellow.
"One car left at a shopping plaza parking lot,
or two cars cooling down before a motel door
—these seem to be the only ways to go."
He's arguing for better public transport?
Leave it to a New Yorker to want to extend
the subway hundreds of miles to Buffalo.
Exiles do come up with the weirdest complaints.
"*If* the locals have wit enough to screw around."
He grins—and here's the boomerang on schedule,
with bits of scalp, homing softly to his hand.

A bachelor at heart, beyond the fetch of hubris,
and, oddly, the most sociable of lone wolves,
Lionel isn't one of your tender souls,
nor has agonizing over self-complacence
figured among his more remarkable traits.
(He's actually crazed enough to *like* himself!)
And whether he's being modest regarding
his achievements or hyperbolic about
their difficulty, I can't quite decipher.
And one *is* inclined to let him have his say
—before, hair-triggered, his *say* rants off into space.
At least, this Cain has no *sister* to keep.
His grin, having made the rounds, alights on me.
I find I'm grinning back at him, like a damn fool.
Next time I'll duck. For now, I offer, "You're right,
much as I hate to admit it. Statistics show
the incidence of nonvehicular
adultery here to be alarmingly low."
And now I feel my mouth fill up, tongue in mid-pounce.
I savor it—all the sweet tang of a put-down.
So *this* is the cake one eats and has, too!
"Why, you cheeky, old, randy rascal, you,"
I say, "have you been drinking the water here?
You've developed *hardening of the adulteries.*"

Behind the contacts behind his glasses: eye-glint.
His dangled, tacky toothpick lifts in shrewd surmise.
A gross exporter of weapons-grade irony,

for whom the joke is always on *les autres,*
Lionel likes my little sally—suddenly
I see myself dog-paddling into his worldview,
and Being being mingled with my attributes.
Glance weighs me. Toothpick dips in my direction.
He's signing, I take it, in pure New Yorkese.
"So," he says, "you weren't born here, were you?"

They Say and They Repeat

"For now." "For the time being." "While this lasts."
Invoking time's passages (decaying, crumbling
under the lightest, the instant footfall),
they say and they repeat such halfhearted phrases
against the Absolute, which rises newborn
in vows, in devotion, and already has
overwhelmed them and refreshes everything
—even their unbelieving protestations—
with the new life's firstness without end:
for now forever, for the time being
forever, while this lasts forever.

The Parting

Though the heavens shall undergo revision
and new constellations wheel into space
their fresh, unfabulated imagery,
they will not hide the blacked-out sky they brighten.

You Know What I'm Saying?

"I favor your enterprise," the soup ladle says.
"And I regard you and your project with joy."

.   .   .

At Grand Forks where the road divides twice over,
the wet wooden squeegee handle poking out
of the bucket beside the red gas pump tells you,
"*Whichever* way—hey, for you they're *all* okay."

The stunted pine declares from someone's backyard
you happen to be passing, "I don't begrudge you
your good health. In fact, my blessing—you've got it, now."

An ironing board is irrepressible.
"Your success is far from certain, my friend,
and still it's vital to my happiness."

The yellow kernels in the dust, mere chicken feed,
call out, "We salute you, and you can count on us."

We do not live in a world of things
but among benedictions given
and—do you know what I'm saying?—received.

Funny Bones, or Larry Dawn's 1001 Nights in Condolandia

"A funny thing happened tonight on my way
from the grave . . . a *really* funny thing. . . ."

Why, it's Larry Sunrise! (shouldn't it be Sun*stroke?*),
once Chickie Glick (a.k.a. Gary Gallo,
creator-distributor of "Gallo's Humor"
—"I'll Roast You Posthumously. Tactful. Thorough.
Recitation Of *Vitas* A Specialty.
Housecalls. *Shivas.* Wakes. Will-Readings. Twofers.
Pajama Parties. (Doctors In Attendance.)
VISA Only Please. Medicare Accepted").
The Borscht Belt Lazarus (pronounced "La-tsuris"
—don't your old worms grow wings in your tomb, too?),
he's ninth and last life of the rundown Catskills.

("Katz *kills*? Some helluva doctor this Katz is.
May Kevorkian have Katz for *his* physician!")
Larry's just shlepped south to work a condo show.
Resurrected in his agent's microwave,
he's warm-up for the monster act to follow.
Larry's jokes are classics, guaranteed pretold;
have stunk up all they're ever going to stink.
Fifty if he's a day, okay, make it sixty,
and roly-poly pink in a poly blazer
(baby blue, with the wrinkles ironed *in*),
he's already shpritzing the room with punch lines
ack-acked from the Oozy of his dirty mouth,
hacking and yakking off yuks and yechs all around.
Moloch chain-smoking children sounds how Larry sounds.
Then what's to wonder if Larry bills himself
"The Only Comic Who Works With Oxygen"?

". . . So tonight I was on my way from the grave
(like Lazarus said, 'Death? Been there. Done that')
. . . and one baby step I took, one little foot,
and there I was, and here I am: in *Flo-ri-da*.
So I know, maybe I didn't get very far,
but Lazarus himself, was he born all over?
Maybe he never died, he only retired.
Well, what are *you* all doing here? Nice to see yuh!
Hello, campers. Welcome to Camp Condolences!"

✦

To a thousand venues in Condolandia
on Friday nights and Saturday nights in season,
the little stars—wannabe-, almost-, never-was—BIG
(Frankie: *big;* Jerry: *big;* Larry? Gimme a break!)—
they fan out and go to twinkle their shticks in shows
now, tonight—before it's never forever,
and bring them entertainment's empty calorie,
a sweet interim, a nosh of eternity.
And who could be *less* a star than Larry is?
So it's right he's here two steps up on a stage

in a condo cafeteria/clubhouse,
with a standing mike, beside a piano,
taking up jokes against a sea of tsuris.

Larry looks down on the scene swirling at his feet.
At fifty tables, like fifty lifeboats caught
and swamped in strobing, throbbing fluorescence,
bob 500 whitecaps (Larry counts the house):
heads on which Death's dark advance angel swiped
with his chalk, and—*gotcha!*—didn't miss one.
In the surf-wash and storm-froth, Larry sees dreck
from the *New York* wreck, the broken *Brooklyn*,
the capsized *Philly:* crutches and canes and wheelchairs
and walkers pooped out on a Florida beach,
or doing kazatskies in the undertow.
They give Larry bad thoughts, get him talking crazy,
these outcasts of the Great Ceramist (Retired),
who still can't keep his shaky hands from the clay,
trying to get them right, getting them wronger
—the obese, the misshapen, the wheezing, the halt,
the enfeebled, shrunken, depressed, the dotty:
whom Death has stroked but still denies a kiss
—hobbling, bobbling in their waterlogged conga line.

"What am I, stand-up for the lying-down crowd?
But seriously, folks [the voice *serioso*,
then pause, then *socko!*], don't feel too good myself.
Maybe I'm dead—this looks like Death Ghetto.
But go imagine it, at my age a father!
You've all read about the Bypass quintuplets?
I'm the dad. They're close to my heart, those kids.
Here, I'll open my shirt, show you their picture.
Listen, don't mind me, I'm on a roll tonight,
I'm a regular runaway ambulance
—a hundred I'll mow down just to save one!"
Then, mouth sewn shut, he's laughing through stitches,
"But seriously, folks . . . I'm only kidding!"
(He's only kidding, ha ha, he's only kidding.)
"And, hey, trust me. So long as I crack wise,
nobody dies—certainly not from laughing!"

In the house of the drowned, Larry asks for water
("Just a little glass—plain, please, and hold the bubbles").
Or comes with bucket, rags, squeegee, big sponges,
gets busy polishing invisible puddles.
They shine like the sun? Larry only rubs harder,
rubbing it in deeper, down to the bitter end
—because only "innocence" could show such chutzpah,
and he, he's healthy, he's home free. ("Who me? Worry?
About water? I wash my *hands* with water!")

And the more he talks the more it's "only talk,"
and no brazen fact has the strength to barge in.
Let's face it, Larry fears engulfment by seniors
coming to get him with their silvery tide
—and then he'll never leave here as himself again,
as anything but dissolution, water.
"Mistake," he wants to yell, "I'm not one of you!
And what's more [lying, lying], *ha ha, I can swim!*"

Whose cold hand's grabbing his ankle, pulling him down?
Mel Strom for sure, that self-centered meshuggener!
Who's giving him mouth-to-mouth resuffocation?
And out there in the daisy chain bobbing, waiting,
Widow Wheelchair throws wide her horny arms, calling,
"Come dance with me in the foam, my *zieskeit,* my son!"
His last human contact (oh no, he's heard this one
before, and he's trying his best to stop it!)
will be some washed-up comic's stale one-liner,
which, between groans of laughter and glubbed good-byes,
slips away through his poor, his numbed fingers.
Then nothing, nothing to cling to but the sea.

✦

You can't fly? You float. And if you can't float,
you wave your arms and legs like crazy,
to make yourself be stronger than gravity
—well, *funnier* than gravity, anyway.
Truth is Larry could splash a little less,

surfacing right now, kicking up a storm,
"Okay, honk if you hate laughing!
Why is everyone being so quiet?
What is this, a Benefit for the Reaper?
'Death Aid,' maybe? So pledge, pledge something.
Trusses. Bifocals. Dentures. Give so it hurts!"

Larry, god bless him, is being Larry,
outrageous Larry with his zings and zorrows.
Clutches at his chest. Left side? Nope! Right side? Nope!
His liver. A pocket. *Two* pockets. He's frantic.
Quick, his hands carve "curvaceous" out of thin air.
He frisks her all over, the statchoo-esque stripper,
the virtual burleycue blonde, he's created there.
Her boobs—twice, three times, four—he frisks for his heart.
"Think it's better milking *your* little, dry titters?
So, go try squeezing honey from a gallstone!"
Staggers, grins, happy as only a man can be
who's found he's misplaced his coronary.
Comes up for air with his "newborn" routine,
"Hello, campers, welcome to Camp Golightly!
Wish *I* could afford to be a camper here, too.
Got no pot to piss in, no plot to plotz in."

◆

On Larry's lips effrontery is normal,
Unspeakable (the orphan) has a home.
On his tongue a good taste is a scandal,
a kind word (what's that?) is taboo,
and last year's bad jokes are going off
at this year's good prices.
               So, what else is new?
In Larry's eye: the gleam of Top-this-if-you-can
—and Hope Eternal of the next one-liner.
("You didn't like the last? This one will kill you. . . .")
Oh, he'll get on your nerves, all right,
but Larry never hurts anyone's feelings.
He doesn't know from "feelings," doesn't know
from "anyone." Believe it or not,

Larry doesn't know from "Larry."
In fact, he doesn't know from "funny."
What he knows from is if you're laughing.

Then laugh, have a little heart for the guy!
In his shoes, *your* feet would smell sweeter?
Now what's he up to? Down behind the piano
Larry's dragging out a shiny cylinder
—of oxygen! Tenderly, he rockabyes it,
"My baby Seymour—as in 'emphyseymour.'
Next time I'll bring his sister Ivy—I *promise*!
She's all tied up now in the *'I-See-YOU.'* "
He mugs, he blusters, being coarse, acting big
like a bigshot's big, who's telling the world off,
"I don't care how gross your sieve gets. Shake till you break,
I'll be around for the end—and bigger, grosser!"

Even down here, at the level of Larry,
the life force is working the audience:
it keeps on asking can you take a joke.
You can? Well, can you take *another*?
Larry's the kind of nudnik-livewire
who won't let you let him go: a pest with zest.
He's like shaking hands with a short circuit
with juice enough to heckle your heart alive,
or joybuzz it the hell to Eternity.
You know, survival of the—ha ha—fittest.
Tummler, zany, Larry goes like Death goes,
"It's nothing personal, I'm *only kidding*."

And Lazarus? Does it say he was born again
again? For him *one* born-again was enough.
Then what about Larry on the condo circuit,
descending nightly through humongous human humus
—to stand naked before the gums of Death, joking?
Mornings it's harder to lift the earth overhead.
And what pushes up is each time less, and heavier
—the early worm gets the silica special.
Gravesite gravel filling his heart,
from a mile away you can hear, you'd swear,

old Larry rattling and raling like a maraca
while he rumba-shlumps around in Flo-ri-da.
But night after night something in him
is kissing off the same old joke with a first kiss.

◆

Larry with two hands on the mike, doing Humble.
Doing Mensch. Doing Sincere. Plus Compassionate.
"Thank you, all of you, from the bottom of my heart.
You've all been such good sports (may you rest in peace).
I give you, folks, one of the great audiences
of South Florida—truly so, *no kidding.*"
(Shortchanging them ten minutes—wouldn't you know?)
The hand that bid them all stand to acknowledge
their self-applause descends now in benediction.
"God bless you, and see you this time next year, you hear?
And I'll do my best to help you EXIT LAUGHING.

"And if you can't applaud my act tonight,
Miami Beach *mañana*—tomorrow—will do.
Catch me at The Freshfields and at The Fountainblue!"

Exit Larry laughing laughing laughing laughing.

◆

Enter Anna Maria Alberghetti singing singing.

The Retirement

Everyone talks here, nobody listens.
If you didn't talk to yourself, you'd forget
how to listen—going over in your mind
a week ago's bargain you got, murmuring
the story you've been telling the others,
how you're shopping for something else, honest,
when . . . and then . . . and, no, don't jump right in,

make like it's nothing special—"Seen better for less,"
your attitude says, "so where's the big deal?"—
then quick, you go for it, you snap it up.
You *found* that sale, then you *took* advantage.
Luck. Sharpness. Enterprise. The spice of life!
And now when you open your eyes, every morning
you're two sweet bucks ahead of the game
—two bucks, count 'em, that fate forked over.
Just think of it, your beautiful, clear edge,
your piece of sky guaranteed sunny!

At night in your silent rooms it sits with you,
and you remind it, "See, you'd have been spent,
lost in god knows whose pocket—if not for me."
"Yes, it's true," it answers. "I'm deeply grateful."
The two of you there, quiet, talking. Like that.
And it's a mystery how it's never used up,
and present in no matter what you buy with it
—which, three pairs socks, say, and epsom salts,
becomes something extra, something you needed, sure,
and yet a *treat* (no less!), a part of the wonder.

You feel blest you've lived long enough to see this.
A second ago, your life was no big bargain.
Some people thought it wasn't worth two cents.
Now you wouldn't sell for a million whatevers.
And every hour everywhere more prices are coming down!

(Of course you bought the giant size. You had to.
It's nagging on you. Suppose some's left over.
Maybe it wasn't such a bargain after all.
"Oh, what the heck!" That voice doesn't sound
like you—barking like that, desperate, like someone
who knows they're in over their head—for good.
Then you calm down, you think, They'll find it here.
Someone will take it, it won't be thrown away.
Happy? Angry? Sad? You don't know yourself.
Every time you look, the box is staring back.
You pour out exactly the right amount
into the bath, then give an extra shake or two,

and sometimes you put in a little bit less
—as if, in heaven's name, you've gotten into debt
with these epsom salts, and somehow it's up to you
to make things come out even, and end when you do.)

Praising Opens

I praise you and my heart opens.
You are admirable
—and small tender brave mortal.
I hide you in my praises.
I preserve you.
You grow in safety.
And, mortal, my heart opens.

New and Uncollected Poems

For J.M., His Poems

To prove that ecstasy can be kind,
your charm lifts us into new worlds
without demanding
we leave everything behind.

Speed of Words

Unlocalized, without dimension,
and instantaneously and at once
photon and cosmos
—but at speed of words nothing happens.
The helpless, shining sun does not illuminate.
Therefore, cloths have been set out,
and leaves crowded into rustling tenements;
therefore, great magnets of meaning are made to bend
the abstract angels into being.
And see, light returns the greetings of trees,
and, at the height of any flagpole, breaks
into speech.

Dance in the Dark

Circles, doubles back, circles, knocks again.
Can't believe it: this *she* means, actually *means*
to fight him for this body she has,
unfairly, the advantage of inhabiting.
And so ungrateful for the use of it
he's granted her—and pretty much rent-free!
Still, he's willing to share—take turns, say.
And it's not as if she's got to be *in*
whenever he comes around calling.
She can just *go* somewhere for a while,
have herself a nice, little vacation
from standing guard behind those hazel? eyes.

Oh, and yes, *of course*, he'll straighten up after.
Place will look more or less like new, really!
Bet she wouldn't even know he's been there.
Mean no *harm. Tell* her that. Whatever it takes.
Maybe blow some bucks. Help her see it this way.

He's stymied? And she? *She's* perplexed, suspecting,

sensing he's not himself to himself those times
he fails to hold the world out of reach.
And tempting, teasing, pleasing flower, fruit, or jewel
he may let drop her way (by inadvertence?
from slyness?) is paste to him and waste and shade
should fingertip, or lip, so much as graze the glow.
Then what's she worth to him—always after her—
if, accursed, she makes his best goods worthless?
Small, perfect, pure the bauble was, droplet of
all loveliness—and bait that dispossessed her:
tricked out the door to tremble in his cold,
while he in his comfort and almighty glory
sits in the window watching her punishment
—oh, punished because to *blame* for the comeliness
of heart in which she adorns her person!
Trapped inside, trapped outside, she circles,
circles, and doubles back. Knocks. Knocks again.

Briseis

Where Thetis, bustling about, had gripped
her struggling baby's chubby, helpless foot:
the dimple only her downcast eyes could see.
It was then great Achilles, hero, man-
slaughterer, touched his captive's heart.
For where mother went a woman may follow.
And she could see her work cut out for her
—had better be getting busy; in fact,
she had to hurry, if the poor gentleman
ever was going to be made immortal.

Came to Nothing

The waiting in the rain that came to nothing
... or nothing more than a row of parked cars
and a newspaper growing damper ... —this
wet withering I recollect better
than all one summer's entire garden
run wild to spend itself in what seemed
monthslong coupling now run together.

Poem with Refrain

How that night you sought me, slipped from skirt
and blouse, and stole into my bed softly,
and lay touching naked breasts to my bare back,
where I lay wakeful, and feigning sleep;

and how your small kisses caressed, your fingers
drifted over me, and over and over
your murmuring made the repetitious bliss
of wavelets rippling home to mother shore:

"Don't go. Don't leave. I love you. I'm sorry.
I understand now. I promise you I'll change.
Only let me love you, and everything will be
as it was when we were first in love ..."

And how—do you remember?—I was quiet,
and didn't turn to return your kisses.
No, I was staring at the wall, and thinking,
"Where ... where have I heard this shit before?"

And how, though I was stone there, you persisted
until I sensed within your murmur, then *knew*
precisely *where* I'd heard all that before:
my own voice (urgent, honeyed) murmuring

time and again to this woman or that,
who lay—as millennia of women have—

pitiless, chilled, alone, in the dark, thinking,
"My god, no, not the same shit as before!"

Say Pardon

Yes, I pardon you, but—because, offended
and aggrieved, I have been set above you
and made to be and to seem in the right
—I ask you, First, please, forgive me.

Fifteen Minutes

This measly fraction is what Andy prophesied
for each shadow-scarfing media consumer
taking his turn as media fodder: his name
rehashed in rumors, his face a pixel porridge.
Behan taught, however, that everybody *ought*
to know fame for one good, solid hour, and be
the man in person celebrated by pals,
whom he stands, glass upraised, a round and more,
and who grow famous, too, in his company.

Chaos Theory, or *Karmic Chutzpah*

> *Thousands of readers, " 'Howl' changed my life in*
> *Libertyville Illinois"*
> *"I saw him read Montclair State Teachers College*
> *decided be a poet—"*
> —ALLEN GINSBERG, "Fame & Death"

Thermal mounting on thermal and voice
on voice on glorifying voice on wings
of quotes uplifting breath after last breath
—death-bound to his bed in America,
a poet daydreams billowing puffscapes,

crag and dome and tower and crown:
the testimonial-swollen thunderhead
of mourners' throats celebrating now
the swerves he caused, the turns, the turnings-
on-to, the churning . . . making light as if
gravity didn't darken in these
. . . and bursts in broken flashes and
ruptured vortices and raindrops . . .

—and, swept off its orchis petal perch
in Ulan Bator, a butterfly
like a bright idea,
helplessly cartwheeling out of the sky,
has struck the poet Toghun dead.

State of the Union

From their lips pure puffs of plain crap
crowd out the atmosphere—until the mark
of authenticity is murk and fetor.
"If we don't feel we're being lied to,
how can we believe what we hear?"

The Needy Rich Are Always with Us

Much put upon, master went,
"Must *I* do *everything*?
For godsakes, here's the whip
—now beat yourself!"

Ideologue

A windmill, thinking itself a dragon,
went roaring across the countryside after
whatever lance would let out all its air.

Don't You Admire Me?

Pitter of pink feet on the foot-battered path
—hurrying where all the world had rushed before.
Then soundless space space space of his leaping,
treading now the innocuous, soft mid-air,
going nowhere and somehow arriving there
at the bloody mat and doorway's dark downward

—where one iron *thunk* backslapped tremendously
the delicate ears and tender, proffered throat,
the dangled-out tongue, the eye's burst grape,
the head laid careless down in the spilled drink.
"Am I not—confess it, dear little friend—
the marvelous mousetrap you were hunting for?"

[Sic] Transcript Gloria, or The Body Politician

The transcript records that day's dark admonition
(the tape turning from reel ominous to real grim):
in Ehrlichman's cold voice Colson's vision
of Dean, *"He says you got an* ass *on your bosom."*
We have been left to picture the infernal scene.
Here a weasel's, there a wolfish, or woeful, grin
gleams; then all leers dim: the crook of a question mark
is dully chiseling its stigma on the boss's brow
—beneath which one drab eye from its dank crevice now
scuttles, and gapes for light in the nightmare murk.
(The tape skips a beat, then loses heart altogether.)
But, his finger uplifted, his stage hiss at once
apocalyptic, confidential, some damned dunce
sagely explicates: "A *burro* on your breast, sir"
—whose deeper frown demands higher truth, plainer wit.
"Oh, Mr. President—there's a mule *on your tit!"*

When the Lion Dies

When the lion dies, rabbits roar.
So within their littleness they hear
resound the murmur of the breath
they dared not breathe before his death.
Valorous with vanity now,
they raise aloft impudent ears.

Gigsburg

"Poet Rebel Bohemian Survivor"
—the ad's ejaculation went leapfrogging toward
self-transcendence, its final spurt its farthest.
"Make the scene! Meet the man! Be there!"
And now two hundred college kids are looking at
a seventy-year-old chanting poetry man.
"Man," their brains are going, "all the *shit* he's done!"
Up onstage, swaying in a three-piece business suit,
that's History, son—cool relic of the days
when buddysattvas roamed the urbs of Earth,
and fought and wrote for freedom and the good.
"Man, oh, man," the kids can't believe their eyes,
"all that shit—and, like, none of it *shows!*"

The Return of the Repressed

Really, it was nothing.
Just a few gray guys in fatigues
back from the fringes of empire,
wandering through the crowds of the capital.
Their war had been over so long
no one remembered it.
Who needed that old crap anyway?

.   .   .

Of course,
the antiquarians made a fuss.
With live specimens and a public issue,
finally they felt
contemporary.
Which just goes to show.

Wars come and wars go.
What else is new?

When they started going ape in front
of the unknown soldier's monument,
we gave them and their wounds
one-way tickets back
and all the old medals lying around.
Really.
I was happy to kick in my last one.

Happening

Soho Saturday night. The Galérie Broome,
whose brutal décor—litter, splinters, dirt—
indicates the street's swept in through the door.
Ditto traffic noise the room is wired for.
Some scattered cartons, bricks, stumps, scrap lumber,
creosoted ties, stove-in sacks of plaster
assert a simple *is*-ness while subtly they
conduct the gallery-goer through their maze:
to this ill-lit, out-of-the-way corner, where,
life-size, a goggle-eyed, waxworks gent
—some jovial, tuxed-up stagedoor Johnny—
examines through a loupe from inches off
the cheek, lovely though averted, of one
who's turned away to regard in her mirror
herself—in gray body stocking, raven hair
pulled back and ash-dusted—Solange Mistral:
celebrity sculptress, here artist-performer.

On the stand nearby a strew of magnifiers,
and card instructing, *Use, Please, and Return.*

—Catatonia, beautifully nuanced,
　　brilliantly wrought: catatonia
　　has found in Miss Mistral its poet.

—Bourgeois rigidity.
　　Simple as that.

—Lust's gaze, in reifying,
　　awards itself the blindness of the thing.

—A Medusa for our time: mirror-besotted.

—Even our narcissism cold-shoulders us.

—Possibility is petrified as
　　this loveliest of monoliths.

—It's all about Time—geologic time
　　pent up inside our human hourglass.

—The static drip of next-to-nothingness.
　　The glacier in the kitchen tap.
　　Can we bear this? Can we bear this?

—Grain by grain, Galatea, homesick,
　　pauses in the portal of stone.

—Less is more? At the very least:
　　esthetics of anesthesia.

—The artist is her medium.
　　The artist is her martyrdom.

—Before it can decay to impatience,
　　then to panic madly dashing for the door,
　　she gathers the fresh sediments of our boredom,
　　compresses them to undivided terror.

. . .

I care no longer.
Say what you will.
Judged always
success, failure,
—each instant a trial,
the trial perpetual—
my soul burned up
in your desire.
Bend close.
Lift the glass to your eye.
See my clay grow harder.

The Interruption

She'd just gone out onto the stoop, and run down the steps,
and into the street, when there was this boy from across the way,
as if he'd been waiting for her to come out of her house,
and playing the puppy who wags tail and tongue, tongue and tail,
showing off its new trick where it can't tell one end from the
      other.
And she was supposed to admire, and stay there and laugh and clap
to encourage it—and then pet the fool until he calmed down?
If he knew how completely rude and ridiculous she thought him,
he would take his shame and go sit himself in a corner.
And she just might tell him a thing or two if he kept it up,
trying her patience like this—because he was *interrupting* her.
He had to be blind not to see that this was something important
that she was out here doing—in fact, it was an *emergency*.
Why else would she have her kitchen apron on in the street?
Or under her arm this old straw basket they used for shopping?
Or these four coins rolled up in a piece of paper in her fist?
And not any paper, but the *list* of things she's going for:
CREAM, a half measure; a nickel-weight of GINGER, or a dime-,
if the nickel-weight was too little, she would see; and EGGS, two;
and RAISINS, as much as whatever was left over would buy.
Word for word she'd written them down just as mother was saying.
And she had to go quickly—to the little store around the corner—

because the rice already was cooking when she and mother realized
they were out of EVERYTHING! So, she'd run out fast, just as she
        was,
not throwing on a light sweater or putting a comb through her hair.
And fast as she'd gone, still she had time to plan and to *foresee*
every step of the way there, every step back. In her mind she saw:
herself coming onto the stoop; herself skipping on the steps;
her white anklets and low black shoes running down the street
all the way to the corner and then around the corner three
        doorways,
and then down six stone cellar steps and into the dark store.
Plain as day she saw behind the wooden counter old Mrs. Gussie
—round and white and small and waiting quietly like a tabby,
with always that same white apron around her fat little middle,
and her white hair up in a knot, her white, soft, wrinkled face,
her eyeglasses without rims, eyes like sapphires that were gleaming
with all kinds of questions, like, What are you rushing about,
        dear?
So, she saw how, gently, she'd have to hurry her, old as she was,
giving mother's regards right off, before she started in asking . . .
All this she had seen, but not *him* lurking noisily in the road
with dumb I-love-you's, and, as if that was the only language
he spoke, understanding nothing *you* said to him, unless it was
this just-as-dumb exasperated I-love-you that you said back,
and even then not understanding *that* really meant, GO AWAY . . .
—because, how else would this whole world and herself moving in
        it,
that she was seeing so clearly and in such wonderful details
and that already existed almost halfway, ever come to be?
How would she know she'd planned things right, and her story came
        true?
—so that, seeing herself there, she'd not pity that blind little
        girl,
that fool who ran out with her white anklets and low black shoes
and, broken-hearted, fetched nothing, nothing at all . . .

Well, that was five minutes ago, and now it was forty years later,
and he gone from in front of her, and her little girls grown women;
so, if she hurried and got around the corner before the shop
        closed,

she could be back home before the rice burned and mother, out
of patience, would be angry and blaming her, which wouldn't be
fair.
But she was going quickly, and, yes, she would save the day!
Already she could see herself stirring the little rice children
in their milky stew; how good and heavy the old wooden spoon was,
moving them around and around; now she took it out and held it up
and she blew on it three times so mother could taste the sweetness;
and now she put her own tongue out to touch the milky spoon, too.
And they were appraising the pudding's savor, mulling it over,
their eyes meeting, and each asking the other, Yes? Not yet? Now?
And now nodded together: Yes, it's good, the sweetness, just right.
Then by threes and by ones and by twos from the tidy cup
of her palm she would go ahead and sprinkle the raisins in.

Prometheus at Fourteen

Three kids shove one another across
the lawn toward the pool, hotfoot the cool
sharp turf, feeling, dropped among elders,
unfamiliar and small. Embarrassment flies
before and points behind, accusing
and knocking their naive manhood.
Constricted and pale, their bodies tremble,
"What am I showing? What do you see?"

But three geysers smack up suddenly.
They—their escape made good, their cheap
stupendous laughter, their heroic gabble
—honk in triumph at the plundered shore
from safety where perilously they tread,
"A god's nuts! Fire! That's what you saw, my friend!"

Old Ivy and Arsenic

"My old classmate Ben, you say? Ben?
Sends me his regards? Do I *remember* him?"
Backward his voice scrolled along the years;
his eye, inwarding, darkened to collect
the ghostly coinings memory remits.
"Ben. Ben. Ben *Southend*? Ah . . . yes . . ."
Here at last were file and ledger,
an entry's possibly deceptive glimmer.
His mouth puckered down to a squint,
a prim compression of constatation,
authentication, exacting measurement.
(Such the pin-pursed grimace passed around
the sewing circles of tax collectors.)
The pucker dimpled, the dimple purred,
"There is, I believe, a *little* money there."
Unbound, the soul of Ben fluttered down down down,
pale leaf of tissue torn jagged and quite
precisely, on the perforations.

Man with Blue Catarrh

Astounding! Or *Awesome!* Or *Epochal!*
Some such was the word of his election.
The rooftops and street corners blared it.
Bells told each other, told everyone.
The plaza's hubbubbing hundreds were thousands
suddenly, faces uplifted toward his window,
howling out a curse, a vow, a hope
set throbbing in the high-rises' boombox.
Salvo hailed salvo. Fanfare gloried in fanfare.
Massive thrum-beat of the heavens—overhead,
pigeons, wheeling around, went homing away.
His name emblazoned on the holiday!
As if a giant schwa had swallowed the sky
and sucked out the sense with the savor,

what reached him was dull, a ghostly rumble:
bonging shouts, sort of, or loud shushing
or, stuck in his ear, this unbudgeable thud
too thick to trickle into intelligence.
"Fortune's darling"? Was that it? Or "Fate's fool"?
What annunciation held its tongue in thunder?
"Life eternal?" Beginning now? Begun already?
How many seconds of it had he missed?
Or noose come to catch him up, whispering
the terse rock-a-bye of his last gasp?
Or kingship finally, divinely authorized?
Awful, this hissing *ping ping ping ping*!
Had smoke been detected inside his head?
Habemus what? *Pa* is that? Or *Da*? They say
they have someping? So, he has someping, too.
Or she loved him! No? Not a bit? Not at all?

Well, he'd get around to that by and by.
He was sorry disappointing so much
momentousness, which might make the headlines
of other cosmoses; in this molemound
no "lord of war," no "peace's laureate,"
no "star astonishing the stars"—only
a brow and snout dredging dusk in thimblefuls.
So, on the whole, if they gave him his druthers
—here he was reaching for his handkerchief—
he'd take the hanging, a really good one
that would do wonders for his sinuses.

The Brother

This great man, this fine public figure,
is stealing his portion, gobbling it up
—brazenly, in front of everyone's eyes.
And his swagger and blarney and light fingers
and swell-headed pleasure in who he is
have got them all applauding him for that.
And because he gets them to be brazen, too,

they love him for this, calling out to him,
"Fine for you, man. Now let us *see* you take more!"

But brother (and how his face suffers the face
that likeness nails to it), brother, he gazes
in silence into his empty bowl, and he *knows*.

Culprit Conscience

Sir (if I may sex you so):
Lately you awaken me
mornings four to six to gnaw
my ear, accusing all I am,
my talent, my works, my prospects,
my person, goodness, dress, wit,
intelligence, husbanding and
fatherhood, my discipline,
charity, taste, conduct
and disposition of this too
brief too immeasurable gift
of life; most lately—last straw—
you criticize my manners.
No occasion finds you sleeping:
you vex vexation, celebrate
humiliation, sour triumphs,
discomfort for lacking consolation,
attack alike for too young too late,
too old too soon, brazen, shy,
healthy, sick, slow and quick,
or that I stumble but want the grace
to fly entirely or fall finally.

Do not believe that *you*,
sir, would pass inspection,
being, I think, much like me,
except, unhappily, *I* have
a conscience while you have none.
Collusive with the worst

in me, your pride is over-
weening, arrogance boundless,
attacks violent, licentious,
no weapon beyond you, no part
of me too tender, or exempt
from the warfare of your court.
You even lie about me to myself!
Victim, witness, sleuth,
prosecutor, judge, jury,
you proceed by compulsion
and innuendo, take intention
for act, abstention for worse,
and never acquit. Why, I ask,
this ruffian justice,
this vindictiveness? since
I know neither you nor kin,
living or dead—if any.
Barbarous, what decent person
permits you his society?
Discourteous, unprincipled,
unkind, parasitic, lazy,
squalid in your private habits,
bedbug and bugbed both,
for good reason you hide
yourself from all but me.
That I admit to my company
so humorless a boor is
the worst *I* can say of myself.

You claim to judge me, sir.
Rather, your exclusive attention's
rude flattery is my one
genuine—if painful—vice.
I indulge myself no longer.
I cast you out, and serve
formal notice: I rule here.
You are dismissed, banished
to your own odious company.
Your sentence: Exposure to the light
of pleasure and to gales of laughter.

. . .

("*Ha. You'd have a better conscience*
if you were a better person . . .")

The Weakest Hands Seize the Heaviest Ax

With this one blow to stun into submission
the delicacies of her deciding,
Jake brains her with his big, blunt "But I *love* you!"
The weakest hands seize the heaviest ax.

Armed with humorlessness and One Idea,
Jack hacks at trees until little-he lifts his head
in a metaforest of toothpicks and trash.
The weakest hands seize the heaviest ax.

Jock's art of shock makes of "them" a show—of stupe-
faction—for the pretty few of us in the know,
who smirk, knowing nothing but knowingness.
The weakest hands seize the heaviest ax.

Do we resent what we sense we fail to sense?
So much, there is so much I do not grasp.
I must stay in touch. I must stay in finer touch.
Let not my weak hands seize a heavy ax.

Arslan & Arpad: On the Question of Craft

How does he do it? everyone exclaims
—for no less amazing than the three balls
or bowling pins he keeps circling in the air
(as if they were one ball, one bowling pin)
is the skill of Arslan the great juggler.

How much more astounding, then, must be that
of Arpad who's tossed up that glinting vial.

Look, it's spinning like crazy—it's coming down!
Grandmaster of the Nitro though he is,
somehow Arpad's technique goes unnoticed.

To a Grave, Unquietly

"Roth amused his compatriots by scanning
headstones for Jewish names."
—NEW YORK MAGAZINE

That's true. Often the only amusing thing in a graveyard will be the
 Jewish names.

There they are, in the full sight of everyone, winking from their
 stones, "It's me. Over here. Yeah. Bet you don't believe your
 eyes. I got in!"
Amusing, right?
And if, God forbid, I come up empty now and then, I carry my own
 supply of JN's—you know, family, friends. Then I just *remember*
 them.
That's amusing, too.
So, What do you get when you put a Jewish name on a gravestone?
 A stand-up comic, full of *joie de mourir.*
And when you take the Jewish name away what do you have?
 A Stein is a Stone is a stone.
Our famous Jewish sense of humor.
 Like, Laugh at yourself and the world laughs with you.
Or take a "restricted" cemetery. You know:
 Mingle not thy putrefaction with my clay!
And here these Jewish names are making like they're officers (yet!)
 of Earth's least exclusive club.
I dare anyone not to be amused then!
Other times I ask myself, Is this anachronism never going out-of-
 date? Where's the stone *that* is written on?
You know their antimanna trick? Names and all, they went straight
 up into thin air.
Mark the marble! Engrave the granite!
I used to say mine will read, ONE MORE GAME? Now I'm
 thinking, BE MY GUEST.

Change my name to something *more* Jewish. Owe it to you,
    passerby. What will amuse you?
Waiting to hear, and I ain't got forever.

Here lie under their Jewish names some Jews.

Old Wife Tale

A little while the dream lingered,
then was gone, somewhere in the dark:
again as in its first beauty,
your face above my dreaming face,
whispering, "Irving, such a waste!
You can make it up to me.
It's not too late."

Redemption not less real
for being ephemeral.

Versions of Proteus

Was turning—wasn't he?—when
you grasped him that he was you
were Proteus in the throe
of grasping himself loosing
losing Proteus, weren't you?

NOTES

Some of the poems collected here differ in
small ways from their last appearance in print.

From *WORKS AND DAYS*

"Arabian Night." *page 4*. "And I who sit like night at the window." As this
    volume's title group, from which this poem is drawn, indicates, the
    speaker is the lost crow sent out by Noah in search of dry land.
"The Lost Language." *page 9*. "*O liebe brayt?*" Yiddish: O beloved bread.

From *THE PRIPET MARSHES*

"Song." *page 32*. Originally published as "Orpheus' Song."

From *MAGIC PAPERS*

"Psalm." *page 43*. "The glory of man shall fly away like a bird." See Hosea
    9:11.
"The Father." *page 56*. In memory of Dennie Sutcliffe.
"Elegy for a Suicide." *page 65*. In memory of Merrie Abel.

From *LOST ORIGINALS*

"Birth Day." *page 91*. "And arrives where all are strangers, all / are kind" is a
    version of lines in Edward Thomas's "Over the Hills," from which this
    poem grew.
"Six Sailors." *page 101*. "this john aspiring to mackerel." That is, *"maquereau,"*
    French for pimp.
"Bembú a su amada." *page 103*. "Bembú." "Big lips." The poet Juan Díaz
    Bembú, as well as this poem (and its occasional translation-ese), are my
    inventions.

From *LEAPING CLEAR*

"Beethoven's Bust." *page 117*. "and disappears under the sky's black rock."
    Black Rock is the far west side of Buffalo, New York, and borders on
    the Niagara River.
"The Good Life." *page 126*. Written a year earlier, this poem was first
    published several months before a similar theme park opened (and
    soon closed) in Florida.
"Antonio, *Botones*." *page 129*. "*botones.*" Spanish: bellboy. *"Hacienda."* Spain's
    Department of the Treasury.

"Egg." *page 133*. *"orfèvre."* This corrects the computer-generated pun in *New and Selected Poems: "orf Lèvre."*

"A Player's Notes." *page 141*. The game is squash racquets.

"The Golden Schlemiel." *page 144*. This story appeared in the *International Herald Tribune* in April 1974. Anwar Sadat was then president of Egypt. "Deif" rhymes with "grief."

> "fig": mockery's thumb emerging between the middle and index fingers of the balled-up fist.

From *NEW AND SELECTED POEMS*

"Family History." *page 159*. "night and fog." *Nacht und Nebel*. The Nazi extermination campaign in France.
> The following are Yiddish:
>> *"Mit Dem Shpits Tsung Aroys."* With the tip of the tongue out.
>> *"Arbet macht dem leben ziess."* Work makes life sweet.
>> *"Vos zol ton a Yid? Epes a shneider."* What should a Jew do? [Shrugging.] A tailor.

From *TEACH ME, DEAR SISTER*

"Eberheim." *page 190*. "the novel." William Gerhardie's *Futility*.

"Albert Feinstein." *page 197*. "never rightly named." The playwright Arnold Weinstein.

"Just Another Smack." *page 203*. "Schoolmaster Auden gave them full marks." See his "Musée des Beaux Arts."

"The Grand Magic Theater Finale." *page 217*. Performed in Jean-Louis Barrault's theater-in-the-round in the vacant Gare d'Orsay, Paris, July 1974.

"Talking to Fernando." *page 218*. After Jean Giono.

ALL OF US HERE

"All of Us Here." *page 223*. Set in an art gallery like the Sidney Janis Gallery in New York, where, in December 1978, I first came across an ensemble of George Segal's plaster sculptures.
> "Careers open to idealism!" After Napoleon's "Careers open to talent."
> *"Ils sont dans le vrai."* Flaubert, on seeing his niece and her husband among Rouen's Sunday bourgeois promenaders.

From *THE LIFE AND LETTERS*

"Street Scene." *page 285*. "And runs 'not as one who loses.' " Brunetto Latini, who "seemed like one of those who run for the green cloth at Verona through the open field; and of them seemed he who wins, not he who loses," encountered by Dante in *Inferno*, Canto XV.

"Variations on a Theme by May Swenson." *page 297*. " 'Feel me to do right.' " From May Swenson's poem "Feel Me" *(New and Selected Things Taking Place)*.

"The Little Children of Hamelin." *page 300*. See Robert Browning's poem "The Pied Piper of Hamelin."

"Malke Toyb." *page 305*. Yiddish: Deaf Malke.

From *BEAUTIFUL FALSE THINGS*

"Sono un poeta . . . Scrivo." *page 348*. I am a poet . . . I write. So Rodolfo introduces himself to Mimì in *La Bohème* in his aria *"Che gelida manina."* (How cold your little hand.)

"Beautiful False Things." *page 351*. "Krip" is Albanian for "salt." *"Je est un autre?"* Rimbaud: "I is another."

"These Memoirs." *page 358*. See Harold Norse's *Memoirs of a Bastard Angel* for a similar series of iconic encounters.

"Desiring Power Where Surrender Failed." *page 371*. "How can sharing bread not be true companionship?" "Companion," etymologically: sharer of bread.

"Heavenly Muse." *page 379*. Free Spirit to the poet's peevish Letter, Heavenly Muse can't be bothered to quote correctly. In one instance, however, she appears to misquote deliberately Gerard Manley Hopkins's "The roll, the rise, the carol, the creation." ("To R. B.")

NEW AND UNCOLLECTED POEMS

"Chaos Theory, *or* Karmic Chutzpah." *page 406*. This inverts the common example of chaos theory: A butterfly flutters its wings in America, and in China a thunderstorm ensues.

"[Sic] *Transcript Gloria, or* The Body Politician." *page 408*. "(the tape turning from reel ominous to real grim)." President Nixon secretly tape-recorded Oval Office conversations. One tape contained a suspicious eighteen-minute gap.

   Erlichman, Colson, Dean. Richard Nixon's inner circle of co-conspirators in the Watergate affair.

   "of Dean, *'He says you got an* ass *on your bosom.'* " I can't say at what point "ass" replaced "asp," but so I read it in the *International Herald Tribune* in May 1974.

INDEX OF FIRST LINES

INDEX OF TITLES

About the Author

IRVING FELDMAN was born in Coney Island, New York, in 1928. He was educated at the City College of New York and at Columbia University. He has taught at the University of Puerto Rico, Université de Lyon in France, and Kenyon College, and he is currently Distinguished Professor of English at the State University of New York at Buffalo. Feldman's collections of poetry include *Beautiful False Things* (2000); *The Life and Letters* (1994); *All of Us Here* (1986), a finalist for the National Book Critics Circle Award; *New and Selected Poems* (1979); *Leaping Clear* (1976) and *The Pripet Marshes* (1965), both finalists for the National Book Award; and *Works and Days* (1961), winner of the Kovner Poetry Prize of the Jewish Book Council. Feldman is the recipient of a National Institute of Arts and Letters award and a grant from the National Endowment for the Arts, as well as fellowships from the Academy of American Poets, the Guggenheim Foundation, the Ingram Merrill Foundation, and the MacArthur Foundation. He lives in Buffalo, New York.

A Note on the Type

This book was set in a modern adaptation of a type designed by the first William Caslon (1692–1766). The Caslon face, an artistic, easily read type, has enjoyed over two centuries of popularity in our own country. It is of interest to note that the first copies of the Declaration of Independence and the first paper currency distributed to the citizens of the newborn nation were printed in this typeface.

Composed by Creative Graphics,
Allentown, Pennsylvania
Printed and bound by Berryville Graphics,
Berryville, Virginia